CLIMATE AND CULTURE

A Philosophical Study

Classics of Modern Japanese Thought and Culture

The Ways of Thinking of Eastern Peoples
Hajime Nakamura

A Study of Good
Kitaro Nishida

Climate and Culture: A Philosophical Study
Tetsuro Watsuji

Time and Eternity
Seiichi Hatano

Studies in Shinto Thought
Tsunetsugu Muraoka

The Japanese Character: A Cultural Profile
Nyozekan Hasegawa

An Inquiry into the Japanese Mind as Mirrored in Literature
Sokichi Tsuda

About our Ancestors: —The Japanese Family System
Kunio Yanagita

Japanese Spirituality
Daisetz Suzuki

A Historical Study of the Religious Development of Shinto
Genichi Kato

CLIMATE
AND
CULTURE

A Philosophical Study

by

WATSUJI TETSURO

translated by

GEOFFREY BOWNAS

Greenwood Press
New York • Westport, Connecticut • London

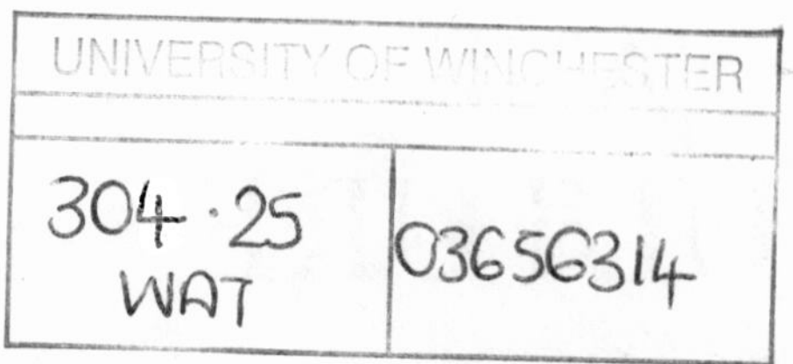

Library of Congress Cataloging-in-Publication Data

Watsuji, Tetsurō, 1889-1960.
Climate and culture.

Translation of: Fūdo.
Reprint. Originally published: Tokyō : Monbushō, 1961.
1. Man—Influence of climate. 2. Monsoons.
3. Human ecology—Japan—Philosophy. I. Title.
GF71.W313 1988 304.2′5 88-21985
ISBN 0-313-26558-5

British Library Cataloguing in Publication Data is available.

Library of Congress Catalog Card Number: 88-21985
ISBN: 0-313-26558-5

First published in 1961

Reprinted in 1988 by Greenwood Press, Inc. jointly with Yushodo Co., Ltd., Tokyo with the permission of the Ministry of Education, Japan

Printed in the United States of America

The paper used in this book complies with the Permanent Paper Standard issued by the National Information Standards Organization (Z39.48-1984).

10 9 8 7 6 5 4 3 2 1

Photo Tanuma

FOREWORD

The Japanese National Commission for Unesco has been carrying out, since 1958, a project of translating Japanese philosophical works into foreign languages and publishing them with a view to introducing Japanese thought to the people of other countries. Under this project, we have so far brought out nine titles; *A Climate* by Watsuji Tetsuro is the third volume of this series.

Nearly a decade has passed since *A Climate* was first published in 1962 and to our regret the publication has long been out of print, even though there were increasing demands for this book.

In order to meet the demands of the readers, the Japanese National Commission has brought out the present revised edition under the new title of *Climate and Culture*, and it is our hope that this edition will be of use for those who are engaged in the studies of Japanese culture and thought.

We are greatly indebted to Professor Geoffrey Bownas, Director of Centre of Japanese Studies, Sheffield University, who willingly took trouble again to review the translation.

March 1971

Ryoji Ito
Secretary-General
Japanese National Commission
for Unesco

Translator's Preface

It was on my third day in Japan—on Culture Day, 1952, in fact—that I first heard the name of Professor Watsuji. A goodly gathering of Japanese Orientalists was celebrating the end of a Culture Day Conference in Kyoto and, across the table, there floated this name, coupled with the question, "Have you ever read any of his works?" The questioner was Professor Kaizuka, the great Japanese historian of ancient China, my teacher and sponsor in Japan.

Since that evening, I have often linked these two names in my memories of Japan. Those who knew Professor Watsuji may well regard this association as a little forced and if they do I cannot but bow to their judgement, for it will be my eternal and sad regret that, from the time when I was commissioned by the Japanese National Commission for UNESCO, early in 1960, to translate *Fudo,* its author never recovered sufficiently from his long ailment to be able to see or talk to me. It is natural, I suppose, that a translator should build some image, however indistinct, of the author he translates: because of this early episode that connected the two, and because of what I regard as a similar breadth of outlook, a similar sympathetic and gentle humanity and a similar incisiveness of thought, I came to construct my image of the unknown in part from my memories of the known.

Professor Watsuji's sharp eye and broad understanding class him among the rarest and most precious of travellers. Again and again, as I worked on my translation and read his accounts of the sights and sounds of Europe often so familiar to me, did I notice something new or come to understand more fully some puzzling aspect of the Japan I saw about me. Even today, eighteen months on, I find myself smiling as I recall the room in which most of this translation was completed, so close to the *densha* route that, as Watsuji argues, the tiny house seemed to be rocked as if by an earthquake and to cower and grovel in the path of the huge onrushing monster of an electric train. Even now I wince as I remember the brash braying of the train horns, so strident in comparison with the poignant sadness inherent in most home-made Japanese noises. And last summer, in England, I felt, for the first time, the "loneliness" of the north European summer evening—no frogs, no cicadas! *Climate and Culture,* I would argue, would be valuable if read merely as a general guide to Japan and her culture and would well repay reading by all intelligent would-be visitors. For one of Professor Watsuji's unique qualities was his deep affection for and sympathetic comprehension of his own Japan, both of which grew with his ever-widening erudition. I feel that perhaps I would not lack supporters if I were to argue that so many of the Japanese I have met,—particularly those of the generations that follow Watsuji's—while they may know just about all there is to be known about their own particular interest in the West, in process of acquiring this alien knowledge have yet grown quite out of touch with their own culture. Watsuji's roots, and those of scholars like him, are all the stronger for the nourishment they gain from a familiar soil.

There are a great many whose assistance I must acknowledge. The staff of the Japanese National Commission for UNESCO were a joy to work with and, from Mr. Muto and Mr. Yamashida down, never regarded any request as too burdensome or trivial; Professor Furukawa of Tokyo University was always ready to spare time and help in the interpretation of some of the more obscure problems. I remember particularly how we met on the morning after the worst of the student riots in June, 1960, (the girl who died was a member of his department) and wondered how Watsuji would interpret what we had seen the night before. Mr. Minamoto of the Education Section in the Shiga Prefectural Office gave much help; Mr. Michael Brown of the Department of Education in the University of Nottingham offered valuable criticism and Mrs. Ruth Sellers typed the manuscript with her customary and outstanding dependability. I thank them all, along with others too numerous to mention, but I claim for myself all responsibility for errors.

Oxford.

December, 1961.

Preface

My purpose in this study is to clarify the function of climate as a factor within the structure of human existence. So my problem is not that of the ordering of man's life by his natural environment. Natural environment is usually understood as an objective extension of "human climate" regarded as a concrete basis. But when we come to consider the relationship between this and human life, the latter is already objectified, with the result that we find ourselves examining the relation between object and object, and there is no link with subjective human existence. It is the latter that is my concern here, for it is essential to my position that the phenomena of climate are treated as expressions of subjective human existence and not of natural environment. I should like at the outset to register my protest against this confusion.

It was in the early summer of 1927 when I was reading Heidegger's *Zein und Seit* in Berlin that I first came to reflect on the problem of climate. I found myself intrigued by the attempt to treat the structure of man's existence in terms of time but I found it hard to see why, when time had thus been made to play a part in the structure of subjective existence, at the same juncture space also was not postulated as part of the basic structure of existence. Indeed it would be a mistake to allege that space is never taken into account in Heidegger's thinking, for *Lebendige Natur* was given fresh life by the German Romantics, yet even so it tended to be almost obscured in the face of the strong glare to which time was exposed. I perceived that herein lay the limitations of Heidegger's work, for time not linked with space is not time in the true sense and Heidegger stopped short at this point because his *Dasein* was the *Dasein* of the individual only. He treated human existence as being the existence of a man. From the standpoint of the dual structure—both individual and social—of human existence, he did not advance beyond an abstraction of a single aspect. But it is only when human existence is treated in terms of its concrete duality that time and space are linked and that history also (which never appears fully in Heidegger) is first revealed in its true guise. And at the same time the connection between history and climate becomes evident.

It may well be that this problem presented itself to me because it was precisely when my mind was full of a variety of impressions about climate that I was confronted with a detailed examination of the question of time. But again, it was precisely in that this problem did present itself that I was made to ruminate over and to concentrate my attention on my impressions about climate. In this sense it would be fair to argue that for my part it was the problems of time and history that brought a realization of the question of climate. Had not these problems acted as intermediaries, my impressions of climate would have stayed simply as such, mere impressions of climate. And, in fact, the intermediary function that these considerations fulfilled indicates the connection between climate and history.

In the main, this work is based on notes for lectures given over the period September 1928 to March 1929. This series was given very soon after my return from my travels outside Japan with the result that, in that I had no leisure to reflect in detail on the problems of time and space in human existence, I took up for discussion only the consideration of climate. The greater part of the contents of this book have been published piecemeal, with my original lecture notes written up and revised as the occasion arose, and only the last chapter retains its basic format. From the outset, the several problems were considered as intimately inter-related and though I am fully conscious that there still remain considerable deficiencies, I have decided for the present to put my thoughts together and publish. I should be gratefull for my colleagues' criticisms and suggestions.

August 1935

I have taken the opportunity of this re-edition to revise the section on China in Chapter Three which was written in 1928, when leftist thinking was very prevalent. I have eliminated traces of leftist theory and now present this chapter as a pure study of climate.

November 1943

CONTENTS

Chapter 1 The Basic Principles of Climate

(1) *The Phenomena of Climate*

I use our word Fu-do, which means literally, "Wind and Earth", as a general term for the natural environment of a given land, its climate, its weather, the geological and productive nature of the soil, its topographic and scenic features. The ancient term for this concept was Sui-do, which might be literally translated as "Water and Earth". Behind these terms lies the ancient view of Nature as man's environment compounded of earth, water, fire, and wind. It is not without reason that I wish to treat this natural environment of man not as "nature" but as "climate" in the above sense. But in order to clarify my reason, I must, in the first place, deal with the phenomenon of climate.

All of us live on a given land and the natural environment of this land "environs" us whether we like it or not. People usually discern this natural environment in the form of natural phenomena of various kinds, and accordingly concern themselves with the influences which such a natural environment exercises upon "us"—in some cases upon "us" as biological and physiological objects and in other cases upon "us" as being engaged in practical activities such as the formation of a polity. Each of these influences is complicated enough to demand specialized study. However, what I am here concerned with is whether the climate we experience in daily life is to be regarded as a natural phenomenon. It is proper that natural science should treat climate as a natural phenomenon, but it is another question whether the phenomena of climate are in essence objects of natural science.

By way of clarifying this question, let me quote as an example the phenomenon of cold, which is merely one element within climate, and is something distinct and evident as far as our common sense is concerned. It is an undeniable fact that we feel cold. But what is this cold that we feel? Is it that air of a certain temperature, cold, that is, as a physical object, stimulates the sensory organs in our body so that we as psychological subjects experience it as a certain set mental state? If so, it follows that the "cold" and "we" exist as separate and independent entities in such a manner that only when the cold presses upon us from outside is there created an "intentional" or directional relationship by which "we feel the cold". If this is the case, it is natural that this should be conceived in terms of the influence of the cold upon us.

But is this really so? How can we know the independent existence of the cold before we feel cold? It is impossible. It is by feeling cold, that we discover the cold. It is simply by mistaking the intentional relationship that we consider that the cold is pressing in on us from outside. It is not true that the intentional relationship is set up only when an object presses from outside. As far as individual consciousness is concerned, the subject possesses the intentional structure within itself and itself "directs itself towards something". The "feeling" of "feeling the cold" is not a "point" which establishes a relationship directed at the cold, but it is in itself a relationship in virtue of its "feeling" and it is in this relationship that we discover cold. The intentionality of such a relational structure is thus a structure of the subject in relation with the cold. The fact that "We feel the cold" is, first and foremost, an "intentional experience" of this kind.

But, it may be argued, if this is the case, is not the cold merely a moment of subjective experience? The cold thus discovered is cold limited to the sphere of the "I". But what we call the cold is a transcendental object outside the "I", and not a mere feeling of the "I". Now how can a subjective experience establish a relation with such a transcendental object? In other words, how can the feeling of cold relate itself to the coldness of the outside air? This question involves a misunderstanding with regard to the object of the intention in the intentional relationship. The object of intention is not a mental entity. It is not cold as an experience independent of objective cold that is the intentional object. When we feel the cold, it is not the "feeling" of cold that we feel, but the "coldness of the air" or the "cold". In other words, the cold felt in intentional experience is not subjective but objective. It may be said, therefore, that an intentional relation in which we feel the cold is itself related to the coldness of the air. The cold as a transcendental existence only exists in this intentionality. Therefore, there can be no problem of the relationship of the feeling of cold to the coldness of the air.

According to this view, the usual distinction between subject and object, or more particularly the distinction between "the cold" and the "I" independently of each other, involves a certain misunderstanding. When we feel cold, we ourselves are already in the coldness of the outside air. That we come into relation with the cold means that we are outside in the cold. In this sense, our state is characterized by "ex-sistere" as Heidegger emphasizes, or, in our term, by "intentionality".

This leads me to the contention that we ourselves face ourselves in the state of "ex-sistere". Even in cases where we do not face ourselves by means of reflection or looking into ourselves, our selves are exposed to ourselves. Reflection is merely a form of grasping ourselves. Furthermore, it is not a primary mode of self-revelation. (But if the word "reflect" is taken in its visual sense, i. e., if it is understood as to dash against something and rebound from it and to reveal oneself in this rebound or reflection, it can be argued that the word may well indicate the way in which our selves are exposed to ourselves.) We feel the cold, or we are out in the cold. Therefore, in feeling the cold, we discover ourselves in the cold itself. This does not mean that we transfer our selves into the cold and there discover the selves thus transferred. The instant that the cold is discovered, we are already outside in the cold. Therefore, the basic essence of what is "present outside" is not a thing or object such as the cold, but we ourselves. "Ex-sistere" is the fundamental principle of the structure of our selves, and it is on this principle that intentionality depends. That we feel the cold is an intentional experience, in which we discover our selves in the state of "ex-sistere", or our selves already outside in the cold.

We have considered the problem in terms of individual consciousness in the experience of cold. But, as we have been able to use the expression "we feel cold", without any contradiction, it is "we", not "I" alone that experience the cold. We feel the same cold in common. It is precisely because of this that we can use terms describing the cold in our exchange of daily greetings. The fact that the feeling of cold differs between us is possible only on the basis of our feeling the cold in common. Without this basis it would be quite impossible to recognise that any other "I" experiences the cold. Thus, it is not "I" alone but "we", or more strictly, "I" as "we" and "we" as "I" that are outside in the cold. The structure of which "ex-sistere" is the fundamental principle is this "we", not the mere "I". Accordingly, "ex-sistere" is "to be out among other 'I's' " rather than "to be out in a thing such as the cold". This is not an intentional relation but a "mutual relationship" of existence. Thus it is primarily "we" in this "mutual relationship" that discover our selves in the cold.

I have attempted to define the phenomenon cold. However, we do not experience this kind of atmospheric phenomenon in isolation from others of its kind. It is experienced in relation to warmth, or heat, or in connection with wind, rain, snow, sunshine, and so forth. In other words the cold is simply one of the whole series of similar phenomena which we call weather. When we enter a warm room after walking in the cold wind, when we stroll in the mild spring breeze after a cold winter is over, or when we are caught in a torrential shower on a boiling hot summer day, we first of all apprehend ourselves within such meteorological phenomena, which are other than our selves. Again, in changes in the weather, we first of all apprehend changes in ourselves. This weather, too, is not experienced in isolation. It is experienced only in relation to the soil, the topographic and scenic features and so on of a given land. A cold wind may be experienced as a mountain blast or the cold, dry wind that sweeps through Tokyo at the end of the winter. The spring breeze may be one which blows off cherry blossoms or which caresses the waves. So, too, the heat of summer may be of the kind to wither rich verdure or to entice children to play merrily in the sea. As we find our gladdened or pained selves in a wind that scatters the cherry blossoms, so do we apprehend our wilting selves in the very heat of summer that scorches down on plants and trees in a spell of dry weather. In other words, we find ourselves—ourselves as an element in the "mutual relationship"—in "climate".

Such self-apprehension is not the recognition of the "I" as the subject that feels the cold and the heat or as the subject that is gladdened by the cherry blossoms. In these experiences we do not look towards the "subject". We stiffen, or we put on warm clothes, or we draw near the brazier when we feel cold. Or, we may feel more concern about putting clothes on our children or seeing that the old are near the brazier. We work hard to have the money to buy more clothes and charcoal. Charcoal burners make charcoal in the mountains, and textile factories produce clothing materials. Thus, in our relationship with the cold, we come to engage ourselves, individually and socially, in various measures for protecting ourselves from the cold. In the same way, when we rejoice in the cherry blossoms, we do not look to the subject; rather it is the blossoms that take our attention and we invite our friends to go blossom-viewing, or drink and dance with them under the trees. Thus in our relationship with the spring scene, either individually or socially we adopt various measures for securing enjoyment from it. The same may be said of the summer heat or disasters such as storms and floods. It is in our relationship with the tyranny of nature that we first come to engage ourselves in joint measures to secure early protection from such tyranny. The apprehension of the self in climate is revealed as the discovery of such measures; it is not the recognition of the subject.

The various measures which are thus discovered, such as clothes, braziers, charcoal-burning, houses, blossom-viewing, dykes, drains, anti-typhoon structures, and the like, are of course what we ourselves have devised at our own discretion. It is not, however, with no connection with such climatic phenomena as the cold, the heat, and the humidity that we have devised them. We have discovered ourselves in climate, and in this self-apprehension we are directed to our free creation. Further, it is not only we ourselves who today cooperate to defend ourselves or work against the cold, the heat, the storm or the flood. We possess an inheritance of self-apprehension accumulated over the years since the time of our ancestors. A house style is an established mode of construction, and this cannot have come into being without some connection with climate. The house is a device for protecting ourselves both from cold and from heat. The style of architecture must be determined most of all by the degree of protection required against cold or heat. Then a house must be so built as to withstand storm, flood, earthquake, fire and the like. A heavy roof is necessary against storm and flood, though it may be disadvantageous in the event of an earthquake. The house should be adapted to these various conditions. Furthermore, humidity imposes severe limitations on residential style. Where the humidity is very high, thorough ventilation is essential. Wood, paper and clay are the building materials that offer the best protection against humidity, but they give no protection at all against fire. These various restraints and conditions are taken into account and accorded their degree of importance before the pattern of the house of a given locality is finally established. Thus the determination of the architectural style of a house is an expression of the self-apprehension of man within climate. The same may be said about clothing styles. Here again, clothing styles have been established socially over a long period, styles being determined by climate. A style distinctive to a certain locality, perhaps because of the latter's cultural supremacy, may be transplanted to another locality with a different climate. (This can occur more readily with dress than with architectural styles) . But to whatever locality it may be transplanted, the fact that the style is conditioned by the climate which produced it can never be effaced. European-style clothes remain European, even after more than half a century of wear in Japan. Such climatic conditioning is even more obvious in the case of food, for it is with climate that the production of food is most intimately connected. It is not that man made the choice between stock-raising and fishing according to his preference for meat or fish. On the contrary, he came to prefer either meat or fish because climate determined whether he should engage in stock-raising or in fishing. In the same way, the predominant factor governing the choice between a vegetable or a meat diet is climate, rather than the vegetarian's ideology. So our appetite is not for food in general but for food prepared in a certain way which has long been established. What we actually want when we are hungry is bread or rice, a beef steak or raw fish. The way that food is prepared is an expression of a people's climatic self-apprehension and is something which has taken shape over many generations. Our ancestors ate shell-fish and seaweed long before they mastered the skills of the farmer.

We can also discover climatic phenomena in all the expressions of human activity, such as literature, art, religion, and manners and customs. This is a natural consequence as long as man apprehends himself in climate. It is evident, therefore, that climatic phenomena understood in this light differ from phenomena studied by natural science. To consider a sea-food diet as a climatic phenomenon is not to regard climate merely as natural environment. To interpret artistic style in relation to climate is to indicate the inseparability of climate from history. The most frequent misunderstanding about climate occurs in the commonplace view that influences exist between man and his natural environment.

Here, however, the factors of human existence and history have been excluded from the concrete phenomena of climate, which are regarded merely as natural environment. It is from such a standpoint that it is often said that not only is man conditioned by climate, but that he, in his turn, works on and transforms climate. But this is to ignore the true nature of climate. We, on the other hand, have seen that it is in climate that man apprehends himself. The activity of man's self-apprehension, man, that is, in his dual character of individual and social being, is at the same time of a historical nature. Therefore, climate does not exist apart from history, nor history apart from climate. This can only be understood from the fundamental structure of human existence.

(2) *Climatic Limitation of Human Existence*

I have defined climate as a means for man to discover himself. But what is this "man"? If one is to interpret climate as one of the forms of limitation on human existence, one should attempt to state, in broad terms, the place this limitation has in the general structure of human existence.

By "man" I mean not the individual (anthrōpos, homo, homme, etc.) but man both in this individual sense and at the same time man in society, the combination or the association of man. This duality is the essential nature of man. So neither anthropology, which treats man the individual, nor sociology, which takes up the other aspect, can grasp the real or full substance of man. For a true and full understanding, one must treat man both as individual and as whole; it is only when the analysis of human existence is made from this viewpoint that it becomes evident that this existence is completely and absolutely negative activity. And human existence is precisely the realisation of this negative activity.

Human existence, through fragmentation into countless individual entities, is the activity which brings into being all forms of combination and community. Such fragmentation and union are essentially of a self-active and practical nature and cannot come about in the absence of self-active entities. Hence, space and time in this self-active sense, form the fundamental structure of these activities. It is at this point that space and time are grasped in their essential form and their inseparability becomes distinct. An attempt to treat the structure of human existence as one of time only would fall into the error of trying to discover human existence on the level only of individual consciousness. But if the dual character of human existence is taken as the essential nature of man, then it is immediately clear that space must be regarded as linked with time.

With the elucidation of the space-and time-nature of human existence, the structure of human association also appears in its true light. The several unions and combinations that man fashions evolve intrinsically according to a certain order. They are to be regarded as not static social structures but as active and evolving systems. They are the realisation of negative activity. This is how history took shape.

Here the space-and time-structure of human existence is revealed as climate and history: the inseparability of time and space is the basis of the inseparability of history and climate. No social formation could exist if it lacked all foundation in the space-structure of man, nor does time become history unless it is founded in such social being, for history is the structure of existence in society. Here also we see clearly the duality of human existence—the finite and the infinite. Men die; their world changes; but through this unending death and change, man lives and his world continues. It continues incessantly through ending incessantly. In the individual's eyes, it is a case of an "existence for death", but from the standpoint of society it is an "existence for life". Thus human existence is both individual and social. But it is not only history that is the structure of social existence, for climate is also a part of this structure and, at that, a part quite inseparable from history. For it is from the union of climate with history that the latter gets its flesh and bones. In terms of the contrast between spirit and matter, history can never be merely spiritual self-development. For it is only when, as self-active being, the spirit objectivises itself, in other words, only when it includes such self-active physical principle that it becomes history, as self-development. This "self-active physical principle", as we might term it, is climate. The human duality, of the finite and the infinite, is most plainly revealed as the historical and climatic structure.

It is here that climate is revealed; for mankind is saddled not simply with a general past but with a specific climatic past; a general formal historical structure is substantiated by a specific content. It is only in this way that the historical being of mankind can become the being of man in a given country at a given age. Again, climate as this specific content does not exist alone and in isolation from history, entering and becoming a part of the content of history at a later juncture. From the very first, climate is historical climate. In the dual structure of man—the historical and the climatic—history is climatic history and climate is historical climate. History and climate in isolation from each other are mere abstractions; climate as I shall consider it is the essential climate that has not undergone this abstraction.

Such, then, is the place of climatic limitation in the structure of human life. It will no doubt be evident that there are certain points of similarity between the problem of climate and that of "body" in traditional anthropology, which took as its study the individual nature abstracted from the duality of the individual and the social. It then endeavoured to treat man, divorced from his relationships, as a duality of body and spirit, but all efforts to clearly grasp this distinction between body and spirit led to a final disregard for the unity in this distinction. This was essentially because the body was taken as equivalent to a "material body" and divorced from concrete self-active principle. It was for this reason that anthropology was divided into spiritualist and materialist camps, the one developing from psychology towards epistemology, the other moving in the direction either of anthropology as a branch of zoology, or of physiology and anatomy. But the philosophical anthropology of today is attempting to heal this division and again treat man as a duality of spirit and body. So the crux of the problem becomes the realisation that the body is not mere matter; in other words, it is the problem of the self-active nature of the body. Yet anthropology will always be the study of "individual man" rather than of "man in his social relationship". We, in this enquiry, are pursuing a problem of a similar nature, although ours, that of the duality of human nature, is the more fundamental. The self-active nature of the body has as its foundation the spatial and temporal structure of human life; a self-active body cannot remain in isolation for its structure is dynamic, uniting in isolation and isolated within union. When various social combinations are evolved within this dynamic structure it becomes something historical or climatic. Climate, too, as part of man's body, was regarded like the body as mere matter, and so came to be viewed objectively as mere natural environment. So the self-active nature of climate must be retrieved in the same sense that the self-active nature of the body has to be retrieved. It would be fair to say, then, that, in its most fundamental significance, the relation between body and spirit lies in the relation between the body and the spirit of "man in his social relationships", the individual and social body-spirit relation which includes the relationship with history and climate.

The problem of climate affords a pointer for any attempt to analyse the structure of human life. The ontological comprehension of human life is not to be attained by a mere transcendence which regards the structure as one of time, for this has to be transcendence in the sense of the discovery of the self in the other and the subsequent reversal to absolute negation in the union of self and other. In this case, the relationships between man and man must be on a transcendent plane and the relationships themselves, the basis for the discovery of self and other, must already be essentially on a plane which "stands outside" (ex-sistere). Transcendence itself must have assumed some historical significance, as being the temporal structure of such relationships. It is not something in the individual consciousness but the relationships themselves that constantly reach into the future. Time in individual consciousness is a mere abstraction on the basis of the history of the relationships. Transcendence also "stands outside" (ex-sistere) climatically. In other words, man discovers himself in climate. From the standpoint of the individual, this becomes consciousness of the body, but in the context of the more concrete ground of human life, it reveals itself in the ways of creating communities, and thus in the ways of constructing speech, the methods of production, the styles of building, and so on. Transcendence, as the structure of human life, must include all these entities.

Thus climate is seen to be the factor by which self-active human beings can be made objective: climatic phenomena show man how to discover himself as "standing outside" (i.e., ex-sistere). The self discovered by the cold turns into tools devised against the cold, such as houses or clothes, which then confront the self. Again climate itself, the climate in which we move, and in which we "stand outside", becomes a tool to be used. The cold, for instance, is not only something that sends us off for warm clothes; it can also be utilised to freeze the bean-curd. Heat is not only something that makes us use a fan; it is also the heat that nourishes the rice-plants. Wind has us scurrying to the temple to pray for safety through the typhoon season; it is also the wind that fills a sail. So even in such relationships we "stand outside" in climate and understand our selves from it, our selves, that is, as consumers or users. In other words, this self-comprehension through climate at the same time leads us to discover ourselves as confronted with such tools.

There is much to be learnt from the thought that such tools are to be found very near to hand in human life. A tool is essentially "for doing something". A hammer is for beating, a shoe for wearing. But the object that is "for doing something else" has an immanent connection with the purpose for which it is employed. The hammer, for example, is a tool for making shoes, and shoes, again, are tools for walking. The essential character of the tool lies in its being "for a purpose", lies, that is, in this purpose-relation. Now this purpose-relation derives from human life and at its basis we find the climatic limitation of human life. Shoes may be tools for walking, but the great majority of mankind could walk without them; it is rather cold and heat that make shoes necessary. Clothes are to be worn, yet they are worn above all as a protection against cold. Thus this purpose-relation finds its final origin in climatic self-comprehension. As well as understanding ourselves in cold or heat, we take measures, as free agents, for protection. We should not devise clothes completely spontaneously in the absence of the factors of cold or heat. It is when we proceed from "for our protection" to "with what" that climatic self-comprehension becomes express. Hence clothes are devised to keep us warm or cool; they are of every style and thickness. Such stuffs as wool, cotton and silk come to be socially recognized as materials for clothes. It is clear, then, that such tools have a very close relationship with climatic limitation. To say, then, that tools are to be found nearest to hand is, in fact, to say that climatic limitation is the foremost factor in objective existence.

Climate, then, is the agent by which human life is objectivised, and it is here that man comprehends himself; there is self-discovery in climate. We discover ourselves in all manner of significances every day; it may be in a pleasant or a sad mood, but such feelings or tempers are to be regarded not merely as mental states but as our way of life. These, moreover, are not feelings that we are free to choose of ourselves, but are imposed on us as pre-determined states. Nor is it climate only that prescribes such pre-determined feelings, for our individual and social existence controls the way of life of the individual, which is dependent on it in the form of pre-existent relationships, and imparts to him determined moods; it may sometimes impart to society a determined mood in the form of an existent historical situation. But the imposition of climate, united and involved with these, is the most conspicuous. One morning we may find ourselves "in a revived mood". This is interpreted in terms of specific temperature and humidity conditions influencing us externally and inducing internally a revived mental condition. But the facts are quite different, for what we have here is not a mental state but the freshness of the external atmosphere. But the object that is understood in terms of the temperature and the humidity of the atmosphere has not the slightest similarity with the freshness itself. This freshness is a state; it appertains to the atmosphere but it is neither the atmosphere itself nor a property of the atmosphere. It is not that we have certain states imposed on us by the atmosphere; the fact that the atmosphere possesses a state of freshness is that we ourselves feel revived. We discover ourselves, that is, in the atmosphere. But the freshness of the atmosphere is not that of a mental state, as is shown best by the fact that the morning feeling of freshness is embodied and expressed directly in our mutual greetings. We comprehend ourselves in this freshness of the atmosphere, for what is fresh is not our own mental state but the atmosphere itself. So we do not need to go through the process of examining others' mental states to be able to greet each other with "Isn't it a lovely morning?".

Such climatic burdens or impositions occur very frequently in our life. The feeling of exhilaration on a clear, fine day, of gloom on a day in the rainy season, of vitality when the young green bursts, of gentleness when the spring rain falls, of freshness on a summer morning, of savageness on a day of violent wind and rain—we could run through all the words that *haiku* uses to denote the season and still not exhaust such climatic burdens. Our life is thus restricted by a climate possessed of a limitless range of states. So not only the past but also climate are imposed on us.

Our being has a free in addition to this imposed character. What has already occurred happens in advance; what suffers imposition is at the same time free; in this we see the historical nature of our being. But this historical nature is bound up with climatic nature, so that if the imposition contains climate in addition to the past, climatic limitation lends a certain character even to man's free activities. It goes without saying that clothes, food and the like, as being tools, assume a climatic character; but, even more essentially, if man is already suffering climatic limitation when he attains self-comprehension, then the character of climate cannot but become the character of this self-understanding. It is existentially evident to us that according to the changes in the climate in which man lives, he reveals all sorts of distinctive characteristics in the expressions of his existence.

So if climatic character becomes the character of man's self-understanding, it is this climatic character that we need to study and discover.

What, then, should be our approach to such a thing as climatic character?

The climatic limitation of human life is a problem of the whole climatic and historical structure; it is not a concrete or specific problem of man's way of life. In the latter case, the limitation only takes a distinctive form in a given country at a given age and this is a distinctiveness that we are not concerned to study. Man's way of life understood ontologically does not lead directly to a comprehension of the distinctive character of being; all it can do is to act as go-between for such comprehension.

This being so, for an understanding of life lived in this distinctive mould, we must apply ourselves to a direct comprehension of historical and climatic phenomena. But would the latter understood merely as objective lead to a full comprehension of climate in the sense in which I have used it above? We must accept that it is only through the interpretation of historical and climatic phenomena that we can show that these phenomena are the expression of man's conscious being, that climate is the organ of such self-objectivisation and self-discovery and that the climatic character is the character of subjective human existence. Thus as long as this enquiry is directed to the distinctiveness of distinctive being, it is an existential comprehension; but in so far as it treats this distinctive way of life as the condition of man's conscious being, it is ontological comprehension. Thus a grasp of the distinctive historical and climatic make-up of human being becomes an ontological existential comprehension.

In so far as climatic character is the subject of enquiry, it cannot help being so.

Our enquiry will, therefore, proceed from observations of distinctive climatic phenomena to the distinctive nature of human life. In that climate is essentially historical climate, climatic types are simultaneously historical types. I do not seek to avoid this aspect, for it is one that cannot and should not be avoided. But I shall attempt to treat this enquiry specifically from the aspect of climate, in part because it has been conspicuously neglected, a neglect which no doubt arises from the difficulty of handling the problem in a scholarly manner. Herder attempted a "Climatic Study of the Human Spirit" from an exegesis of "Living Nature" and the outcome was, in Kant's criticism, not so much the labour of the scholar as the product of the poet's imagination. This is a hazard that confronts anyone who dares to delve into the depths of the climatic problem. But I feel that it must be faced, for the problem of climatic characteristics should be put under the searchlight of radical research and be thoroughly clarified in all its aspects, if only that historical enquiry might acquire a proper concreteness.

(Drafted 1929; redrafted 1931; revised 1935.)

Chapter 2 Three Types

(1) *Monsoon*

The word "monsoon" is said to have come from the Arabian *mausim,* meaning "season". As a result of the peculiar relation between the continent of Asia and the Indian Ocean, during the six months of the summer, when the sun, after crossing the equator northwards, turns south and crosses it again, the monsoon blows landwards from the south-west; but in the winter season, the monsoon blows seawards from the north-east. In the warm ocean belt, during the summer monsoon a strong current with a very high humidity content blows towards the land and gives rise to a climate unique in the world. Broadly speaking, the whole of the coastal belt of east Asia, including Japan and China, can be described as belonging climatically to the monsoon zone.

The monsoon is a seasonal wind. But it is specifically a summer-season wind which blows landwards from the warm ocean zone. Hence, the climate of the monsoon area has as its distinctive characteristic a fusion of heat and humidity. I wish to treat the monsoon as a way of life—something that a hygrometer cannot do.

As every traveller in the Indian Ocean during the monsoon season has experienced, however hot be the cabins on the windward side of the ship the portholes cannot be opened. To open the portholes and give a free passage to this wind with its intense heat means nothing more or less than to render the cabins inhabitable. Humidity is at once far more intolerable and more difficult to resist than heat. There is no remedy for an atmosphere with such a high degree of humidity as to rust a piece of iron and discolour a gilded plate contained in a leather portmanteau in a cabin with its porthole closed tight—no remedy but to distribute through the steel-pipes a cool air that has been baked dry by the heat and then re-cooled by ice. To withstand humidity, one must summon up a two-fold energy, for resistance to humidity calls for measures taken against both cold and heat. Yet, the inhabitants of the monsoon zone are by nature weak in resistance to their climate in comparison with those of either cold or desert zones. Where twice the resistance is required, they barely summon up the single strength mustered elsewhere.

The reason for this can be understood from the nature of humidity itself. For while it is difficult both to tolerate and to take measures against, it does not arouse within man any sense of a struggle against nature. One reason is that in the eyes of those who live in the monsoon belt, humidity, or moisture, is nature's gift to man. In fact, the same monsoon that is intolerable on the ocean is nothing other than a vehicle for the sun to convey sea water to the land. As a result of this moisture, the hot countries directly underneath the summer sun are carpeted with lush vegetable life. At this season of heat and moisture, all manner of grasses and trees germinate, grow and mature. And when the land everywhere is shown to contain plant-life, animal life also flourishes. Thus, to these people, the world becomes a place teeming with plant and animal life; for them, nature is not death but life, for death stands, instead, by the side of man. Hence, the relation between man and his world is not that of resistance, but that of resignation. The drought of the desert produces a relation which is the exact opposite.

The second reason is that this humidity typifies the violence of nature. Humidity often combines with heat to assail man with violent deluges of rain of great force, savage storm winds, floods and droughts. This power is so vast that man is obliged to abandon all hope of resistance and is forced into mere passive resignation. The drought of the desert may hound man with the threat of death, but it does

not assail him with the very power that gives him new life. In the desert, man can resist the threat of death with the resources of his own life; there, resignation is resignation to death. But the violence of nature typified in the form of humidity holds a threat filled with power—a power capable of giving life. It is not the threat of a death that stands by the side of nature, for death stands by the side of man. This force that teems with life tries to push out death, the death that is latent within man. With his own resources man cannot hope to withstand this force that is the source of life; so, in this case, resignation is resignation to life. In this sense also, the monsoon zone is the exact opposite of the drought of the desert.

The distinctive character, then, of human nature in the monsoon zone can be understood as submissive and resignatory. It is the humidity that reveals this character.

However, humidity can be further divided into various characteristics. Japan, with its distinctive rainy season (the "plum rains") and its typhoons, is particularly humid; her first ancestors recognised this when they called it instinctively the "Land of Rich Reed Plains and Fresh Rice Ears". However, this humidity is revealed also in Japan in the form of heavy snow falls. It is Japan's fate to suffer very facile and drastic seasonal variations. Hence the distinctive monsoon characteristics, passivity and resignation, can be expected to undergo further specific limitation in the case of Japan. South China, also, with its huge rivers, such as the Yang-tse, as long as any in the world, is a humid area. Yet in the case of this wide continent, with deserts to the north and the humidity of the south typified, as it were, by the long course of the Yang-tse, the climate is quite different from Japan's; for this variety of humidity contains a fair degree of dryness. So we must seek for true and typical humidity in the monsoon zone proper, that is in the South Seas and in India.

The heat of the South Seas is nothing strange to the Japanese. Anyone who knows the height of Japan's summer would not discover there anything which he could say he had never experienced. Naturally, the varieties of the plant life are strange; yet, from a distance, the coconut groves of the south are very similar in colour and appearance to Japan's pine forests, nor are rubber plantations so very different from the deciduous forests familiar to the Japanese. On the whole, the natural features are not unlike those of the height of Japan's summer. Especially is this true when summer is regarded from the point of view of human livelihood; in this aspect, the monsoon area conforms closely to the Japanese experience.

Summer is one of the seasons; but a season is also a way of human livelihood. You do not define summer by mere statements of the height of the temperature or the sun's strength. On a mid-winter day with the temperature abnormally high, people may say "It's just like summer." But they are not, in spite of such statements, conscious of being in the middle of the summer. This is also the feeling, as they near the South Seas, of travellers who have left Japan in mid-winter. A day or so after the ship leaves Hong Kong, the ship's company suddenly appears in white tropical uniform. The sun glints and flashes on the deep-blue sea, the thermometer rises, and people begin to perspire. Everyone thinks that here at last is a place where the summer never ends. However, it is when the traveller reaches Singapore, drives in the evening into the city, sees the luxuriant grasses and trees and hears the noisy hum of the insects; or when he watches a street scene on a summer's night with cool-enjoying people coming and going between rows of open-air ice-stores and fruit shops that, for the first time, he gets a strong feel of "summer" and is once more astonished when he thinks back to the contrast with the "winter" in Japan which he has left behind so recently. The lush luxuriance of the plants and the trees, the buzz of the insects, the cool of the evening—these, for such a traveller, are more essentially the tokens or the organs of "summer" than the height of the temperature or the power of the sun. Yet, without this "feeling" that it is "summer", there is no summer. Man has a well-defined way of living in regard to summer; so what he finds in the South Seas is no other than this way of living he has already and for a long time associated with "summer".

Yet what the northern stranger regards as "summer" in the South Seas is not "summer" to the people who live there. For the former, the notion of "summer" and the humming of insects already of themselves prompt thoughts of the coming autumn; *shoji* removed for the summer months prompt thoughts in the Japanese mind of the coming winter wind. Summer, for the Japanese, is linked closely with visions of young leaves, of bamboo sprouts, of the shrike and of persimmons. But in the South Seas there is only a straightforward summer which contains no similar points of comparison with autumn, winter or spring. In other words, there is only a single type of season, which, in fact, is not summer. There is no fixed time for plants to change their leaves. In early March, the red leaves of the rubber trees fall at the same time as fresh green leaves and buds burst; at the end of June, similarly, the four seasons all merge into one. Fruits, too, except for a very few varieties, never fail throughout the year. A constant and determined climate of this nature is not the same as a seasonal summer, for "summer" as experienced by man cannot be other than a seasonal variation as experienced by him in his mental state or condition, a variation of the kind that the people of the South Seas do not experience.

This factor helps us to understand why the people of the South Seas have never made any appreciable cultural progress. The climate of the South Seas affords man a rich supply of food; hence his attitude is that all is well as long as he is blessed with nature's generosity. But, here, the relationship between man and nature contains no variety and, as a result, man is moulded to a passive and resignatory pattern. Not even the struggle against savage animals or deadly snakes can damage this mould. There is no incentive to stimulate the development of productive capacity. Hence, apart from the rare occasion when huge Buddhist pagodas were built in Java under the spur of Indian culture, the people of the South Seas have given birth to no cultural monuments. So they became easy prey for and ready lackeys of the Europeans after the Renaissance.

However, it was not so much the Europeans as the Chinese who were in effect able to tolerate the monotony of the climate of the South Seas. European intellect opened up the natural resources of the South Seas, but Chinese merchants gradually amassed the wealth of the area and still continue to do so. An understanding of the distinctive nature of the Chinese would no doubt lead to the realisation of how this could have happened.

But the monotony of the South Seas does not stem from insubstantiality. It is rather a monotony full of content, of power. The monotony, again, is not that of insubstantial feelings on the part of men who take interest in nothing; it is rather that of people who are ever agitated and burning with violent passions. There would indeed be startling advances if some way were found to break this mould and set this teeming power in motion.

Let me give a concrete example. The Botanical Gardens in Penang differ from those in Singapore in their location. They are built in a valley between low hills. But the impression of the broad-leaved trees ranged on these hills is exactly like that of Japan in mid-summer; there is the same feeling of strength and power as the pasanias and oaks of Japan give when they grow luxuriant in a mere two or three weeks during the hottest season of the year. However, in Penang, this process continues throughout the year. But when you leave the gardens and, going through the forest of broad palms, begin to climb the hills, there are grasses with white heads like the pampas, and small purple flowers like autumn grasses; between them, the fresh green or the reds of the attractive, tidy rubber trees. At the top of the hill, the atmosphere is even cooler and trees similar to the Japanese cypress or magnolia have the same sad shape of branch or trunk as those of any Japanese garden. No doubt, these trees do not change their aspect all the year round; but their effect, as contrasted with the "mid-summer" of that luxuriant growth at the foot of the hill, is exactly that of "spring" or "autumn". Hence, even though there are no alternations of season here, yet there are included within the "climate" various transformations corresponding exactly to the effects of such alternations. In other words, although there is no temporal variation, there is spatial variation. And, for such as can resign themselves passively to this, the monotony of the South Seas is one of season only; it is not a monotony of content.

The Indians are pastmasters at this art of resignation. Hence, in India, alongside an extreme lack of historical awareness, there stands an astonishingly rich insight into the many facets of human nature.

India is the most faithful example of the monsoon pattern. There, there are three seasons, a comparatively cool and dry period, a hot and dry period and a rainy season. In Calcutta, the mean temperature in January, the cool season, is 18.1°; in March, the hottest month, the average temperature is 28.4°; and the average temperature for the year, 24.8°, is almost the same as the average summer temperature in Kyushu, Japan's southernmost island. Even in a place like Lahore, where there are great variations of heat and cold, the average temperature over the whole year is 23.9°. This is indeed a land of eternal summer in the eyes of the northerner.

Although, seasonally, India is monotonous, in comparison with the South Seas there are far more variations of heat and cold. Hence while the fullness of being of the South Seas type does exist here, yet, at the same time, there is a loophole for an escape from the set pattern of being of the latter.

However, it is the rainy season, brought by the monsoon, that has done most to create the resignation of the Indian. Over two-thirds of India's 320 millions (a fifth of the world's population) are farmers and grow their crops thanks to the monsoon. In general, apart from the few areas where there is a plentiful supply of water, the food of the household and the fodder of the animals depend on the monsoon; whether it is late, whether it lasts its due time and brings its due amount of rain are matters of great moment. If the monsoon is abnormal, then a bad crop ensues, bad enough to bring calamity. Anciently, there were famines whenever such frequent bad years occurred. In recent times, with modern transport facilities, such famines can be forestalled. But there is no remedy for the hardships of India's farmers. Malnutrition reduces the power of the body's resistance and plagues rage. At the time of the "Spanish Influenza" in 1918–9, 115 million people are said to have come down with the disease and of them seven and a half million died. Even today there is no means of resistance against nature, no escape for India's people from such insecurity of life.

It is just this condition, the coexistence of heat and humidity, which appears to the full in nature's power in India. At one and the same time, it grants and menaces life. In the islands of the South Seas, there was no such peril and men could be completely resignatory; but in continental India, this resignatory relationship with nature must always contain some measure of anxiety and unrest. There is resignation; but, for all that, there is something that stirs and animates this resignation and turns it into a keen sensibility or impressibility. Here, the fullness of nature's power becomes the fullness of man's feeling.

The fullness of feeling of the Indian comes out of this attitude of resignation. The attitude of resignation is at the same time one of submission. The same nature that gives life presses down with a power so huge as to overwhelm all human resistance. The continental heat itself already tests the power of this resistance to the very limit; but when this heat is linked with humidity, man can no longer do anything but submit. Thus, nature withers and relaxes man's energies and slackens the tension of his will. The fullness of feeling of the Indian is not accompanied by any unifying will power.

The structure of the resignatory type, in the case of the Indian, is set in the mould of a lack of historical awareness, a fullness of feeling and a relaxation of will power. This is exemplified in both the historical and social aspects of India's cultural pattern.

The Indian, as revealed in these twin aspects of his culture, is said to share a common linguistic and racial origin with the Greek; in spite of this, the distinctive natures of the two are completely alien. For it is India herself that has given individual shape to her culture, has given direction to her strivings and has put spirit into her ideals. It was the north-west area of the Himalayas and the valleys of the great rivers that flow out of the Himalayas that give its distinctive nature to Indo-Aryan thought and completely shaped the Indian attitude to life. This was the Indian Holy Land—and so it remains today. When the Greek first emerged as such in the island-dotted seas of South Europe, he was already a man of a *polis*. Homer's epics picture both gods and men as *polis*-minded. But when the Indian emerged as such, he is seen to be one who from the first abhorred the restraints of *polis* livelihood and loved the independence afforded by agriculture and a communal village structure.

The art of commerce, which the Greek regarded as one of his great achievements, was here held in scorn. Originally the Indian also, as the invader and conqueror of India, was in one aspect a fighter. However, his fighting was not of a physical type; his victory was won not so much by his bodily power as by his surpassing mental power. India's warriors may have had a sword in one hand; but in the other they held a spade. The Vedas, poetry and philosophy, are the most outstanding example of the common livelihood of the agricultural community, the product of this culture of the warrior-poet or the warrior-philosopher. The warrior was at the same time the priest, worshipping the mysterious power of nature. Gradually, priest grew independent from warrior and became more influential than the latter. The Brahman who chanted psalms of praise at the sacrificial festival of the tribe presently became the repository of esoteric wisdom, the teacher of man and his spiritual guide.

Man as a social being in India, the product of the communal village structure is quite distinct from man as a social being in the desert. The essential point of difference is that the former lacks warlike attributes and volition. His spirits are never manifested as those of a single tribe or community only, for the forces of nature which bless all men equally do not evoke resistance in men and so cannot develop to become the war-god of a single tribe. This is not to say that in the Vedas of the earliest period we do not find a type of man fond of active fighting—the psalmist of the Rig Veda often prays to the spirits for victory in battle. However, the spirits of the Rig Veda are not the product of the straining of the will towards an escape from the distresses of life; they take on a mythical aspect moulded by the forces of benevolent nature. The majority of the hymns of praise are offered not to a "spirit" but to nature itself, or at least, to one aspect of nature; not to the spirit of the sun, for example, but to the sun itself; not to the spirit of water, but to the flowing stream, to the rain falling from the cloud. The Rig Veda itself is evidence of the development of this mythical essence from the personification of the forces of nature. Hence man's relationship with the spirits is one in which he asks for nature's benefits; it is very different from the relation of absolute submission in the desert. There is here nothing of the trembling adoration or the rock-firm faith of the psalms to Jehovah in the Old Testament. Nor does the prayer to the spirit spring, as in the desert, from the very depths of the soul. The psalmists of the *Vedas* are, instead, much more intimate with their gods; they do not seek their god's aid by bending to his will or vowing submission to him. Rather they anticipate the blessings of earthly riches in return for mere admiration of their god. "God, rich in grace, if you are the giver of all blessing, you would bless and create joy in those who praise your name". One who sings this hymn of praise does not dread his god; his faith is based on an attitude of the "embrace" of grace. Even if the gods who are the objects of a faith of this nature have become personified, they still do not become the 'man-gods' of the desert; the latter assume this attribute in virtue of their constant association with human personality. So, already in the earliest philosophic psalms of the Rig Veda, there appears the concept of these spirits as absolute in virtue of their life-giving power. This pantheistic thinking becomes *Brahman* and Ahtman in the Brāhmana and the Upanishads. These are un-personified creative principles. Philosophically, they become 'being' and 'non-being'. The theory of 'being' in Uddaraka, the peak of the *Upanishads,* is based on a refutation of a postulation of 'non-being' as the first principle.

The *Vedas,* as hymns of praise, have the least content of historical narrative of all the world's literature of their type. The Old Testament, of course, is eminently rich in historical narrative material, and the Homeric Epics cannot be said to be lacking in such content. But the *Vedas* have no such material. They do take up the accomplishments of gods and the doings of man, but these are not presented objectively; they are merely admired. These texts, as their name indicates, describe wisdom, in its relation to the gods and to men. And, in addition, this description is not conceptional but lyrical. The four types of *Veda,*—Rig, Atharva, Sāma and Yajur—are confined to matters of the practice of the ritual; they are wisdom imbued with religious sentiment. Hence, the style is marked by a fullness of feeling and there is a marked difference from the tone of the Old Testament historical narrative or the sculptural epics of Homer.

This "wisdom of admiration" gives us a simultaneous insight into the two aspects of the distinctive nature of the Indian. One is his power of imagination, the other is his reflective thinking. The two are intimately related in the *Vedas* and they are often similarly revealed in combination in later aspects of Indian culture. We, however, can understand the identical product both from the artistic and the philosophical aspects. The comprehension gained from such a distinction would also lead to the realisation why the two were both so readily unified and so difficult to isolate.

The power of conjecture in the *Vedas* indicates the high degree to which Indian sensibility was fined. All the forces of nature were deified in virtue of their mysterious character. Sun, moon, sky, storm, wind, fire, water, dawn, earth, anything similarly conspicuous and attractive, as well as the forest, the plain, animals and everything, provided only that it obliged a sense of some aspect of its power in resignatory humans, became a spirit or a demon. Hence the world of Brahman myth is probably more richly inhabited than that of the myths of any other culture. However, this vast concourse of deities is not systematised into a single family by blood connections, nor can the relationship of natural phenomena be taken as a basis for the unification of these deities within a single lineage. One might even argue that at the base of the various deities there is a uniform "one-ness" or "being" or "non-being"; but this kind of philosophical unification has no control on their form. So the world of deities becomes gradually more and more complex and even penetrates the fantasies of Buddhism.

However, it is the theory of transmigration that gives by far the most vivid picture of the Indian strength of imagination. All living beings, including man, share the same life spirit. All living things—whether in heaven or in hell, whether domestic or wild animal or even insect—are the site of our being; we, now human, may be reborn as cows in the next life, we may have been serpents in the last one. Hence, what is now a cow or a serpent may once have been or may on another occasion be re-created as man. Thus, all such living beings, although they may well differ in respect of their phenomenal form, must all be of the same basic nature. The differences in phenomenal shape are on more than a representation of the variant fortunes of the same 'being'. In this particular, it can truly be said that the imagination behind the theory of transmigration has succeeded in doing way completely with the temporal vicissitudes of human history—of 'being' as restricted to man, that is—and, at the same time, has really grasped the essence of the problem of the spatial vicissitudes of being. The snake crawling here was once man, or cow, or bird; it has experienced all manner of loves and hatreds. Such past experiences have determined its present manifestation as snake. In the same way, the present form of every living creature is conditioned by its past being. If this is the case, then the whole of "being" that made up the past at any given time forms the present also. The only difference is that the individual constituents have changed in form, for the present aspect of all living creatures comprises the entirety of "being" in the past. Rather than trace historical development, then, all one need do is to distinguish the various formal transformations of the present. Thus, according to this conjecture, in the bearing of the snake as it glides across a path, in the expression in the cow's eyes, one can read also its past being as man. Thus, in his daily life, man is intuitively surrounded by a true wealth of "being". Should he take a single step and crush an ant to death, he thereby becomes a significant partner in the destiny of the "being" of an entity that was once human.

This theory of transmigration is the common product of the swiftness of Indian receptivity and the fullness of feeling; together they have created a world of fantasy far more fantastic than a dream The literary arts of this culture fit the same pattern. The most significant example of this form is the Mahayana sutras. Here, sensuous images are exhibited one after another without limit and there are pictures of the exploits of the myriad *Bodhisattvas* complete to the last detail. This is a torrent of imagery fit to inundate man's powers of comprehension, for even though the picture is painted by the agency of words, it has an impelling fullness comparable only to that of a gigantic symphony. We are drawn into this dream world intoxicated by the fullness of the imagery. Yet this total effect is only realised through complete indifference both to any unifying rule of composition and to the statuesque distinctness of form of the individual. In other words, this art-form is the product of a fullness of feeling with no sense, generally speaking, of order. At this point, man completely transcends any sense of the unity of time and space.

There is an even more apposite and concrete example of this form in Indian art. Whether in sculpture, painting or architecture, alongside an astounding wealth of detail stands a great weakness in unity of composition. The reliefs of Amarāvatī and Sānchī, for example, are chiselled so replete with human bodies in different poses as almost to stupefy the onlooker. Hence, as a whole they lack clarity of structure. There is no vividness of form such as might strike the viewer profoundly in the very first moment he looks at the reliefs.

It is pleaded in their defence that India's artists group together the forms of all "being" with the motive of symbolising its one-ness. It is this that prompts the Indian sculptor to pile up image after image to the utmost possible degree, or the builder to place spire upon spire and to break up these spires into innumerable surfaces or resolve a wall surface into countless irregularities. This is his symbolisation of the universal precept "the one in the many". Yet although such unity might differ from the artistic unity of the humanistic West, it is clearly one kind of unifying principle. One cannot charge Indian art with a lack of unity simply on the grounds of the absence of the classical purity of the West. Because of the Indian concept of unity, in spite of this astonishing detail, each small part is given its place and retains its due balance. It is the mark of the Indian to fell conscious not only of man but of all being in general as one. His ready receptivity works to exclude all sense of resistance. But it is precisely for this reason that this unity born of receptivity differs from an active or dominating unity achieved by an effort of the will. Artistic unity is only effected through the latter. To say that there is a unity born of receptivity in India's art is quite different from saying that Indian art possesses a formal unity. For it is not necessary to go to the lengths of grouping together innumerable images to symbolise the sense of the unity of all being. An artist who understood the function of symbolism could achieve this by grouping only two images. Even though he does use grouped figures, the unity of the artistic product is achieved by a perfect control of detail and by distinctness of form. However the ideal which compels the Indian to sense the one-ness of all being is not in itself control of detail. In that India's sculptors and architects lack such control of detail, the whole becomes merely a clutter of such detail,–it is not a whole born of true unity. Thus, no amount of quibbling can conceal the fact that Indian art lacks both perspective and clarity. Its fascination lies in its ability to carry you off intoxicated by its wealth of detail and then, through this intoxication, to tempt you to its seductive esotericism. If it is approached in an attitude which demands above all distinctness of form in the whole, then Indian art only gives the impression of decadence. It is here that the fullness of untutored passion is revealed at its height.

It is precisely the same with Indian thought. The "thought of feeling" evident in the Vedas is not lost even in the golden age of

Indian philosophy. This "thought of feeling" gives Indian philosophy its distinctive character, for it relies not on inference but on intuition, on direct appreciation. It is founded not on the universal concept but on the type or the figurative concept. It is particularly notable that it acts not as historical awareness but as a physical or a phenomenological awareness of being.

One could point to a number of points of similarity between the natural philosophy of the early Greeks and that of the Upanishads. Both are feeling for the one-ness of creation; so both enquire into the state of things in the beginning. The answer to this kind of investigation is given in terms of 'water' or 'fire' or 'being' or 'non-being'. It may appear natural that Deussen should have found a fundamental identity between the thought of Parmenides and Plato and that of the Upanishads. However one thing should not be disregarded; the Greek philosophers were seeking the 'beginning' of the world that confronted them and attempted to grasp it by argumentation. Thus, once the atom was discovered as the world's essence, the principle of 'being' was also discovered on the same grounds. From the outset, this relation of confrontation with the world was objective; it was neither practical, nor hostile nor antagonistic. However, in the case of India's philosophers, no such relationship of confrontation existed, for what they sought was the beginning of the whole, a whole that included themselves. Hence, before it could be explained that in the beginning there was 'being' and that this 'being' became 'fire' and 'water' and 'the universe', this beginning is already *Atman* and *Brahman*. In other words, it is sentient beings; it is we ourselves. If we are the basis of the world, this does away with any confrontation between ourselves and the world; the appreciation of this fact is the departure point of Indian philosophy. Indian philosophers merely describe this appreciation; they use neither argumentation nor universal concept in explaining it.

Uddáraka thoroughly rationalised the *Atman* cosmological myth. According to him, in the beginning there was only "being" (equivalent to *sat* or τὸ ὄν). Since this is no other than *Atman,* the "I", it is also something intelligible to the "I". But one should not ask by what processes this "being" or "I" was attained. It is a truth that is seen and sensed so the concern of the philosopher is to interpret particular phenomena from his experience of this truth. This being so, how does this universal 'being' evolve the variety of particulars?

The first stage consists in being conscious of the fact that 'being' can be manifold; this consciousness then creates "fire". Here, what is meant by "fire" is neither a principle of mutation nor an indestructible element; it is "being in the form of fire". Something which burns or glitters, something red, and so on, anything in fact, which can be understood through the figure of expression of "fire" is what is meant here by "fire". Thus "being", in the first stage of particularisation is determined in the aspect of fire; but, here again, we cannot question the inevitability of such determination, for it exists only in the intuition of the philosopher living by a long tradition of sun worship.

Water, similarly, is "being in the form of water". Anything that flows, or is of bright colour, is indicated by this term "water". This second stage of particularisation is based on a familiar illustration from daily life. Perspiration—water, that is—is born of heat, i.e., fire; clouds or rain are produced by solar heat. In the third stage, when "being in the form of water" becomes conscious of the potentiality of particularisation, then food (the earth) is created. This likewise, is based on an example near at hand; food can only be produced by rain. So, in this light, Uddaraka's theory of the particularisation of "being" in fact expressed in figurative terms his personal experience in regard to the lifegiving force of nature.

Such ways of thought existed not only in the early period but even at the zenith of Indian philosophy. Buddhist philosophy rejected metaphysics based on *Atman* (the "I") as the basic principle and set out to discover the real state of present "being". This is the principle of viewing things as they are. Here the fundamental intuition, in virtue of its rejection of the metaphysics of the "I", is altruistic; it also takes due account of change, for all phenomena are mutable. In addition, the view of pain here, in that all is regarded as pain, clearly owes much to the distinctive "feeling of thought" we have discussed above. What is here understood by pain is not simply pain experienced, but the whole of pain, known intuitively from a particular instance of such pain. It is pain regarded from the aspect of an actual, universal law. Such intuition itself reveals the fullness of feeling of the Indian and the Indian character further stands out in the method of treatment of this intuition. For here one can substitute the universal concept for the example. It should not be forgotten that the various "laws" which comprise the "system of the law" are derived from such intuition. Thus, for example, the law of "death in old age" is not the "age" and the "death" of the individual; it is mutability intuited from a phenomenal example. Again, the "eye" is not the visual organ of the individual; it is the "whole of seeing" intuited from the particular example. This distinctive trait of Indian thought accompanies a poverty of argumentation and logical thinking. There is no attempt, for example, to subsume a variety of special characteristics under one universal concept and so reduce complexity to simplicity. The array of the various laws often degenerates into a complete absence of system; ultimately, then, we reach the point where only the "number" of laws fulfils the function of unification. The philosophy of Abhidharma is an apt example, for it was not easy even to arrange the various laws in a hierarchy of five degrees. Even where reasoning is at its most penetrating, the demonstration of externality to the self of the various laws is reiterated individually in the case of the five aggregates, the six spheres, the six elements and the various laws in the array of the Abhidharma philosophy. Worse than this: when we come to the parts of the canon other than the treatises, philosophical thought is quite devoid of logic and is expressed only in terms of intuition and imagery.

Indian logic is no exception; here, also, intuitive illustration lies at the core. Classified inference is regarded as based on intuition, for what is grasped by the latter is clarified by the former. The method of proof is not to lead to induction of the unknown from a premise already known; the process is to put up a conclusion at the very start and to proceed to prove it by reason and by analogy. Thus the three-part process of the new logic is exactly the reverse of the process of inference in formal logic. Further, the proposition corresponding to the major premise includes analogy. From the very first, analogy was accorded great weight in the development of Indian logic, and, even at the latter's most sublime heights, analogy was still counted as the one indispensable constituent. In this particular, then, it would be no exaggeration to argue that Indian logic is intuitive.

After brilliant developments of every nature, Indian philosophy finally degenerated into the esotericism of Buddhism and the symbolism of Hinduism. This can be viewed as the path that the "thought of feeling" would naturally follow. In spite of the Indian's strong imaginative disposition, he finally returned to his magic and superstition; in due course, Buddhism was driven beyond the frontiers and the philosophy of the Vedanta yielded place to ritual. It could well be argued that learning was stifled to death by fullness of feeling and laxity of will.

We have seen above how his imaginative powers and his thinking, as revealed both socially and historically, are characteristic of the Indian; his nature is receptive and resignatory and is exemplified as a fullness of feeling which is possessed of neither control nor historical sense. It was just such Indians who crossed the Himalayas and invaded

China and Japan. Yet in this case also, their invasion was not that of the overpowering warrior. It was true to type, receptive and resignatory to the utmost degree. For it was through the agency of Buddhism that the Indian attracted China and Japan, and drew to himself such things as were of the Indian pattern there. In contrast, India herself suffered the invasion of the desert in the form of the aggression of the overpowering warrior. It was not, as with India's invasion to the north, that elements of the desert type latent within the Indian were drawn out by this invasion; it was, instead, the overwhelming of the desert from the outside. As a result, the Indian became all the more receptive and resignatory. Under Mohammedan subjugation, Indian fullness of feeling was subject to unification of the desert type. This relationship is exemplified by the architecture of Muslim India. It is debatable whether this architectural style was in fact no more than an import of the Byzantine-descended mosque or whether this style was evolved by the adoption from Indian architecture of the pointed arch and the circular, turnip-shaped roof.

The European conquest followed that of the Mohammedan; but the Indian, until recently, was quite incapable of assuming his invaders' warlike and aggressive style. Instead, the long period of subjugation apparently turned his fullness of feeling into a cringing sentimentalism. Even such adventurous Indians as penetrated into the South Seas were, in the majority of cases, the very personification of docility and devotion; in their voice and in their manner, there is always that sentimentalism which gives the impression of faintheartedness. This is just the feeling given by Indian deck passengers travelling between the South Seas and Ceylon. The great majority of families do their cooking on deck, eat their food, play and sleep there. You can watch a mother fondling her child, little brothers or sisters dandling a baby, and there is in these episodes a fullness of sentimentalism such as to bring tears to the eyes of one who watches.

Glimpses of Ceylon give the same type of impression; simple country scenes as you travel—mothers fondling their babies in front of hovels set in the midst of the palm-groves, old men with white hair, children back from school dangling their satchels, whole families cooling themselves at night, sitting outdoors on stools under avenues of broad-leaved palms. Such glimpses are none of them, intrinsically, of the kind to stir the heart of the traveller; yet they do evoke intense feeling. And even in the case of night festivals, behind the gay bustle of the crowds or of the processions of a myriad lanterns, there hovers a plaintiveness which cannot be disguised. This fullness of feeling, instead of prompting our admiration as in the case of the India of the past, for example, simply pains our hearts in respect of the lack of will and the submission to oppression that we see here. Although we may well see no actual evidence of oppression, we feel that the Indian himself is in a way a symbol of suffering from oppression. In Shanghai or Hongkong, the power of the European is openly flaunted, yet the Chinese, far from appearing oppressed, is strong and energetic; one feels almost, in fact, that he was the victor. One cannot fail to notice the difference in the case of India. Because of his receptivity and resignation, or, to put it in another way, because of his lack of an aggressive and masterful nature, the Indian, in fact, prompts in us and draws out from us all our own aggressive and masterful characteristics. It is on such grounds that the visitor to India is made to wish impulsively that the Indian would take up his struggle for independence.

In this sense, although his cotton may well glut the world's markets, the Indian is receptive and resigned as ever;—witness his policy of non-resistance and passive obedience. The physical strength of the Indian labourer is said to be far less even than that of the Chinese, and no more than a quarter or a third of that of his Western counterpart; but neither this, nor his distinctive nature can be transformed overnight. For this distinctive nature has been moulded by climate, and change depends upon the conquest of climate. This latter can only be achieved by a climatic path—by the attainment, historically, of an awareness of climate. This done, man may surmount climate.

(Drafted 1928; revised 1929.)

(2) *Desert*

The word *sabaku* is usually used to mean 'desert'. I shall use it in this general sense, to convey the very distinctive climate of Arabia, Africa, Mongolia and so on. But a moment's reflection on the meaning of these terms, *sabaku* and desert, would no doubt reveal that they are intrinsically quite distinct. The use of the two words to describe the same climate, like the description of one and the same diagram as an equal-sided or an equal-angled triangle, arises from a difference in the point of apprehension. And the simple fact that such a difference in the angle of approach can exist in itself indicates the human element within the phenomenon we call *sabaku*.

The word *sabaku* came to Japan from China. There is no indigenous word in Japanese that corresponds to it, for *sunawara* is not identical with *sabaku* and, strictly speaking, the Japanese knew of no *sabaku*. Nowadays, the Chinese use their term *sabaku* in the sense of desert as a result of a reverse influence from Japan; but in its early usage, it was intended as a description, purely and simply, of the Gobi Desert. *Sa* is frequently used to signify 'flowing sand' and *baku* also indicates the sea of sand of the north. The Gobi is a vast sea of sand, lifted and, it seems, made to flow by savage winds. The Chinese, in that they lived outside this climatic zone, looked on it as a vast sea of sand—for this was its distinctive feature when viewed solely from outside.

But the *erēmia* of the Greeks, the *deserta* of the Romans and more recent terms, such as *Wüste, waste, wilderness,* indicate more than merely a sand-sea. They signify a place where no-one lives, where there is no life, a violent and hateful place. Those who employed such words in description of the desert viewed it not in terms of its climate but in terms of the absence of life there. In their eyes, the desert is not merely a sand-sea; it is a range of bare hills, their beetling crags exposed; or it is a great water-less river bed. Here, among such hills and valleys, is a world where nothing, neither plant nor animal, can live. Such a climate is desert; like a house with no-one living in it, it has no life, it is empty and barren. Yet when a climate is termed desert in this sense, the point of reference is not merely the external aspect. The word denotes a relation of unification between man and his world. For just as any house or town can become 'desert', so can a climate. Desert is a condition of mankind (the latter understood not merely as man but man in his dual role of individual and social) ; it is not an aspect of nature regarded in isolation from man.

When 'desert' came to be used as a geographical term, men believed they could treat it to describe a natural phenomenon totally divorced from man, an arid and barren area produced by lack of rain. Yet, in this usage too, the concept of "desert" was based directly on the model of such arid and barren areas in Arabia and Africa. Arid land with bare and towering crags is rock desert; a 'pebble-sea' is gravel desert and a 'sand-sea' is sand desert. So the word *sabaku* does not correspond to the general term 'desert', but only to the particularised 'sand desert'. *Sabaku,* the object of our enquiry here, is not what is intended by 'desert' in its basic sense and I use *sabaku* only because there is no other more appropriate term.

I propose to treat desert as "a state of man" and I assume in such treatment that man is both individual and social; and that man cannot exist except historically. In this sense, the desert understood as a "state of man" should not be treated in isolation from human social and historical factors. The desert is only exemplified in concrete form within the structure of the social and historical patterns of man. To understand the desert as a phenomenon of natural science, one must adopt the abstract position of rejecting all human elements from this concrete desert or from human society of a desert type. The desert as a natural phenomenon is precisely such an abstraction. Now abstraction is one of the most precious talents of man; by it he comes to know the composition of a concrete object. However, it would be wrong here to confuse the abstract and the concrete. I do not try to discover the influence of the desert in the abstract on the concrete life of man as a historical and social being; rather, my aim is to clarify the historical and social function of the desert—this being the basic sphere of such abstraction.

How, then, can we come to grips with this concrete desert? For the man of the desert himself, this could be called a problem of self-interpretation. But man is not always the one to understand himself best. His awakening to himself is usually realised through the agency of another. This being so, awareness of himself might perhaps be most forcefully effected in the case of the man of the desert if he were exposed to a long and steady downpour of rain. It is the man who is not of the desert who, as a tourist, can come near to an understanding of the concrete desert. For, while in the desert, he becomes aware of the historical and social aspects in which he is not of the desert. However, such understanding is only effected through an understanding of the desert. Even though his understanding is based on only short experience, in so far as it is a true and substantial understanding of the desert, the traveller can henceforth enter into the life of the desert—the desert regarded, that is, historically and socially.

The tourist lives a life of the desert only for a short term of his stay in the desert. He never becomes a man of the desert. His history in the desert is that of a man who does not belong to the desert. But just for that very reason he learns what the desert is, and understands the essential nature of the desert.

"Every soil is the brave man's country". This proverb shows man's broad and free attitude to life. It is not a proposition to do with climate; yet a statement of this sort only becomes possible in that, climatically, every soil is the brave man's country, and hence that a 'soil' in this climatic sense already incorporates the sense of the livelihood within the 'soil'. In other words, any soil can take the place of a man's home country only in the sense that he can "feel at home" in it. Hence, the proverb, in a significance connected with climate also, has a bearing on man's way of life. Let us imagine such a "brave man" crossing the Indian Ocean and reaching the town of Aden at the southernmost tip of Arabia. Above him towers a barren, dull-brown and tapering cliff. Here, there is none of the vitality or gentility, the nobility or freshness, the gradeur or intimacy that the "brave man" is entitled to expect from his "soil"; there is only an eerie, dismal and gloomy atmosphere. No soil in any climate, no cliff or hill crag will prompt a feeling quite so forbidding and gloomy. Here, the "brave man" is given a vivid insight into "otherness"—the otherness not merely of a physical rock but that of another man and the link between the latter and his world.

In abstract terms, this strange soil is without a single blade of grass or tree. A hill covered in grass and trees is mantled with vegetable life; thus its colouring and its aspect also exhibit a plant vitality. Here, there is a close relationship between such life or vitality and wind and rain. The latter have no direct concern with rock cliffs that have no plant life. So a hill without grass or trees exhibits no sign of vitality; wind and rain exert a physical influence only on the cliff surface. This is a skeleton of a mountain; a dead mountain. Its contours, its tapering rocks, its murky colour are all expressions of death. They give no feel of a vital force.

Such a grassless and treeless crag is, in concrete form, dark and forbidding. This darkness is not essentially a property of the physical nature of the crag, but is nothing other than man's way of life. Man lives in relation to nature and sees himself in nature. He discovers a desire to eat in a fruit that seems tasty; he finds his own feeling of ease in a green mountain; and, in the same way, he sees his own ugliness in an ugly mountain. In other words, he discovers here a man other than of a green mountain.

We may understand the distinctive nature of man's way of life here through an investigation of the features of dryness in climate. In Aden in spite of the scorching intensity of sunshine, only on four or five occasions in the year does rain fall. Even while the monsoon is blowing hard in the Indian Ocean, in Aden there are only thin wisps of cloud high in the sky, not enough even to blot out the sun. At other seasons, the sky is completely clear. Every evening without exception, the sun sets in a cloudless sky. But this type of clear sky is not that to prompt a refreshing sense of vitality; its deep blue seems parched and withered, nor does it become any lighter in tone as you look nearer to the horizon. The land that this sky covers, too, is thoroughly parched; there is nothing at all that shows the slightest trace of moisture. Apart from a pitiful little huddle of trees planted here and there in the town by man's hand, the world is only dryness. This dryness turns into the gloomy crag; it becomes the ugly desert, the huge Roman reservoir, the water-carrying camels, nomadism and the Koran. In a word, it becomes man in and of Arabia.

Dryness is the essential constituent of desert; all the latter's remaining features—the absence of inhabitants, of vitality, of gentleness and the like—are derivatives of this dryness.

The essential dryness of the desert is disclosed to the traveller by the dark and forbidding crag of Aden. Yet when this sort of thing has been said so many times of the desert, why should the traveller be made to feel such strangeness and wonder? It is because he has "lived" this dryness for the first time; and now, he understands dryness not as a determined atmospheric humidity, as indicated by thermometer or hygrometer, but as man's way of life.

When our traveller reaches the shores of the Red Sea, and especially the historically famous Mount Sinai or the Arabian desert, he may even be driven by this climate, with its smack of death itself, to re-read the Old Testament. For this was the dread sand-sea and rock-sea that the chosen people crossed. They faced a dead mountain, a range of rock skeletons. The dread revulsion of the desert is something that the sea, however angry, can never attain. For the sea, with its ever-moving waves, the life-like colour of the water and the vitality of the plants and fish that make their home in it, always gives a sense of living. Even the fear of the rare storm-wind cannot deprive us of our intimacy with the sea. But the deathly stillness, the dead colour and aspect of the desert, the lack of all life threaten our life to its very foundations. Even the dark of the desert night, blotting out the shape of everything on land, holds the repulsive touch of death. Only the stars seem to have real life, in complete contrast with this blackness of the desert. This is perhaps the most distinctive feature of the desert night. It is not only that, because of the extreme dryness of the atmosphere, the light of the stars flashes vividly; the ceaseless twinkling of innumerable stars, large and small, their light seeming almost to reflect each moment from one to another, makes you feel that you are listening to a great symphony. Here, in this blue sky, there is vitality and movement. Here, there is escape from the deathliness of the desert. It was over this kind of land that the chosen people wandered—land filled only with the threat of death, a land where for eight months in the year, the sun bakes down from a cloudless sky and where even the shade temperature rises to 45 degrees. The Sinai Peninsula, the Syrian and Mesopotamian deserts, are all of this nature. No relief is given by the Euphrates and the Tigris, for, until they flow into the plain of Babylon, they afford moisture to only a narrow strip of land near to their banks. Apart from these two rivers and those which rise in the mountains of Armenia, there is no other river in the whole of Arabia. Even the rare sharp shower soon disappears down the dry river beds and, after an hour or two, leaves no trace. If it were not for the few oases where the grass grows green, fed by the spring rains, or the rock-springs and human-dug wells, man in Arabia–man of the desert, that is–could never exist.

This life of dryness is "thirst"–a life spent in search of water. Nature seems only to hound man with the threat of death, and offers no water to such as merely wait for it. Man, in his struggle against nature's threats, must roam the desert in search of its jewels–grass and water-springs. For this reason, such oases and springs became the seed of quarrels between groups of men. In other words, to live man was obliged to fight another threat, that of his fellow men. Thus man of the desert came to possess the singular characteristics of the desert. In the first place, the relationship unifying man with his world in the desert is that of resistance and struggle. What man sees of himself in nature is death. And in virtue of this glimpse of death, he is made conscious of life. The whole of life and birth stand by the side of man; there is then no point in waiting and hoping that nature will grant them. Man feeds and breeds his livestock with the aid of oases and wells won from his struggle with nature. "Bear" and "Breed" are his war-cries in this fight of life with death.

Secondly, men come together to fight this war with nature. Man cannot exist on his own in the desert. So a particular characteristic of man in the desert is his propensity for co-operation. For it is in association that men win their oases and springs from nature. But in this struggle, man must further oppose his fellows; the loss of a single well to another tribe imperils the very existence of his own. In both these aspects, then, man of the desert resists and fights.

The struggle against nature takes the form of all-out cultural endeavours of the kind that will make man stand out in contrast to nature. Here, man cannot imagine the embrace of a nature deep in grace; nor, again, does he sense any control of nature as his slave. His aim is to make himself, or his labour, stand as the opponent of nature.

In the desert, man is from the outset an entity outside of and different from nature. A light on the far horizon in the desert night, with the whole land, as far as you can see, dark and revolting as death, gives an extraordinarily forceful reminder of the world of man, of life, of warmth and of affinity. Its impact is even greater than that of island lights seen on the horizon from the sea. Only the man of the desert can know the elation the ancient traveller across the desert must have felt when he saw the lights of the capital—only a day's march away from his night camp at the end of a long and hard journey from Judaea toward Heliopolis.

If it be true that something "of man" makes an impact on man only in that it is "of man", then it would be natural that what is not found in nature but of which only man is capable should become especially attractive in the desert. This is impressed on the traveller by, for example, his reaction to an Arabian town. Our traveller who visited Aden's harbour would no doubt find the Arabian town which faces the sea in the plain to the left of the port no less striking than Aden's crags themselves. The low-lying plain appears as a faint brown line on the horizon, so faint that you can scarcely believe it to be land. The only point of distinction between it and the sea is that of colour. In the centre of this brown line, a cluster of square buildings, seeming almost to bobble in the sea like white gulls, flashes in the sun. Though their white walls and their corners may appear small at this distance, they yet give a vivid reminder of man, of man's hand. Something that is "of man" is floating on the sea of lifeless nature. It seems almost a midday dream—for so vividly does man's town stand out against nature.

The origin of this great contrast can be explained in terms only of shape and colour; for the shapes and colours that go to make this town are not to be found in any aspect of the natural surroundings. A towering mountain is a completely haphazard and unsystematised shape which gives no sense of order or aim. And although the sea or a flat surface of sand do contain straight, transverse lines, they are monotonous and orderless. Only man's houses possess any geometrical method; only they, with their squares and rectangles, obtrude with any sense of completeness. This is man-made form; it is not something which was adopted from nature, nor has it been effected by man by the subjugation of natural form. It is a creation so clearly outside of nature that it stands in contrast with nature. The same can be said of the colour of these houses. The soil is a dull brown; the animals, such as the camel, are of the same dull colour as the land. Only the works of man are a clean white. Thus has man implanted concretely in the shape and the colour of his town his sense of struggle against nature.

The man of the desert's struggle against nature is crystallised in Arabian art. This sense of struggle is evinced in the distinctively man-made character of the sumptuous patterns of Arabian dress, or again in the outstandingly dreamy sense and the remoteness from nature of the simple yet powerful contours of the mosque.

This feature leads to an understanding also of the Pyramids. The ancient Egyptian was not truly of the desert; but, as their very siting indicates, the Pyramids were created in close relationship with the desert. The desert, seeming always about to encroach into and over-run the Nile valley, is an endless series of undulating sand-waves. These are unordered and unplanned. Within the Nile valley too, the Nile itself, dominating the whole plain, is a similar huge and lax undulation. The outlines of both water and fields are everywhere unordered and haphazard. Within this natural scene, totally undisciplined and unregulated, tower high and solid the Pyramids, only they regular and finished. Thus their pattern, not a part of the natural surroundings, gives a very forceful reminder of the power of man, power used by the ancient Egyptians to oppose the desert. Hence, the simplicity and the abstraction of the design of the Pyramids worked as a symbol of the power of man precisely in virtue of such simplicity and abstraction. From the very first, it was essential that the design be of a specific size to enable the Pyramids to stand in opposition to the desert. For the size as well as the shape made possible the exhibition of man's authority in opposition to the vague and vast sand-sea. Not even had they been several times the size of the Pyramids, could constructions of the tumulus style have expressed so vividly man's opposition to the desert.

Nor should we fail to notice the impression of the mysterious given by the Pyramids. It may be thought that, as works of art, they are too simple. Yet, granted their siting, the feeling of mystery that they give is in no way inferior to that of any other surpassing work of art. We are never shown the whole, only the part. We are always drawn by the part that is hidden. Nothing else gives this feeling with quite such force. Normally, granted, we are only shown one surface of an object; yet, in no other case, are we so inevitably attracted by the surfaces we do not see. This is especially true of works of art. Look at one surface of the Venus de Milo, for example, and you are not conscious that the others are concealed from you. But, all the more because of their lack of artistic substance, the Pyramids give this feel of the occult.

These two impressions lead us to the realisation of the inevitability of and the need for the Pyramids as representations of man of the desert. There may perhaps be a tendency to interpret this simplicity of form in terms of the need for some gigantic monument; but the very wish to build such a gigantic monument to stand in opposition to the desert is itself a representation of man of the desert.

However, the most striking example of desert man's struggle with the desert is his mode of production; in other words, desert nomadism. Man does not wait passively for nature's blessings; he makes active incursions into nature's domain and succeeds in snatching a meagre prey from her. This fight with nature leads directly to a fight with the other man; it is like two sides of a coin—on the reverse side the fight with nature, the fight with man on the obverse.

This factor of struggle was the constant feature of desert life from earliest antiquity until the Age of Islam. The various tribes inhabiting the Arabian peninsula, (called the tribe of Shem in Genesis, although this name covers the Arabians, the Hebrews, the Phoenicians and so on) share a common character and spirit, and speak very similar languages. The spiritual characteristics of this tribe of Shem, its thought, its religion, its polity and the like can all be interpreted in terms of desert living conditions. This life pattern is that of struggle.

First, the social structure. The tribe has been moulded in the pattern of a joint association from 1,000 B.C. until the Arabian Bedouin of today. This association is not merely "primitive", but something that is closely linked with the land of Arabia. Viewed from the formal aspect, the tribe is linked by the idea of blood-relationship through descent from a common ancestor. All adult males—those capable of bearing arms—live an associational life, the bond between them fused by strict regulations governing custom, morals, law and the like. But viewed from the internal aspect, this grouping is for purposes of defence. Every member of the blood family is faced by the same peril; it is the duty of each member of the association to help him to ward this off or to exact vengeance. Men thus come together on the basis of this joint duty, and, as the effect of such combination, the interests of the group—and thus of the individual—are safeguarded. The group's oasis or spring, the essential basis of its livelihood, is preserved even at the risk of war with a neighbour tribe.

The livelihood of the tribe reflects this struggle against both nature and man. Man could not exist only by individualism. Since it is this unity of the tribe that in the outset renders possible the being of the individual, loyalty to the whole and submission to the general will are indispensable. And at the same time the fate of the individual depends upon the action of the whole. The defeat of the tribe spells the death of the individual. So every member of the whole must exert every last ounce of his strength and valour. A never-failing straining of the will, with never a moment's thought of yielding, is essential if man in the desert is to stay alive; he can afford no meek docility. It is thus that man in the desert acquires his dual nature—his submissiveness and his aggressive spirit. These, the features that set him off from the rest of mankind, form one of the most vivid of the patterns of human character.

Man in the desert has thus acquired a unique socio-historical nature. But at this point, we should remember that the desert is not just a land-mass itself, it is a very real socio-historical factor. So even if, in a spatial sense, man can leave behind the desert as a piece of land, he cannot leave it and its effects in the sense of its being a socio-historical entity. To be able to leave it, he would need to develop socially and historically into a different person. Even in the event of such development, he does not reject but in fact retains his past. If desert man chose out a site blessed with a rich supply of water and turned farmer, this would merely be the development of the man of the desert; it would not be the development of, or transformation into, another person.

This process can be seen in the history of the people of Israel. To a people traditionally desert nomads, the land of Canaan seemed like paradise. So they fought a long and bitter war to gain this land, and, once established in it, they acquired the arts of farming. With the restraints of desert life removed, the population grew rapidly; branch tribes were founded, alliances cemented, and, at length, a kingdom came into being. This was no longer a society based on the compact unity of the inter-tribal association of the desert. Yet it was not until the people of Israel reached the land of Canaan that their religion was crystallised and that they began to create all manner of religious arts. And the undeniable fact is that it is the qualities of man of the desert that show up most outstandingly in such artistic creations. Attempts were made to realise their one-time tribal social organisation in the form of that of the unified race. The deity that had represented the unity of the tribe became the symbol of the unity of the race. However, complete submission to this deity and war with other races (and so with other deities) remained, as hitherto, the feature of the people of Israel. The climate of Israel encouraged all manner of social and cultural development, yet this was the development not of the new farmer but of the old man of the desert.

Nor should one forget how, even in dispersal, the Jews continued to retain their desert character. The dispersal began several hundred years B. C.. Yet it was in such dispersal that the Jews taught Europe to form closely-knit religious associations. Such an association of the desert type, in an aspect more forceful than yet revealed in man's history, is now demanding, in the name of religion, a supra-national realisation. But the Jews themselves, who were the leaders in the formation of such religious groups are excluded from this association, and continue, instead, to preserve to the last their own national character. Persecution by the Europeans has forced this on them—but it was the Jews themselves, who invited such persecution. Thus, even though the desert, as a socio-historical reality, is set in the middle of Europe's green pastures, and even though it has passed through Europe's historical phases of feudalism, bourgeoisie and the like, it necessarily preserved itself intact. Not only this; as it once attracted them, the submissive and aggressive pattern of desert life continues to attract modern man today.

But this is not the only case where the desert has spread beyond itself. When the people of Israel turned farmer, there were those who sneered at this as being the final degradation of the man of the desert. For the latter's pride is to roam free and unfettered as a wild beast. He prefers valour to easiness of life. In his eyes the meanness of the indigenous man who is content to hide himself within the walls and serve his lord is the most despicable on earth. This spirit was even more evident at the beginning of Islam. So the man of the desert, with his submissive, aggressive and particularly his wilful character once more fell on agricultural land and subjugated the people who had opened it up. This was Islam's world conquest.

One can discern the hold that man of the desert has on the world by surveying the religions alive in the world today. If we exclude such as had their origin in India, they are all—Christianity, Judaism, and Mohammedanism—the products of the desert. It would be fair to say that, as a practical religion, Mohammedanism has the greatest power today. But from the historical aspect, the history of that small tribe of Israel—even at its zenith it never had more than a territory of a mere hundred miles in length and from thirty to sixty in breadth—has forced Europeans to believe for over two thousand years that the history of Israel, in fact, reads almost like that of the whole human species. It would be hard to find elsewhere such lasting power. The man of the desert acted as teacher of man: because, in virtue of his own distinctive character, he had a deeper insight into man than the rest of his fellows.

The achievement of man of the desert reached its sublimest point when he gave man a god in his own image. The only achievement to match this was perhaps that of the Indian—his gift of the absolute to man.

However, in the first stage this god in man's image was simply the god of the tribe. His origin lay in the belief that a god-like force permeating the tribe made possible its existence and its growth. So there were as many gods as tribes. Jahve was at first only one of this number. Such gods lived and ate with man, fought at his side and received the catch of the hunt or the spoils of war. At great festivals man offered victims to his god and then divided the flesh among his fellows in the tribe. This joint banquet—the food the flesh of the victims—was a powerful factor in maintaining and renewing peaceful cooperation in the livelihood of the tribe. In this ritual there is no element of awareness of the relation as such between the individual and the tribe; but in that, through this communion of the flesh of the sacrifice, there arises a faith in the blood-relationship of man with god, this is, in fact, the practical gathering of the whole as a unity. Morality is revealed at a very early stage in the form of the god's dictates. God vouchsafes to man rich land and posterity, the extermination of every foe, and the exclusion of all illness—in other words, freedom from care and a thriving material life. But, in return, he lays on man an obligation to observe his moral and sanitary injunctions. In other words, life in the desert is only made possible by recognition of the whole tribe, this recognition being exemplified in the form of the dictates of the god. So, for the man of the desert, such recognition means escape from the distresses of life (*Not-wenden*);

for man of the desert, the tribal god is inevitable and essential (*notwendig*).

It is a general feature of primitive religion and one not limited only to the desert that the one-ness of the tribe is sensed as and through a god. In the desert, however, even when tribal life had developed beyond the primitive stage, faith in the tribal god, because it was essential to life in the desert, was more intense than elsewhere. The singularity of the desert forced the tribal god into a personal man-like mould. God was the realisation of the oneness of man in his struggle against nature, so there are here no marks of the deification of the forces of nature. Nature must take her place subordinate to god. The gods of Greece, in contrast, were deifications either of nature external to man, such as Zeus or Poseidon, or of aspects of his internal nature, such as Aphrodite or Apollo; such gods as symbolised the oneness of the tribe had already been debased to the status of 'hero' when the myths came into being. And the gods of the mysteries, such as Mythras or Osiris, were deifications of nature's forces and not expressions of the oneness of man. In lands where such gods were given being, nature is in every case a conspicuous donor of blessings. But in the desert, nature is death. Life is to be found only at the side of man. So it was essential that god be in the image of man.

But how did Jahve, from being only one of such tribal gods, become the supreme god in man's image? In this respect, tradition talks of the work of Moses; Jahve, working through Moses, made the people of Israel the greatest of the tribes. Yet if, as the scholars aver, "Israel" was the name not of a single tribe but for a tribal alliance, (in other words, if Israel was a military and religious alliance with Jahve as protecting war-god) then at the time of the origin of this tradition Jahve had already accomplished the unification of the tribes. This is not a rare occurrence. Those gods of whom man is made most forcibly conscious assimilate within themselves other tribes' gods of the same character. In this way Jahve, from being the god of a single tribe, became the god of man of the desert. His form became much more distinctly crystallised as a result of the distresses of the people and the burning faith of a long line of prophets. Yet this crystallised form, through the agency of one man in the Hellenistic world, transcended the desert and penetrated far and wide. So Jahve became mankind's god. It mattered not that he was the product of the desert; it made no difference how a man made his living or what were the methods of production and their relation to the natural world in a particular country. Europe stopped to ask no such questions but was content to believe that here was the god she had been seeking. God here, of course, through Christ, became the god of love; but this notwithstanding, it was only man of the desert—and he because he was of the desert—who could have discovered god in man's image.

It was Mohammed who showed most forcefully of all to what extent this god in man's image is of the desert. Setting himself against the idolatry of the day in Arabia, he crusaded for a return to faith in "the God of Abraham". But his revolution was not made from the standpoint of opposition to the tribal livelihood of his time, for, just as in old times, man could not resist the menaces of nature without the backing of the solidarity of the tribe; submission to tribal unity, just as before, was the essential basis of living in the desert. Mohammed revivified this god in man's image as unifying symbol of the whole tribe. He put great stress on submission to the tribe as being submission *(islam)* to god. Like Moses before him, he brought about submission *(islam)* to god within his own tribe and with this power behind him began the fight against other tribes. He fought persecution not as an individual but, as in antiquity, as an inter-tribal struggle. He won his wars and brought about the unification of the Arab nation through submission to god. Thus it was as a single tribe that the whole Arab people reached the goal of unity in Islam (submission). Thereafter, the submissive, aggressive Arab reached swiftly beyond the desert and subjugated the greater part of the civilised world. It would not be unfair to say that in Mohammedanism the "God of Abraham" was revealed as possessed of the two characteristics born of the desert—submission and aggression.

I have attempted to indicate the structure of man of the desert. The desert is characterised by dryness and it is this dryness that first sets up the relationship of opposition and struggle between man and the world and, second, fosters the individual's absolute submission to the whole. This can probably be made a stage more distinct by a contrast with Egypt in antiquity.

Egypt's climate is a curious blend of the dry and the humid. Rainfall is very slight—Cairo's rainfall is said to be one-seventieth of Japan's—so that the atmosphere is extremely dry. It is only natural that, surrounded by the desert, this narrow river valley—the plain near the estuary is no more than twenty miles across, and the widest point in the upper reaches does not exceed five miles—should be conditioned in pattern by the dryness of the vast desert. Yet this valley has a rich supply of moisture from the river flowing right from the hinterland of continental Africa. All manner of cereals and vegetables flourish in the fields; between them, prosper South-Sea type trees. The green of this fertile plain is like that of the humid Far East and the moist South Seas. It was no boast on the part of the ancients when they called this land the most fertile in the world.

Thus, though there is neither rain nor humidity, Egypt's climate is moist. It is a "dry" humidity. So the character of the ancient Egyptians was formed on the basis of a distinctive combination of both opposition to the desert and, as well, attachment to the Nile. In their opposition to the desert, these people no doubt conformed to the pattern set by desert man; however attachment to the Nile made them the very opposite of the latter. To the Egyptians the Nile is as the unity of the tribe in the desert. Even in these modern days, when the Nile's flow is regulated by man-made dams in the upper reaches, a drop of a mere five feet below the normal flow brings fearful devastation to the delta area. How much more then, when the river was permitted to take its own course, did the livelihood of the ancient Egyptians depend solely on the blessings of the Nile. So the culture of ancient Egypt developed round the core of a passive concern for the waters of the Nile; there was no aggressive address to nature— the Egyptian merely watched passively. Thus, while he can be aggressive and wilful in regard to what is beyond himself, in his own everyday experience the Egyptian is contemplative and emotional. Here, there is an intellectual development and an aesthetic sense not evident in the desert. Men believed in immortality with a rich tenderness and prayed for an eternity of love. This was exemplified in their knowledge of embalming, and in the mummy. In the exquisite statue of Prince Rheotep and Princess Nophret, man and wife, we see a combination of the gentlest wish for an eternity of love and a keenly graphic picture of a life-like couple and their love. This most distinctive feature of the Egyptian, the combination of gentleness of feeling with clarity of perception, can only be understood from this attachment of the heart to the bounteous Nile. It is precisely these characteristics that are lacking in the desert.

What Spengler meant by "nature" was experience saturated with human content. Hence, there could be no general or universal nature, only a particular Greek or Arab or German nature. He attempts to place the problem of space at the root of culture, but he is not able to treat space as man's way of living, as living climate. Thus he tries to explain the Faustian spirit of western Europe or the incantatory spirit of Arabia together by talking about world space as an abstraction in isolation from its concrete particularisation. Hence he fails to notice the fundamental differences between Arab and German nature.

Edward Meyer pointed in a much more concrete way to the characteristics of desert man. First, a dryness in his thinking and a penetration of observation and of judgement in practical matters. But this is calculating and interested, allowing no intellectual vision or sentimental fancy; for contemplation and passivity spell ruin in the desert. Secondly, firmness of will. When called on, the man of the desert rushes in recklessly with bestial savagery and no fear of the consequences. His success as a merchant is accountable to these qualities. Thirdly, the intensity of his moral inclinations. Attachment to the whole is the altar on which the individual is sacrificed and the source of his sense of shame. Hence, man of the desert has again and again been revealed in the person of the bold idealist, the prophet, Mohammed, and the Islamic hero. Yet these idealists, too, had both of the first two characteristics in their make-up. Fourthly, Meyer points to an emptiness of emotional life. There is a lack of gentleness and warmth of heart. So there is little creative trend of the imaginative power. Literature is shrivelled; art and philosophy—where, too, imagination is called for—were stillborn.

These characteristics can be summed up as wilful realism, the opposite of the visionary and the emotional. The desert itself gives an understanding of man in the desert. But this is not simply the nature of those who inhabit the desert, for they do not live isolated from the desert nor does the desert exist as a natural phenomenon independent of man. Desert man is fundamentally of the desert; the desert is a socio-historical phenomenon. And the nature or the character of a people is, after all, its historically and climatically distinctive way of life.

(Drafted 1928; revised 1929.)

(3) *Meadow*

a)

The Japanese word *makiba* is a translation of *Wiese* or *meadow*. But it is quite inappropriate. *Maki* is an enclosure for livestock; but *Wiese* is for the cultivation of grass fodder for livestock, and is, further, general grassland. But again the Japanese word for grassland (*sogen*) does not have the intimate relation with livestock fodder that Wiese has. In fact, Japan has no term corresponding to the latter. So translators of the late nineteenth century used the word *makiba* (with its livestock connotation) in the sense of *sogen* (grassland). Here I shall follow this now normal usage.

The fact that there is no term in Japanese corresponding to the word *Wiese* indicates that there is nothing in Japan to correspond to *Wiese*. Japan's *sogen* has no utility value—it is, in fact, discarded land. However, *Wiese*, while in fact grassland (*sogen*), has a similar function to *hatake* in that while *hatake* produces food for human consumption, livestock fodder is grown on *Wiese*. *Wiese* is not tilled where *hatake* is; yet the two are of the same nature in that both provide a nutritional crop. There are both natural and artificial *Wiese,* but they can always be turned into *hatake*. The artificial *Wiese* corresponds to one phase in the normal rotation of crops of the *hatake*; it is the exact equivalent of the wheat *hatake* in the year when it is sown to clover. So, to imagine a *Wiese*, one should think of a very extensive *hatake* just before the clover flowers. Of course, the grass of the *Wiese* differs from the clover-*hatake* in that it is not of a single variety. Apart from grasses of the clover type like the Chinese milk vetch, there is a considerable admixture of varieties of what are called in Japan "winter grasses". There may perhaps be as many as ten or twenty varieties; but these are all soft grasses like our "winter grass" and are not uncomfortable to the naked body. It would be no exaggeration to liken the green *Wiese* to a carpet, as in fact the Germans do in their term *Wiesenteppich*. Thus, the grass of the *Wiese* is clearly very different from Japan's grass.

I shall use the term pasture for this *grüne Wiese* and I wish to use it as a basis for the elucidation of the particularity of Europe's climate. It may at first sight appear inappropriate and perhaps even a little sentimental to pin the distinctiveness of Europe—the cradle of modern industry— on its green pastures. However, the cold facts of industry too, its iron, its coal or its machines, are the extension of this green pasture. In other words, the factory also is pastural. I propose here to consider in general terms to what extent the European and his culture are pastural.

It was Professor Otsuki of the Department of Agriculture of Kyoto University who by a chance remark set me on to this study. We had gone from the monsoon area through the desert and had entered the Mediterranean. We passed to the south of Crete and then, on the morning when we came in sight of the southern tip of Italy, the first thing to strike us was Europe's green. This was a green of a very special colour such as we had not seen either in India or in Egypt. It was late March, just at the close of the "Sicilian Spring". The corn and the grass seemed almost to be growing as we watched. But what surprised us most was that even half-way up the mountains (a continuation of the Magna Graecia chain) where the limestone crags jutted out, there grew this grass, green as on the plains. Even on the top of these crags, sheep can find grass between the rocks. I had never known such mountains before. Then Professor Otsuki said something quite astonishing. "There's no weed-grass in Europe, you know". This was something very near to a revelation to me; and it was at the point that I began to grasp what it is that distinguishes Europe's climate.

b)

If you set out from Japan and travel with the sun from east to west, you experience first the intense humidity of the monsoon zone then the absolute opposite of humidity, the dryness of the desert Then, when you reach Europe, you find a climate neither humid nor dry but something of a combination of the two. In terms of figures, whereas Arabia's rainfall is only a fraction of Japan's, Europe's varies between a seventh and a third of Japan's. In terms of my own impressions, this is a synthesis of humidity with dryness.

This dialectic is, of course, not that of historical development; it is, first and foremost, based on traveller's experience. However, humidity becomes human experience in the monsoon zone and expresses itself in a certain cultural pattern. In the same way, drought is part of the experience of man of the desert and is exemplified in the cultural pattern of the desert. Whether or not such cultural patterns exert any reciprocal influence historically, they are always interacting agents within the structure of world culture in the matter of the contrast between cultures based on climatic patterns. So the dialectic of the synthesis of humidity and dryness could be termed such in the matter of the structural connection of world culture. Again, the facts of cultural history can be interpreted in this light. For example, when Paul's Christianity, with its Jewish content, was growing up in the European world, although there was a rejection of the dryness of Judaism, the product of the desert, the moral passion of the prophets came to be more and more an integral part. And at the same time, in that the dampness that is not found in the desert became the feature of Christianity in Europe, the gentleness of the religion of love grew very strong. It would not be untrue to say that the worship of the Virgin Mary is much more of monsoon than of desert pattern. This characteristic, the synthesis of the humid and the dry, is not exhaustively explicable in terms only of historical development. It could be claimed that the latter is based, in the case of Europe, on the personality of the European; but when we call this personality European, we are already speaking in terms of climate.

So the climate of Europe can be defined as a synthesis of the humid and the dry. But this humidity is not, as in the monsoon area, brought by the heat of the sun. Summer is the dry season—although there is none of the baking drought of the desert—and winter is the wet season. And in spite of considerable variations between north and south, this pattern holds good for the whole of Europe. The difference between north and south (within the framework of this basic identity) is exemplified by the weakness or the strength of the sun, or by variations in the amount of clear or cloudy weather. In the matter of rainfall, in spite of a general overall similarity, the summer of the southern Europe, where sunshine is more richly supplied, is characterized by a higher intensity of dryness and the winter by a higher degree of humidity. While the southern winter is often marked by clear skies, the northern winter is almost continuously cloudy. Europe's climate, then, can be separated on such counts into north and south. And since, in the matter of cultural history, Europe was, in the very first, the south, we too will begin our discussion of European climate from the south.

c)

Southern Europe is dominated by the Mediterranean. The Mediterranean, as its name indicates, is not a case of sea enclosing continent or of land being encircled by ocean. It is the only sea on the earth that is surrounded with three continents. So not only is the Mediterranean a superb stage for the enactment of cultural history; it is also, as a sea, quite distinct and separate from an ocean. First, in that there is no influence from the Ocean, the water temperature is very high; even at its deepest parts, it is said to reach 12 or 13 degrees. The tidal ebb and flow also is very slight; at seasons of high tides, such as the new and full moon, the general variation is only about a foot and it barely reaches a yard at Venice where the tidal variation is the greatest. The cause of all these phenomena is the extreme narrowness of the Straits of Gibralter which are not wide enough to permit a free flow; so the Ocean is held back at this western inlet. Further, little river or rain water empties into the Mediterranean—not enough in fact to counteract the evaporation of the sea water. This latter is one of the main factors contributing to the uniqueness of this sea.

In my direct experience of the Mediterranean, in neither March, May nor December was it what I would normally imagine as sea. This, you may think, is merely the vague impression of an individual; nevertheless, it is one that I did feel extremely strongly. I travelled from Marseilles by way of Nice and Monaco and then went on to stay in Genoa in the middle of December and early January. Even in mid-winter, this Riviera Coast was so warm as to remind me of the south; in places bamboo groves, apparently transplanted from the East, were to be seen, together with a variety of other tropical plants. You came out in perspiration when you walked at mid-day even without an overcoat. But this south coast of the Mediterranean is quite alien in tone to Japan's southern coastlines. The pure white sand of the beach in the vicinity of Nice and Monaco, skirted by a concreted and buttressed road, had not one piece of dirt or rubbish on it; someone might just have swept it. There was a novel sensation about this sand stretching far into the distance for, while in the south of Japan the beaches are pretty enough even in winter, my feeling is that they are washed and covered much more by the tide. It is the same with the sea wind. Here, in the Mediterranean, the wind is much drier than would be expected for an off-sea breeze. Presumably the tang of the beach is not as strong in winter as in summer, yet I felt that the scent of the sea is stronger in Japan than here. This sensation that here was a sea that gave no feel of the sea was so strange that I once walked about scrutinizing this clear, transparent water. The sea-bed close in to the shore or the rocks on this sea-bed bore no sign of plant life or of shell-fish varieties. It should not be thought for a moment that such things do not grow at all here, but I must admit that I never saw any. So, it struck me that the sea-water here seems to be coloured by plain chemical colour, which strikes us with the difference as compared with the colour of sea-water of our southern part which has a more complex colour tone. Japan's women divers plunge into the winter sea to peel off laver from the rocks and to collect turbo shells. In Japan, if you are fond of winter-laver or a turbo shell roast, you can even have a strong and unmistakable tang of the beach at your city dinner table on a mid-winter night. But there is none of this feel about the Mediterranean; it is a sea with little life in it, a sea where marine plants do not flourish. I do not remember on a single occasion seeing boats putting out to fish in this sea. The sea itself was always calm and still and yet I never caught sight of even a single sail. There was an air of desolation about this scene. To someone who knew the brave sight of winter fishing for tuna and bonito in Japan's southern seas, this was truly a sea of the dead.

My impressions from a day or two's meandering round the Italian coastline were exactly the same. I looked down over the sea from the cliff road to Amalfi and saw no trace of either marine plants, shell-fish or fishing boats. It was no different when I went round Sicily; no fishing boats, plants or shell-fish either on the east, the south, or the north coasts. In the seas around Japan you can tell at a glance whether a rock has been brought to the sea recently or whether it has been steeped in the water over a long period. But on this Sicilian coast rocks washed by the sea were as smooth and free from marine plants as if they had just been placed there. This does not happen even with Japan's lakes.

With this in mind, I began to see just what this Mediterranean was! It was sea, I supposed; but it was quite different from the sea where the warm Black Current flows north to Japan from the equator.

The latter has every manner of living thing from microbe to whale. But in the Mediterranean there are few living things, so few that it might well be called a sea of the dead. Japan's Black Current is infinitely fertile, but the Mediterranean is a lean sea. It was no mere chance that the Mediterranean gave me this impression of desolation; you might call it a sea-desert, for the harvest of the sea here is indeed meagre. So it is natural in the extreme that there has been no development of either a fishing industry or of fish eating habits. The fish dishes of Marseilles or Venice leave a strong impression on the traveller—but he should not forget that along the whole of this coastline these two towns, and they only, are the exceptions. This is because there are only two rivers worth the name—the Rhone at Marseilles and the Po near Venice—that empty into the Mediterranean from the European continent; thus only in the area of these two estuaries does the sea produce anything near a copious catch of fish. This explains why the Greeks, who were so intimate with the sea, yet existed in the main on animal flesh. In comparison, Japan's seas are affected by the fertile Black Current and are also fed constantly by innumerable rivers, so that it is not unjust that Japan's islands should be without a par in the world as fishing bases. The number of Japan's fishing boats and of her fishermen rivals that of the whole of the rest of the world put together; it is only natural, then, that Japan should have regarded animal flesh as not indispensable.

So we can say this. From ancient times, the Mediterranean has served as a route of communication; this has been its sole gift to Europe. The saying, "Mountains separate; the sea links" is indeed true, if in no other case, of the Mediterranean. By contrast, the seas about Japan were never a means of communication but were first and foremost the fields from which the Japanese obtained his food. Until modern times, they served not so much as a means of communication as a barrier to separate an island kingdom from a continent. Hence, it would be improper to try to apply the Japanese concept of the sea directly to the Mediterranean, for as a historical stage it does not have the function that a Japanese would expect of the sea. Already by the time of the *Odyssey* there was a highly accurate knowledge of the navigation of the Mediterranean, so convenient and simple was it to sail on. There are numerous islands, numerous harbours; no mist impairs vision; for seven months running the weather is good and direction and position can easily be plotted by the stars. Winds are predictable and maintain a regular pattern, even to the point of the alternation between off-shore and off-sea winds. So, to a sea-faring people, the Mediterranean is something of a children's playground. For the Greek, who planted settlements in all the coastal areas (with a climate on the Greek style) from Italy westwards to southern France and Spain, the Mediterranean was truly a means of communication. And the bitter dispute between Rome and Carthage would not have arisen had this sea served a different purpose.

This function of the Mediterranean is closely related to its parched and barren nature. If the Mediterranean had been humid like the Pacific, offering nutriment to all manner of living things, the inhabitants of its coasts would not have been so prone to and fond of movement. And because it was parched, it could not provide food for marine life and in addition shrivelled up the islands and the shores that it washed. The small islands in the Bay of Marseilles, just like the crag of Aden, are bare rocks with not a single tree. The coastal mountains are not very different; for while, on the Riviera coast, tropical plants flourish in the low-lying areas, the mountains which rise sheer behind these plains are shrivelled crags the like of which is not seen in Japan. The coastal mountain ranges in Italy are far more bare and bald than those of the hinterland and invariably end in rocks and crags beyond a regular height of about four hundred metres. Thus the coastal areas were fit only for development as trading ports; or, to put it another way, the only benefit that these coastal areas gained from the sea was that they looked out on this route of communication. This sea, with the vast Sahara to its south and again the Arabian desert to the east, has not enough evaporation to moisten the atmosphere and as the humidity of the Atlantic is hindered by the various mountain ranges—the Pyrrhenees, the Alps and the Atlas—during the hot season (when sea-water evaporation is at its highest) the humidity is counteracted most by the dry atmosphere of the desert. Thus, in this area, the hot season is also the dry season; the Mediterranean fails to provide rain for land baked by the summer sun.

d)

Drought in the summer;—here we come face to face with "meadow". There are no weed-grasses in Europe; this indicates, in other words, that summer is the dry season. Weed-grasses have no nutritional value for livestock but they grow and spread very rapidly and can overrun and choke pasture grass. These weed-grasses are what the Japanese know as "summer grasses" and, as the term implies, the essential conditions for their growth are heat and humidity. In May they begin to sprout at roadsides, on embankments, in waste land and in dry river beds; then in July, nourished by June's "plum rains", they grow to a height of several feet almost as you watch. These grasses are tough and obstinate, tough enough even to flourish on the parade ground! Whether the ground be cultivated, or even part of a residential area, if neglected for a year or two, this sort of weed-grass takes possession and turns the place into a complete jungle. But it is this combination of heat with moisture—the "plum rains" and the subsequent sunshine—that gives this weed-grass such tremendous vigour. However, Europe's dry summer fails to provide this moisture just when weed-grasses need it, so that they cannot sprout.

It is quite contrary to expectation, but neverthless true, that summer grasses do not flourish in a place like Italy, in spite of its abundance of sunshine. Maremmen is an appropriate example. Maremmen, strictly, is the coastal area between Pisa and Rome, but it is used in a broader sense to include the whole coastline from north of Pisa down to the vicinity of Naples. It includes the well-known Campagna plain, in the Roman suburbs and the Paludian and Pontine marshes which skirt the sea south-east of Rome. In summer these areas were notorious for malaria already in Roman times; people withdrew to the hills choosing not to live in such low-lying districts. If it were Japan, such discarded land would soon have become irrevocably overgrown. Yet in Italy neither these marshes nor the low hills above them have been taken over by weed-grasses. Of course it would be rash to claim that there are none at all; here and there, they do grow, slender and weak; but they are neither strong enough to choke the tender winter-grasses, nor sufficiently luxurious to rob this area of its pastoral aspect—for this whole district is an excellent sheep pasture from October until April or May. In other words, even discarded land that never has a hand laid to it is "meadow".

Thus, since the dry summer does not allow summer grasses to grow or thrive, the grass is primarily of the winter variety—pasturage. This tender winter-grass covers Europe's fields in summer, the Mediterranean being the only exception. At the end of May, both in the south of France and in Italy the grass begins to yellow and turns the hills and fields into a browny yellow rather than a green. Of course, in the hills there is the silvery green of the olives or of other small deciduous trees; but Italy does not have many trees and it is the yellow of the grass that sets the tone for the hills and fields. These pastures, yellow as a corn-field, only begin to regain their green colour with the start of the rainy season in October. Then, as winter advances, the meadows revert to their beautiful emerald colour.

At this point we come upon the function of the winter moisture of the Mediterranean vis-a-vis the drought of the summer. Europe's

October rains are the equivalent of Japan's "plum rains"; although they do not bring as much moisture—there is only the occasional shower as in the case of Japan's spring rains—the winter grass varieties, not requiring heat, begin to sprout once they obtain such gentle autumn rain. Then this tender winter grass begins to grow not only in the fields but—and here is the surprise—between rocks on the mountain sides. To quote two examples that will be familiar to the traveller, on the hill of Notre Dame in Marseilles, or Mount Tivoli in Rome, where six or seven parts of the hill surface is taken up by hard limestone, the nicks between these rocks are covered with this tender short grass. It would be hard to find any crag in Japan with such a gentle carpet, for, even if anything were to grow between the rocks, it would be something like a miscanthus variety or a baby pine or an azalea, but never such winter grass. So the green of Europe that surprised me when I first saw it from the ship was this winter grass standing out against its frame of white rocks. This winter grass grows even on high crags and of course it flourishes on rolling foothills. It is not rare in the case of a hill that is not too high for the whole surface to be mantled in corn or winter grass. The gentle mountains in the south of Sicily, for as far as the eye could see, were bathed to their very summit in green grass; the only trees here were fruit-bearing, and they only in the depths of the valleys.

The dry summer and the moist winter thus combine to drive out weed-grasses and turn the whole land into meadow. This fact conditions the character of the farmer's labours. "Grass pulling"—the extermination of weeds—is the core of the farmer's work in Japan; if it is once neglected, cultivated land turns almost at once into jungle. This "grass pulling", especially in the case of the rice paddy, assumes the significance of a ceaseless struggle against tough and unyielding weed-grasses at the most trying season of the year (and the season which has determined the pattern of Japanese domestic architecture),

the hot Dog Days of midsummer when these weeds are at their most rampant. Neglect in this battle is practically the equivalent of the abandonment of farming. But in Europe there is no call for such a battle with weed-grasses; once land is cleared and cultivated it submits meekly to man for all time and does not seize the chance to revert to waste land. So in southern Europe the farmer's labours lack this feeling of struggle with nature; he ploughs, sets his wheat or his grass and simply waits for them to mature. He is not obliged to build up his seed rows into ridges so that they escape the effects of moisture; he merely scatters his corn over a whole field, as if it were pasture. Even if other grasses grow among his corn, they are weaker than it and are choked by it. Like meadows, such cornfields demand little labour. If you look from even a short distance, it is hard to distinguish between cornfield and pasture, though the two become best distinguished in late April or in May. Then as the corn begins to yellow, the hay is cut and dried; and after that, the corn harvest. There is no defensive spirit to the labours of the European farmer; he ploughs, sows and harvests all the time on the offensive.

There is an explicit contrast here between the farmer's summer and winter work, which is the basis of the distinction of labour expended on staple foods. In the Mediterranean area summer tasks are concerned with olive or vine culture, not with staple crops. In addition, fruit culture is long-term, with little of the sense of urgency that runs through the tasks of rice cultivation. As the dry summer season begins, the vines bud and start to spread their tendrils; all the farmer need do is to wait until the blossom flowers and the fruit matures. Italy's grape crop is said almost to match the wheat harvest in quantity but, by comparison, the labour is nowhere near as intense. Indeed, in this case the struggle is not so much against weed-grasses as against insect pests. However, the dryness of the summer does not offer ideal conditions for insects. In fact, to one who knows an insect-ridden country like Japan, there is even a certain loneliness to the Mediterranean coastline, so few insects are there. So the vineyard fight against insect pests is less of a struggle even than that against malarial mosquitoes in the low-lying areas. In districts where the low-lying plains are left simply to pasture, the whole of the hillsides which rise from these plains is made into rich cultivable land. The slopes of Mount Alban or Mount Tivoli near Rome, for example, turn a beautiful green after the moistening of the gentle winter rain; then, with the dry summer they become luxuriant olive groves and vineyards. So those who farm these hillsides live a peaceful and balmy life, spending their days in idle gossip as they drink their own rich wine. Italians are said to be lazy idlers; one of the reasons for this is the lightness of their farming tasks. And agricultural labours are light because here nature is subservient.

e)

In such summer dryness and winter moisture—the absence, that is, of the combination of heat and humidity—we find subservience of nature. But weather phenomena indicate this submissiveness of nature far more bluntly than grass! Humidity, when linked with heat, is exemplified in all manner of natural violence, such as torrential rainstorms, floods and hurricane-strength gales. But humidity in isolation from heat rarely engenders such savageries.

The yearly rainfall in the Mediterranean is only about a third or a quarter of that of Japan. It is of a different nature also in that winter is the rainy season and in that the rain falls gently, merely moistening and not washing away the soil. If, as happens in Japan, a vast quantity of moisture, built up over the warm ocean, were to turn into violent rainstorms pelting down on the soil, Italy's hill-slope cultivation could never have acquired its peaceful tenor. On the Sicilian hillsides the grass would be washed away, roots and all, after only a few such storms, and would be shrivelled and killed by the subsequent heat; similarly, the soil of vineyards and olive groves would be washed away. So the main reason for the fertility of this land is the almost complete absence of storm rains.

The river embankments are forceful evidence of the rarity of torrential rain. In places where there is danger of rapid rises in river water level after heavy rains, the banks are built high and firm. But I hardly ever saw any such in Italy. The Po, Italy's biggest river, does of course have embankments in its lower reaches; but considering that it rises in a lake in the Alps and is well-known for the abundance of its flow, these seemed almost negligible. The thawing of the Alpine snows often causes a rapid and appreciable rise in the water level, yet, nonetheless, the banks are thought satisfactory as they are. When I visited the Po valley in March, there had been a rare succession of rainy days and the floods in the Po catchment area were the topic of all the headlines. Yet when I went to see for myself, though the river was up to the top of the banks, there was a tranquillity and a leisureliness about the flow which made it difficult to believe even that there was any movement. Where the banks were lower than usual, the river was quietly overrunning them and flowing over the fields just as the water of a mountain-spring welling forth over the brim of its surrounding rocks without making any noise. The low-lying arable or pasture areas were standing in this water and looked just like huge pools of rain water. Yes, these were flood waters; and the flooded land, because of difficulties of drainage, would no doubt be completely ruined. But suddenly it all struck me as a great joke and I could not help bursting into laughter. To a Japanese, floods mean a rampaging and turbid torrent crashing through dykes and surging over the fields. There was no such savageness about these Italian floods, yet they were the effect of long-continued rains the like of which had not been known for several decades. One can judge from this just how calm and tranquil must be the Po's flow in the normal year.

Generally speaking, the wind is only slight. I was told that very occasionally, and especially in winter, the Sirocco comes blowing off the Sahara desert; but I never met it once in the hundred days I was in the area. The shape of the trees tells how gentle the wind is, for they are as precise and regular as botanical specimens. I remember especially the conical pines and pencil-straight cypresses. There were any number of regular and symmetrical trees not only in the parks but in the fields and even on the hilltops. Only the lower branches had been cut away; the rest of the tree had not had a hand laid on it, yet the branches spread regularly in each direction from a perfectly vertical trunk. To Japanese eyes, accustomed to pines with undulating trunks and uneven branches, this precision of form appeared artificial. The tall, slender cypresses, straight as a die, were just the same; it was as if a nurseryman had laboriously trained them so that the boughs should branch from the trunk with fine precision and delicacy. There was a spontaneous and natural regularity to all manner of other trees, just like the effect of symmetric precision that a Japanese gardener will give to a cypress. There is to be found in the way of the spreading branches a regularity such as described in a book of botany. This struck me as not only artificial but also, in view of the regularity of shape, as rational and logical. But when I stopped to consider, I realised that this feeling of artificiality arose from my being conditioned by the irregularity of tree shapes in my own surroundings; for, in Japan, such precision is the product only of man's hand. In Europe, however, the natural and the regular go hand in hand; irregularity of form is unnatural. Whereas in Japan the artificial and the rational go together, in Europe it is the natural that goes with the rational. The symmetrical trees that form the background of an Italian Renaissance painting, while natural to Italy, give a sense of rationality; but the winding pines of a Momoyama period screen, though natural to Japan, have a unity of irregularity.

These art forms model living nature, yet they picture a different nature. This difference stems from the force of the wind, for where there are few storm winds, the shape of the trees is logical. In other words, where nature shows no violence, she is manifested in logical and rational forms.

There is a link between the lenience and the rationality of nature, for where she is lenient man readily discovers order in nature. And if in his approaches to nature he takes due account of such order, nature herself becomes even more lenient, and man, in turn, is led further to search for the order in nature. Thus, Europe's natural science was clearly the true product of Europe's "meadow climate".

f)

We have interpreted the peculiarity of "meadow climate" in terms of dry summer. Because moisture does not combine with heat, nature is bright, lenient and logical. Italy is a representative example of such a nature, particularly Italy proper, by which I mean Italy south of the Appenines. Now "Italy proper", in this sense, was the cradle of modern Europe, the cot in which the child with all the European attributes lay. Because in Italy nature was subjugated and because here attractive meadows made their appearance, presently the plain forests of northern Europe were cut down, opened up and converted to pasture land. To state this in another way, the Latin language, born here, spread to every corner of Europe; Roman law, codified here, became the legal system of every European country.

But this cradle of Europe only became such in virtue of its Greek education. This is evident from the fact that it was only Italy proper that received Greek settlements. The Greeks, with uncanny intuition, only built towns on sites which had a Greek character. And it was precisely because the Greeks had planted such settlements that they eventually attracted the Romans and made them grow to maturity. In other words, because the Greeks had hunted the

Mediterranean coastline in search of places with a Greek climate, this climate itself came to play a particularly conspicuous and significant role in the life of such places. So we must trace the source of "meadow climate" further back—to Greece. What are, then, the characteristics of the Greek climate?

The Greek peninsula, and particularly the Aegean coastline—the stage of ancient civilization, is protected to the west by a mountain screen and isolated from the open sea to the south by the slim island of Crete. So its dryness is much more intense than Italy's (its rainfall is only one half of the latter's), and, again, its atmosphere is much clearer than Italy's. Even on a winter's day—and winter is here the season of rain—there is a blueness to the clear, bright sky quite peculiar to Greece. It is because there is no humidity in the atmosphere that these special epithets, "Greek noon" and "Greece without shadow", can be and are applied. This clarity of atmosphere makes Greece's mountains, her soil and even her clouds vivid and clear-cut. The azure sea, the green fields are clear and limpid, with nothing about them that is turbid or impure. Even Italy's well-known clarity does not touch the standard set by Greece.

Let me quote a few figures for Attica to indicate how clear and dry is Greece's climate. There, 179 days in the year are fine and another 157 are semi-fine; this leaves a mere twenty-nine that are dismal and gloomy. This count is by Greek standards; if the word 'fine' is given its usual significance, there are three hundred such fine days in the year, and only a mere ten when the clouds fail to clear for the whole day. This is about the greatest contrast imaginable with northern Europe where the weather is gloomy for the whole of the winter half of the year. It is no mere chance that Hades as pictured in the *Odyssey* bears a strong resemblance to the English winter. If a Greek had sailed beyond the Straits of Gibraltar and had been cast up on the English coast, he would truly have felt that

England's gloom made it the land of the dead. In Greece such dismal days all come in the winter rainy season. Yet, according to Prof. Yoshishige Abe's diary for his visit to Greece at the time of this rainy season, out of a fortnight's stay there were seven days of fine weather, three that were semi-fine, three dull and one on which rain fell. Even so, on one of the dull days, he could write of the morning sea, "Its tint is really bright"; on another he noted that the moon came out after dinner, and on the third there was merely an afternoon shower after which it turned clear; but it drizzled all through that night and into the next day. On two of the three rainy days there was a fairly strong wind, perhaps the Sirocco. Now this is the dullest season in Greece; so we can safely conclude that even Greece's most dismal season is brighter than the brightest part of Japan's year.

Fine day succeeds fine day; but this does not lead to a lack of variety. Seasonal changes are comparatively well defined, the beautiful spring from March until June and the hot summer lasting from mid-June until mid-September when, in the normal year, there is not a single drop of rain. Except when the Sirocco blows dust from the desert, the hot sun, shining down from a blue sky, bakes up the land and plants and springs are parched. But the beautiful autumn begins with the refreshing showers of September and plants start to turn green again. From November to March, the rainy season, south winds bring moisture and grass and corn grow green. Even though one calls it winter, this is far more mild than Japan's winter and, in fact, more akin to her spring. Between beautifully clear and mild Indian summer weather, there are a few cold and sodden days. But when the Sirocco blows, winter seems to have disappeared.

Such is Greece's climate. Because of the unremitting dryness of the summer, Greece is unsuited to trees. Though it shrivels, grass revives again, but this is not the case with mountain trees. So the hills are nearly all crag and rock. Apart from the hillside olive groves, there are few trees other than the occasional pine, willow or cypress. So the most predominant of Greece's crops is its winter grass. It is calculated that, even today, about one third of the cultivable land is given over to pasture; in ancient times three-quarters was, or could only be, utilised for meadow. The area of arable land is nowhere as extensive as pasture, for wheat, vines, olives and figs combined total only about a half of the pasture land. The area sown to wheat is especially small, the yield insufficient to meet domestic demand. So the farmer's main labours are divided between stock raising on the pastures and fruit growing. His work is never menaced by climatic vagaries, for the rotation of the seasons is regular and once the rain arrives he can grow his crops. He may never have either bumper crops or lean year, but at least his livelihood is comparatively secure.

Climate, then, ordains that the meadow be the means of producing necessities of life. Since nature's bounties are not over-generous, there is no call for a submissive and resignatory wait for them. Nor, at the same time, are nature's threats to man of the kind to spur ceaseless and all-out opposition. If nature is once brought under man's control, a modicum of tending ensures her permanent docility. It is this docility of nature that above all directed production to the pastures.

This docility of nature has even made acceptance of nature pastoral. Man can sport himself naked on the soft grass, he can give himself over to nature's promptings with no demurs and still suffer no real peril—in fact he gains only enjoyment thence. So Greek clothing contains little element of the need to protect the body from nature. It is in this sense that his naked sports or his nude statues should be interpreted. Thus acceptance of nature was pastoral. The Greek's creative work too was pastoral so that not only the necessities of life but cultural products too were set in a pastoral mould.

So meadow culture, having its origin in Greece, came into being, adapted specifically to Greece's climate. The feature of the latter, as I have said, is clarity, the absence of gloom, the feeling of unchanging noon. Hence everything is open and candid. Where there is a high humidity content in the atmosphere, even on a clear day there is a shadowy gloom and it is hard to escape a feeling of oppressiveness; but there is none of this about Greece's brightness. So there was no strong inclination to seek for the unseen, the occult, or the illogical within nature. Of course, there is "night" too in Greece, so that it would be wrong to pass over the sombre aspect of, for example, the worship of Demeter. But it is the spirit of the sunshine, the brightness of Greece, that has had the most significant influence on world history, for it was by assimilation with his climate that the Greek rose to the heights. In the very beginning, sensing the menace of the unseen or the illogical, he would pray only for blessings from nature. But when the sunshine of Greece's nature became a part of him, he began to learn how to "observe" from this unconcealing nature. In Greece, nature reveals everything and hides nothing, and such a relationship—where not a thing is veiled—is the most intimate of all. Man sees eye to eye with and thus becomes one with nature. Thus was the Greek made capable of finding the logical order within nature and of becoming one with her. When Greece's climate became manifest in the distinctive essence of the Greek spirit, then did Greek culture also put forth its first buds.

Of course I am not attempting to argue that an objective climate, in isolation from human existence, could exert such an influence on a national spirit devoid of any climatic element. Climate works subjectively as a factor within human existence, and, just as the various factors in human life sometimes work powerfully and at other times assume a minor role, so this climatic factor also at times acts forcefully and on other occasions is reduced in power. But while a culture is still at the formative stage such climatic influences are at their most active. Hence, to say that in modern Greece there is no longer any of the atmosphere of the old Greek "never-ending noon" is tantamount to saying that there is none of the old-style Greek culture in the Greece we know today. This is not a refutation of the contention that Greece's culture has, to a remarkable extent, a climatic nature; the problem is rather by what processes and at what stage these climatic influences were at play. So we must turn our eyes to the period when the Greek first became Greek.

g)

Nature is docile, bright and rational in Greece. But these characteristics were not evinced from the very first in the form of the "endless noon" and the logicality of Greece. It was when man became conscious of his control over this docile nature and began to formulate his activities as nature's controller that such climatic attributes became a part of the Greek spirit. An awakening of this kind is often spoken of in terms of man's 'emancipation' from the restraints of nature. But in cases where nature wielded the tyrant's whip, man's emancipation was not achieved by such means; it was because nature was docile and hence already in primaeval times there was technical control over nature that this realisation came; for nature was made man's lackey. Nature was humanised because the Greek felt at one with her. This was the starting point of Greek humanism. The Greek thus founded a standpoint with man standing at the center exercising its control over nature. Emancipation from nature became emancipation from the struggle with nature, the intensification of human activity. Man's struggle with man, the friction between men that is born of the desire for power or competition, the increase of creative power and so rational development through a thirst for knowledge and artistic production through the urge to create—these are all characteristics of the new situation brought about by this new standpoint in relation to nature.

The race speaking the Greek tongue is said to have come to Greece as early as about 2,000 B.C.; but it was not this race's culture that dominated the Aegean until about 1,300 or 1,200 B.C.. The move to Greece was a longterm tribal transfer, not the mass migration of a whole people. These tribes gradually filtered into the peninsula as nomads but, once there, they learnt the arts of farming or fruit husbandry. The tribal life of such herdsmen-farmers lasted for some centuries after the arrival in Greece and (according to Murray and Harrison) the religion of these tribes was a type of totemism. We think of the Greeks, however, not as a tribal people, but as the race that formulated the *polis* and excelled in the arts. So the race that spoke Greek merely came to Greece; the Greek race, in its full and proper sense, did not yet exist. This formation occurred in the age of the great migrations, lasting for several centuries from the fourteenth century B.C..

This people led a bucolic life amidst a docile nature. What, then, was it that induced them to cross the sea to the coast of Asia Minor? One reason advanced is that this unfertile land was unable to support an increase in population. Such an increase there may well have been—there is no proof either way—but if there were, it would, in the first place, have led to fights between tribe and tribe. For, although the land is not fertile, it is yet not so wild that one must devote one's entire effort to the fight with nature. So in the event of want, one must turn to plundering the pasture and the stock of a neighbour tribe. When these fights between men, starting from such seeds, became gradually more intense, then, for the first time, there arose conditions such as might drive a race of farmers and herdsmen to the sea. When the sea became the scene of their livelihood, then only did this people of primitive farmer-herdsmen begin to change. The effect of these changed conditions was that the Aegean became the kernel of Greece.

It seems that these sea-borne migrations began when, as a result of some tense situation, the men rowed off in small boats, leaving behind women, children and livestock. Or it may have been that reckless young bloods first set out over the sea in a spirit of sheer adventure. Whichever be the case, this was certainly no mass migration but, instead, a fragmentary roving of some small groups detaching themselves from the tribal community. Such fragmentary groups, pressed by want, spontaneously turned pirate, obliged, to get food, to set upon some island or coastline. Their struggle while on land, though derived from insufficiency of food, yet had not been that of the man who must plunder to live. But, once they had taken to the sea, plundering became the mainstay of their livelihood and the whole of their life became a fight. The approach to the sea and the conversion to soldiering were one and the same. But since these fragmentary groups could not, alone, attempt effective warfare, they leagued with other such groups to form a union large enough to attack fertile islands or coasts. If they won, they took control of the land and possession of the womenfolk and the livestock. Blood was thus intermingled, rites and festivals of different tribes were confounded, old traditions were violated and lapsed. At this point there began a new way of life completely alien to the traditions of the farmer-herdsman. Formerly, old family conventions had been maintained by such women as wept bitterly at the sacrifice of a bull-which was regarded almost as a blood brother—over its death. Now, new lands had been won by strength and they had women who spoke a strange language, who practised different rites and whose husbands or fathers they had just murdered. Day and night they were haunted by the fear that these women might take vengeance against their new husbands, the slayers of their own menfolk. Before, they had lived by tending their flocks themselves; now, they tasted for the first time the fruits of the labours of others, the indigenous people made to toil for them after submission to their superior strength. Now, their new task was to preserve themselves by cultivating this strength; this was best achieved by the manufacture of arms and training in the military arts. Thus began the life of the warrior.

The Greek *polis* came into being with this conversion of farmer-herdsman to warrior. To young bloods with different ancestry and different rites who had come together for purposes of warfare or plunder, joint defence against a common enemy was more vital than any difference of blood or ritual. When they took possession of a territory, they chose out a strong-point, enclosed it with stone fortifications and made provision against the common enemy. In this process, men cast aside the traditions they had brought with them and built a new, common livelihood. Thus began the new life and the new rituals of the *polis*; and thus it was on the shores of Asia Minor, to which these immigrants had moved, that the first *polis* came into being and developed.

With the building of the *polis* one may begin to use the word 'Greece'. If this be correct, Greece began with the conversion of the farmer-herdsman to a warrior life once he had taken to the sea. Divorced from the land and cut off from their earlier livelihood, these one-time farmer-herdsmen gained freedom from the restraints of nature. This freedom has a twofold significance. In the first place, man cast off his old means of securing his resources by tending nature and sailed the seas instead; and, further, man began to go beyond the point where he produced only the bare necessities of life—food, shelter and clothing—and moved in the direction of a higher standard of living. It may well have been insufficency of such necessities that drove him to the sea in the first place, but this only explains the origin of the movement and does not help in understanding its eventual and real significance. Even if it was to obtain food that men turned to adventure, to conquest and to power, these presently came to have a much greater significance for them than the food itself and eventually dictated their whole livelihood. When they fought to get flocks it was not that these flocks had such an exalted value that they were worth the risk of one's life. It was rather the very activity of gambling one's life and the mastery and power over one's conquests that were held in high regard in and for themselves. This is not what might be called a realistic and calculating attitude to life: it may well have been a desperate undertaking, but it never lost its sportive element. The wars in the Iliad show the warlike spirit of the Greek as the most striking element in his make-up.

A warlike spirit, as Nietsche observed, endorses war. In Hesiod's poems, there are two contesting goddesses on this earth. The one, cruel and brutal, counsels evil wars and battles; no man is fond of her, yet he is obliged by necessity to listen to her. The other is far more gentle and kind to man; she was put by Zeus at the root of this world and by her grace even the unskilful apply themselves to their work. The poor, seeing those with wealth, urge themselves, "Should I not, in the same way, plant my seeds and build up my house?" and neighbour vies with neighbour to gain good fortune. The potter hates or envies his fellow as does the carpenter or singer. Now Hesiod admired as good and noble the goddess who engenders such rivalry and envy. Cruel and merciless war should be thrust aside by man as mere destruction; but rivalry and contest spur men on to loftier creations. Creation through competition was the spirit that such rivalry fostered. So jealousy, as long as it inspired in the individual an effort at bettering himself, was not an evil in the eyes of the Greeks. It was the same with ambition. There was loathing of being merely another's equal, and ceaseless straining to come out on top of him. So the more grand or noble a man, the stronger his ambition and the greater his endeavours. This was why Greece produced so many men of genius and why, again, there was general loathing of despotism. When they exiled Hermodorus, the Ephesians said: "There should on no account be one who is supreme among us. Sould such a one appear, he must depart from us". In other words, a permanent position of superiority is the denial of the spirit of competition, and invites the drying-up of the well-spring of *polis* livelihood. However brilliant his talents, one man should not be allowed sole power. So once one man of genius showed up, a second such was sought for without delay, for once the spirit of competition were destroyed, all that remained would be the viciousness of malice and delight in destruction.

So Greek creativity sprang from this spirit of rivalry. But the latter was dependent on emancipation from the life of the farmer and the employment of a slave class to produce necessities. The full citizen of Greece—the small number of warriors who lived by competition—was able to exist only because of the subservience first of nature and again of the man who tended her. Where nature is severe, a nomad people never submits to the domination of an alien race; thus, although the Israelites lived through a long period of servitude, they never, to the very last, became servile. But the slave class in Greece was treated on a par with the livestock—as living tools. The bullock, in fact, is the slave only of the poor man! The slave's life comprised work, punishment and food, little different, in principle, from that of the field-tilling bullock. With a slave system as thorough-going as this, the small number of people who comprised the *polis* were freed from the labours of the herdsman-farmer.

So it can be argued that the meadow, because it was overcome by man, stimulated in particular his creative life. Docile nature, in the form of beautiful green meadows, developed an attitude of competition which made man absorbed in his life, yet, at the same time, it thrust man back to nature. Men were divided into the god-like citizen and the bestial slave. Probably nowhere in the ancient world except in the Mediterranean was there such a thorough-going cleavage. The phenomenon of the black slave in North America in modern times is slightly akin; but black slavery is the product of the European following the old world's concept of slavery and is little more than a copy of the Greek model. In places where the might of nature—or her blessings, for that matter—overshadows men, they cannot be segregated so absolutely; and it was only the foundation of this out-and-out division that enabled the creation of Greece's brilliant culture. Nor should one forget that both the Greek's unity with nature and his humanistic outlook concerned only a small number of citizens and slave-employers. Of Athens' population of half a million at her most flourishing, only a mere twenty-one thousand possessed citizen rights. It is of special significance that in the Greek *polis* there was such a great number of slaves treated as such and made submissive.

h)

Thus did the Greeks make themselves into Greeks. Hence, the advent of the Greek cannot be divorced from the Greek climate; or it might be better to say that according as the Greek became Greek, so was Greece's climate evinced as such. The *polis* with its slave class enabled the citizen, freed from labour directed to gaining the necessities of food, clothing and a roof, to "observe" such labours at a distance. But when the Greek citizen became such, he was already imbued with a spirit of competition, so that his "observation" was competitive observation rather than mere indolent inactivity. This was bound to give rise to a flood of artistic and intellectual creation. I remember once hearing a painter speaking to beginners. "If you imagine that is what you are going to paint", he said, pointing to a plaster-of-paris head, "You are sadly mistaken. What you are doing is observing it, examining it. In the course of this examination, all manner of things will appear, and the more you are astonished at there being such subtle images, the more will such new aspects appear. Then, while you are observing intently, your hand will begin to move of itself". These words held a sigificance a little more weighty than even the painter himself perhaps realised. For "to observe" is not simply to mirror something already formulated; it is to discover an infinity of new aspects. So "observation" is directly linked with creation. However, one's attitude must necessarily be that of 'pure' vision; observation for an end will not take one beyond the sphere of limitation by the objective. Unrestricted development of observation demands as a prerequisite liberation from any sense of striving for a specific end; thus observation itself becomes the objective. This was precisely the standpoint of the Greek citizen in his competitive observation.

Hence the Greek climate offered a unique opportunity for the furthering of such unrestricted observation. The Greek looked at his vivid and bright world, where the form of everything was brilliant and distinct, and his observing developed without restriction in that there was mutual competition. This is not to say that objective nature was observed down to the minutest detail; what did happen was that the subject who was observing himself developed through his observation. The observation of a bright and sunny nature automatically promoted the development of a similarly bright and sunny character in the subject. This came out as a brightness and clarity of form in sculpture, in architecture and in idealistic thought.

This attitude of the Greek gives an understanding of the distinctive character of his culture—the culture that, in a certain sense, governed the destiny of the whole of Europe. But the Greeks did not throw down work completely because of this attitude of "observation"; rather it was through it that they began a new calling, the production of purely man-made, artificial goods. The tasks of the farmer-herdsman had been in the manner of trailing along behind nature rather than of applying the hand to nature. But through their observation of form the Greeks began a new occupation, that of stamping this form on natural material. In other words, the production of man-made industrial products became work to the Greeks. Weapons and other metal implements, textiles, pottery and so on were produced first on quite a flourishing scale in the various Ionian cities from the seventh century B.C. onwards, and these techniques soon spread to Attica and Argolis. It was thus that the Mediterranean coast came under Greek influence. One reason, no doubt, lies in the high demand there would be in the newly-settled areas on the coast of the Mediterranean; a more vital reason is the development of control over the materials on which man's hand impressed form. Fine quality potter's clay, copper and iron ore could all be found in rich quantities, provided only a man looked for them. In the seas there were rare oysters for dyes; from the pastures there was an endless supply of sheepswool. The impression of form on such raw materials came to dominate the Greek's intellectual and artistic concern. Such activities are seen at their purest in the manufacture of pottery. Just how flourishing this industry was can be judged from the incredible volume of the finds of this Greek ware in Italy. Next, came metal wares, which flourished first in the Ionian islands and then spread to the mainland by the sixth century B. C. in the form of iron smelting and bronzework. The dyeing industry centred on Miletus was so advanced that even as early as the sixth century B. C., dyed fabrics from there dominated Italian markets. Encouraged by the spirit of competition, such manufacturing industries began to flourish in almost every city. Citizens turned to handicrafts, and passed their skills down to their sons. Almost every sculptor until quite late in the classical age came of such craftsman ancestry—even Socrates being such. Nevertheless, demand was greater than could be met, so these technical skills began to develop through the employment of slaves and the importation of a foreign labour force. Hand in hand with this development, of course, went a prosperous overseas trade. So this pattern of *polis* life, built more and more round a core of skilled technical labour, came to dominate the Mediterranean, and was to become a potent factor in guiding the destinies of Europe.

Thus if his attitude of observation determined even the Greek's modes of production, it is only natural that it should have become the most prominent aspect of his contemplative learning. Aristotle says that man, by nature, desires to know, witness his delight in sensation. It is not that the latter is merely useful for an end; man delights in it in and for itself. Especially does he take delight in his sense of sight; he does not "observe" merely for a purpose, for even when he contemplates no action, this "observation" is in itself more gratifying than anything else. This is because "observation" is superior to the activities of the other senses in making things intelligible and in differentiating between them. In one stroke, Aristotle thus indicates the superiority of "observation" and cognition over practice. This delight in sensation was not the fulfilment of sensual desire, but was pure "observation". When Aristotle goes on to explain the development of "observation" into learning, he gives an important role, as before, to technique. For technique is in itself true knowledge, a universal judgement, acquired by experience and based on an awareness of origins. Learning is merely technique purified. When learning came to be considered in the light of the individual consciousness, technique was no longer accorded so much weight. But it was something very essential to the Greek, who viewed technique as the development of "observation", with no basis in utility. So Aristotle says, "The man who first discovered a technique far transcending man's everyday perception was highly admired by his fellows". Such admiration was not solely on the score of the utility of the invention; it sprang also from the thought that the inventor was far more wise than the rest. Thereafter, many techniques were invented, some of them directed at providing the necessities of life, others its joys; but in that the latter were not aimed at utility, they were always regarded as more shrewd than the former. Hence, when in the end man began to acquire leisure, there was the discovery of pure learning, aimed at neither the necessities nor the pleasures of life. In this environment the standpoint of "observation" in the matter of the techniques developed still further to reach that of 'pure' observation, that of *theōria*. *Theōria* was something that monsoon or desert area could not produce.

The pith of this Greek attitude of observation lay in the object observed. Greek nature, bright and clear, hiding nothing and well regulated, thus became the essence of this attitude of observation. The idea that nature displays all and is well ordered directed the natural philosopher and inspired the artist. The outstanding feature of Greek sculpture is that the exterior surface is not just a means of enclosing whatever is inside but is given the function of revealing and displaying the internal contents. The external surface is not simply a horizontal extension; it presents to the viewer a vertical unevenness. Every part of or point in the external surface is directed actively at the viewer and acts as the point of exposure of the life within. So although one only looks at the exterior, one feels that in it one can see all of the interior. The sculptor achieved this by deft touches of his chisel. In the reliefs of the Parthenon friezes, for example, there are still clear traces of the chiselling on the surface area of the clothing where there has been a hollowing and where it was clearly not intended to leave a smooth surface. As a result, one is given a vivid impression of the soft touch of the woollen clothing. There are no strong chisel marks on body surfaces but at various parts of the skin there are distinct traces of hollowing by the chisel, always on surfaces that are vertical. By this technique the complete contrast between the living flesh and the woollen garments is pointed up very sharply.

Such delicacy of feeling is almost lost in Roman copies, where the horizontal extension surface only is stressed and the relationship between external surface and interior, so intimate in the Greek original, is lost. Further, the form itself is incapable of conveying through the exterior the otherness of its inner essence and, as a result, such imitations appear completely hollow and empty. However these hollow imitations do give an outstanding impression of the regular proportion of the human body. From before the time of Pheidias, there was a close connection between Greek sculpture and the Pythagorean mathematical and geometrical theories. Proportion was of vital concern to the sculptor, for the orderly precision in nature lay at the very centre of his "observation". The logic in art and the rationality grasped through technical skill furthered mathematical studies. So in Greece knowledge of geometry did not lead the way to a geometrical precision in technique, for the artist had already discovered geometrical proportion before the birth of geometry.

Where nature conceals elements difficult to estimate and where she is revealed unsystematically, such logical method would not be readily developed. For not only are the mountains, the fields, or the plant life irregular in shape; the human body also has no symmetry or proportion. So the artist, unlike his Greek counterpart, cannot seek unity in his work by proportion and by regularity of form. The latter were replaced by a unity of temper, which cannot be other than illogical and unpredictable. In that it is hard to find any law in them, techniques governed by temper never developed into learning.

The logic in Greek art and learning was the second vital factor governing Europe's destiny. This spirit was born of the trends of Greece's technical skills. I do not maintain, however, that such trends produced logical results everywhere and in every single case, though there was this potentiality within the Greek climatic area. But I do maintain that the genius of Greek art and learning lies not so much in its logic as in its vivid delineation of external as internal. But in that such surpassing art and learning were based on logic, the development of logic itself was promoted. The Roman imitation, as has been said, failed to maintain the artistic excellence of the original. But the Roman copyist did retain the latter's logic. This is true of the whole of Rome's civilisation, for her great achievement was the rationalisation of life by law. So through Rome, Greece's reason settled the fate of Europe.

i)

When the Greek first emerged as such, he had already built any number of *polis*. But when the Roman first emerged as such, he built only one *polis*, Rome. There is great significance in this distinction.

The way to Rome's world dominance opened up after she had withstood Hannibal's invasion and had gone on to overcome Carthage. Thus it would not be unfair to claim that the Hannibalic War was one of the points of crisis determining the course of ancient history. The question was not (as Beloch notes) whether the world should turn Punic or Latin, for even had Hannibal won the victory, the Semitic Carthaginians would probably not have set out on the path of world domination. For Carthage fought her wars with foreign mercenaries. For almost half a century in the earlier part of this conflict the Romans fought pitiably badly, not because their troops were not of fine quality but rather because the statesmen who took command by turns knew nothing of the art of tactics. Even after Hannibal had penetrated into Italy, the main reason behind his victories must be traced to the incompetency of the Roman command. Flamminius or Varro, for example, were little other than smooth-tongued demagogues. The Carthaginian army command, by contrast, had no hand in and was not affected by politics; generals were specialists with a long training in tactics. So during his invasion of

Italy, Hannibal easily got the better of the Romans on all counts, in the disposition of his mercenaries, the training of his cavalry and in the matter of strategy. But however supreme his war-craft, Hannibal's mercenaries were, after all, mercenaries, with no spirit for an all-out assault on Rome. So the rout of Carthage is to be put down, in the last analysis, to them. Why, then, was Carthage forced to employ mercenaries? In the first place, she was faced with a population shortage; secondly, the Phoenicians were essentially merchants. Hannibal was able to attract fine quality mercenaries from Spain because the Spaniards were fiery and warlike and were suffering some distress because of the Carthaginian capture and monopoly of their rich deposits of silver ore. Thus even had he gained the victory over Rome and gained control of the Mediterranean, Hannibal would never have tried his hand at political domination as the Romans did. Thus, the Greek polity would have continued unaltered, Etrusca would have developed in independence and the Mediterranean coastline would have seen the emergence of a variety of cultures of a variety of peoples in competition. The decay of culture brought by Rome's world domination would not have occurred, or, if it had, it would have been considerably delayed. Rome's victory, however, gave her the mastery of the Mediterranean; thereafter, every land within reach was incorporated into the Roman *polis* and a stop was put on the emergence of individual cultures. A hollow universality won the day.

In that this was of intimate concern to the fate of Europe, the Hannibalic War is one of the watersheds of world history. It may be suggested that this problem had already arisen in the Alexandrine concept of world empire. But Alexander's universal domination had been opposed tooth and nail by men like Demosthenes, on the grounds that it violated the Greek spirit. Nor did the Greeks retain Alexander's conquests after his death. Bactria in the east and Egypt and Syria in the west each became independent kingdoms and gradually there were found outlets by which local and individual Greek cultures might develop. Thus, if Rome had been defeated by Carthage, the Mediterranean coastline might never have been unified under a single *polis*.

I do not mean by this, however, that there is no connection at all between Alexander's achievements and Rome's sudden rise to prominence. The reflection that the two series of events were simultaneous is somewhat surprising; in fact, Rome's expansion beyond the confines of her narrow kingdom and her first contact with the Samnians occurred at the same time as the rapid rise of Macedonia. Previously to this, of course, Rome had emerged from a primitive tribe to the status of a kingdom of eight thousand square kilometres; in the three centuries that had passed, there had been a transition to *polis* structure. But this was no more than the unification of insignificant tribal groups living in the plains and hills around Rome. Now, however, Rome had taken her first step on the road to overseas expansion and in no time at all, utilising her ascendancy as a unified kingdom, she extended her control as far as the Bay of Naples. Thus, a newly-risen power with half a million men and a territory of twelve thousand square kilometres, she had her first hostile contact with Greek colonial territory at exactly the same time as Alexander was setting out on his eastern expedition.

The most striking aspect of Rome's history is that whereas Greece's *polis* had been multiform, that of Rome from the very first tended naturally towards unification. From being a petty tribal settlement on the banks of the Tiber, Rome gradually grew so that the town on the Palatine, old Rome, was already too constricting as early as the sixth century B. C.. When the neighbouring hills and the Tiber valley between them were covered over with houses and ringed by a wall, this was the birth of the "city of seven hills". Presently, as it grew to become a state, the town even exceeded these limits; and it was just as Rome began to advance beyond the limits of this kingdom that Appius Claudius led the first aqueduct into Rome.

Here there is a very intimate link with climate. The visitor to Rome is impressed most deeply, among all the remains, by the aqueducts and by the inseparable relation between them and the Roman. Now why should they be so conspicuous? For one thing, of course, they are huge artificial constructions. And again they are the symbol of man's breaking through the bonds of nature's restraints by means of his own labours. For it was the aqueduct that enabled Rome to become a great city the like of which had not been and could not be seen in Greece. They were, at the outset of the great adventure, a signal that Rome had achieved, in a way that the Greeks never did, a breakdown of the restrictions imposed by the land, and had succeeded in building a vast *polis*.

After a visit to Greece, Professor Kamei posed the question whether the size of the *polis* was conditioned by restraints imposed by a shortage of water. This I found a discerning and highly entertaining thesis. There were aqueducts already in the Cretan royal palaces, and in Athens ducts led from the waters of the Hymettus and the Pentelicon; there are traces of such works at Thebes and Megara also. But the Greek never contemplated building aqueducts on a scale great enough to discount the restrictions of a water shortage. Rather, he regarded his *polis* as a unit that was and should be restricted. Aristotle fixed its limits on the basis of the duties inherent in the ethico-political structure; the *polis* should be small enough for its citizens to be acquainted with each other's characteristics. So, in the nature of things, the *polis* should not develop into a large city, and there was thus no call for piercing the barriers imposed by water supply. Such a conception of the *polis* necessarily recognises that *polis* can be ranged alongside *polis*. Rome, however, once it became a unified kingdom, immediately began to overthrow all such limitation. Here the Romans were not learning from Greece, but were acting under the inspiration of their own genius. But it would be wrong to ignore the difference of environment, for whereas it was not easy to hit upon the notion of breaking down water's restraints in Greece, this idea presented itself much more readily in the Tiber valley. Rome is nowhere near as dry as Greece; the Tiber's flow is more copious than that of the Cephissus. So it would be fair to argue that while the Romans learnt from the Greeks how to set man's hand to subduing nature, they achieved this subjection by the man-made aqueduct—a method that the Greeks could not use—precisely because they lived by the banks of not the Cephissus but the Tiber.

Rome's aqueducts, then, symbolise the negation of two of the features of the *polis,* its restrictions and its multiform nature; they demanded, in other words, out-and-out unification. Here, in essence, is the Roman tendency towards unification in contrast to the Greek diversity. The latter, however, is grounded on Greece's nature, where all things are isolated into a variety of forms. Could it, then, be argued that Rome's trend to unification is similarly grounded in the nature of Italy? Does everything in Italy's nature, then, appear to be reducible to a single principle?

Let us infer from a number of factors of this pattern. Could it not be said, for instance, that there is a local Italian flavour to that part of Greek culture that was born in Italy? In the matter of philosophy, for example, the Eleans are a true Italian product. Xenophanes, who had lived both in Elea and Sicily, set himself against polytheism and showed a very clear trend towards monotheism. Parmenides' "being", too, clearly reflects a demand for absolute unity, and there is an outstanding instance in Zeno's penetrating indication of the contradictions in diversity. Sicily's literary product, the bucolic, stands half-way between epic and drama. The bucolic gives neither the complete image of the epic, nor the character delineation of drama. It fuses, if you like, heroic tales with a spirit of lyricism. Now cannot such literary and philosophical styles be said to have their basis in the nature of Italy? Sicily is more moist and so greener than anywhere in Greece; it is entirely proper that the bucolic should have been born there. On one part of the Elean coast near Paestum, with the six thousand foot Chervati to the east and Sicily just over a hundred miles south over the sea, there are still the remains of Greek mansions. Of the Mediterranean coastline cities settled by Greece, this is the most northerly, with, no doubt, a tranquillity of its own which far surpassed the rest, albeit the beauty of their scenery. To me, at least, it is perfectly appropriate that this should have been the birthplace of the philosophy of being. Such places, with their Italian nature, were far more fertile than Greece because of their moderate degree of moisture; to men seeking to produce food, they would be a stage more docile than Greece. It does not seem too fanciful to suppose that with such characteristics, these places would give an air of tranquillity to literature and philosophy.

Italy's climate was, in other words, a degree more rational than Greece's. Unlike the latter, Italy was at first covered with natural forests. But as these were cleared and gave way to arable fields, orchards or meadow, so control by human labour could gradually be achieved more effectively. It would not be unfair to argue that in Italy, there was a technical and rational control over nature greater than was possible in Greece. This no doubt induced the Roman to extend his technical control without limitation. So during the long period from the first Greek settlement in Italy, in the eighth century B. C., during which Greek culture made itself felt in every cranny of Italian life, it was not Greek expression but Greece's logic and her joy in technique that the Roman learnt and adopted. In religion, in art, in philosophy, in language, in writing, in fact in almost every walk of life, Rome merely absorbed the Greek original and failed to find any way to give expression to herself. But in subjugating nature by reason, Rome succeeded where even Greece had failed. The expression of Rome's vast architectural constructions is hardly worth mentioning, but they far outdo Greece in technical power. The idea of a wall two or three yards thick with rich natural mortar binding bricks as thin as tiles would probably never have entered the mind of the Greek, fixed as it was on giving shape to stone. Again when Rome conquered Greece and became heir to the riches of her sculpture, all that she could find there was a joy in rational technique; she was quite incapable of sensing its rich expressiveness. Then, when this joy in rational techniques came to be applied to human affairs, there came the crystallisation of common law, Rome's historical contribution.

So Rome's predilection for unity must be understood in the context of Italy's climate. *Civitas Romana* was a true child of Italy, unrelated to the Greek *polis*. Then, as a later expression of Rome's unifying power, came the Catholic Church, a universal and unifying church that was to dominate Europe for more than a thousand years.

j)

As central and western Europe gradually developed under Rome's tutelage, so did the focal point of European culture slowly move to the west. Since the Renaissance, the Mediterranean coastline has become almost a historical backwater, a site of relics of the past. When a culture expands thus, the factor of changes in locale plays a very conspicuous part. So one could examine from the standpoint of climatic change (that between south and west Europe) time differences (ancient contrasted with modern) in a culture. What such differences would climate effect?

Baek employs seven categories to analyse the contrast between ancient and modern culture.

ancient	*modern*
1. control by nature	control by mind

2.	restraint	freedom
3.	individuality	universality
4.	diversity	unification
5.	realism	idealism
6.	extraversion	introversion
7.	objectivity	subjectivity

There may be all manner of objections to this classification in the matter of detail. This is especially true of art; there is a certain degree of affinity between classical and baroque styles, so the constituents of a culture of one period do have aspects that can be placed in both categories. Now to some extent can the contrast between Greek and Roman culture, both of which belong to the ancient period, be interpreted by these categories. On the other hand, such similarity is natural if Rome's spirit permeated western Europe along with her laws. Again, in the sense that the classical style of the Italian Renaissance was a Greek revival, it is not without good reason that there should be this affinity. In general terms, the Italian Renaissance was a revival much more of Greece than of Rome. The Roman concept of empire had long since crossed the Alps to the north and the cities growing up in Italy towards the end of the Middle Ages had little similarity to the *Civitas Romana* but were much more akin to Greece's *polis.* As in Greece, there was keen competition between these cities; their politicians and artists, like the Greeks, were driven by intense ambition and the arts they produced, as in Greece, showed a marked tendency to expressiveness and rationalism. So elements classifiable as 'modern' in this table are posterior to the baroque style and the prosperous state of Italy's cities at the time was usurped by those on the Atlantic coastline. There is no reason then to regard Baek's categories as other than not far wide of the mark at least in the matter of a comparison between the Greek old and the West-European new world.

But from our own point of view, Baek's categories also give a precise indication of the contrast between the Mediterranean and the Atlantic coastlines. This can be summed up broadly in terms of the distinction between Greece's brightness and western Europe's gloom. But it must not be forgotten that this is only a local difference within the general meadow climatic area, for western Europe's gloom is of the meadow, not of the steppe. Hence to understand this gloom we must first look at the meadow qualities of western Europe's climate.

k)

I have shown that western Europe's climate is of the meadow type, with a combination of humidity and dryness (a summer dryness) similar to that of the Mediterranean. But because the sun here is not as powerful as in the Mediterranean, the temperature is far lower. The winter cold, in particular, is of an intensity unknown in southern Europe; yet even so, the climate of western Europe can be said, I believe, to have the same—if not a greater degree of—distinctive docility of nature as the south.

Western Europe's winter temperatures are far lower than Japan's. Daytime temperatures of six or seven degrees below zero are not unusual; in Germany, at the coldest period, the temperature falls as low as seventeen or eighteen degrees below zero. But, in proportion to the temperature, the cold is not difficult to tolerate; since there is little humidity in the atmosphere, it is merely a pure and simple cold not of the kind that chills the bones. Again, in that there is little variation between day and night temperatures, there is no feeling that the body is a mere plaything of the cold. Thirdly, a really biting cold wind is rare so that the cold does not seem to make aggressive inroads. If a distinction between cold and chilling is permissible and meaningful, even the most intense part of western Europe's winter is cold but not chilling. There is a stagnating cold to the atmosphere but there is none of the savage chill of the kind which assails a man and does not leave off until he is withered. This kind of cold can be withstood fairly easily by an effort, or a strain from within; and this effort even becomes, in a way, something attractive. Germans call the cold *Frische* (which could be translated as cool or refreshing) and take delight in the bracing and crisp feeling that it brings. Even when the cold is at its most severe, there are not a few who go to bed without heating the bedroom; this, of course, is partly because rooms are constructed and equipped with an eye to retaining warmth but in any case the latter is a comparatively simple matter when one is dealing with a type of cold that contains little humidity and is not accompanied by strong winds. Man can build his house making no provision against unbearable heat or humidity and concerning himself only with the cold atmosphere. There is no need to provide against a stagnant and immobile humidity by means of the continual circulation of air as in Japan; thus the warmed air is separated from the world outside by thick, dry walls and remains in the room a long time before it is emitted artificially. A cold atmosphere, then, is much more readily overcome than a heat combined with humidity. Nor do provisions for retaining the heat need to be more than elementary; I doubt whether, in fact, much more heating fuel is used in England and France than in Japan. In a word, the cold of western Europe enlivens rather than shrivels. It stimulates and entices a spontaneous energy that sets man on the road to resisting and overcoming the nature that is exemplified by this cold and leads him to render this nature docile. House construction and equipment designed to retain warmth leave not the least dread of the cold.

This kind of docility of nature exemplifies at the same time a certain sameness in nature. The western European winter is very different from what a Japanese normally conceives as winter. In Japan we have one day a cold and bitter wind which cuts you to the bone; then, the next day, there is the pleasure of sun bathing. One day large snow-flakes fall steadily and lie overnight; then, the next day, it is bright and clear and there comes the quiet drip of the thaw. This is not the product of cold alone but stems rather from a fusion of humidity, sunshine and biting cold. Where there is little humidity it rarely snows even with the temperature down to ten or more degrees below zero. Where the sun's rays are weak, with no more power than the moon's, even though on rare occasions the sky should clear the sun has not sufficient force to melt the previous day's snows. Such infrequency of change in itself indicates the docility of nature. So the feel of winter in western Europe is that of the hearth, of the theatre, of the concert hall or of the ballroom; in other words, it is artificial, in the sense that nature has prompted man to stress his own self-expression. It may well be that this spontaneous self-expression on man's part within his house or indoors is responsible for mechanical invention; the latter is related to a sense of resistance to the gloom of winter.

Intense heat is not overcome as readily as this, for man cannot take measures against heat as he does against cold. Again, heat cannot be ignored to the point that one can devote oneself to something in the matter of artificial invention or production. It would not be wrong to argue that western Europe's climate has a readily tolerable cold in place of the southern heat that is hard to bear. So though there is here a cold winter of the kind that is not experienced in the south of Europe, there is nothing like the intensity of the latter's summer. Italy's February corresponds to April or May in Germany or northern France; the former's May to the latter's midsummer. So the corn that ripens and is cut and harvested in May in Italy is not brought in until the end of July or August in Germany; the grass of the meadow which disappears with the corn in Italy remains green and fresh throughout Germany's summer. So summer in western Europe is no hotter than late spring or early summer in the south.

Even on days which are felt to be hot, the temperature does not rise above twenty-six or -seven degrees at best. One can go the summer through in winter dress, and not a few do! One even notices old people in winter overcoats, and women wear silk dresses lined at the collar with fox furs. What passes here for summer dress could be worn in Japan's November. It goes without saying that there is no element of the intolerable in such a summer.

This docility of summer depends on the absence of violent change brought by humidity and heat. This was the basic condition that drove weed-grass from Europe and turned the whole land into meadow. It was this, too, that eliminated from western Europe's summer those elements that a Japanese thinks of as summer—the cool of the morning and evening, the fresh breeze that relieves the heat, the pleasant evening shower after the heat of the day, the chirp of the cicada and the hum of the insect, the dew on the grass. This is not merely the feeling on the part of an Oriental traveller accustomed to climatic change that there is something lacking and incomplete about the summer in western Europe. Because of the deficiency of humidity in the atmosphere and the consequent insignificance of day and night temperature variation, one can walk in the meadows early in the morning and not wet one's feet; for the same reason, the farmer can leave his tools in the fields when he goes home at night. This is something quite unusual for Japanese eyes, accustomed as they are to seeing the Japanese farmer carrying his spade or his hoe home from his paddy, washing off the mud and putting them away in his shed. It is probably quite beyond the imagination of the Japanese that one could leave tools in the fields all night without their becoming rusted. In fact, in Germany, where the distance from farm house to field is often great, it is not an inconsiderable saving of labour if the transporting of agricultural tools can be eliminated.

Again, the fact that few insects are heard does not mean merely that the summer evening is lonely. It means also that there is only a slight danger of damage to crops by insect pests. I walked in the Grünewald and the Thuringian forest near Weimar looking deliberately for insects but the wooded parts here, where there was hardly any grass underneath the trees, did not produce even a single ant. All I did see was a flight of moths, all of the same kind, winging their way in the same direction. This was barely credible at first to one accustomed to watching the illimitable variety of insects on a Japanese hill in the summer. But Japan's insects, next to her typhoons, her floods and her droughts, menace her crops. Western Europe, by contrast, is like heaven on earth.

Since the subject has turned to typhoons and floods, let us discuss western Europe's winds and rainfall. For a Japanese, nature's tyranny reaches its height in typhoons and floods. But it is the gentleness of the wind and the rain in western Europe that makes nature there gentle.

I have several times mentioned the immobility or the "stagnation" of the atmosphere. By this I mean in part the comparative absence of cold winds in winter and of cool breezes in summer; but there is also a positive element in this "stagnation". This is a congelation, an immobility of the atmosphere of a sort only rarely known in Japan and experienced particularly when the atmosphere is either unusually cold or very hot. When a cold or a warm and sultry atmosphere settles on a city and fails to circulate, there is an oppressive feeling of congelation or agglutination in the air. At such times, the smoke from a chimney rises straight to the clouds undisturbed; vapour trails left by an aeroplane retain their shape and do not fade. Such atmospheric stagnation is a distinctive feature of western Europe's climate.

The soil of north Germany offers a concrete illustration of the gentleness and the paucity of the wind. This soil is composed of extremely fine sand, its particles not as large as millet grains and lacking all cohesion. Yet this sandy soil, for all its fineness, is not blown by the wind. When one has seen the sand of Japan's beaches, where the particles are several times greater, being for ever carried up by the wind, this is really unexpected. Yet the pines standing in this sand-soil all stand perfectly upright, as do the deciduous varieties that grow between the extensive meadows. It would not be any exaggeration to claim that all Germany's trees stand perfectly upright. This fact is even more striking in the case of a forest like the Thuringian Forest, a series of row after row of perfectly erect trees, the trunks forming precisely parallel lines. This is rarely seen in Japan even in the case of cedar or cypress trees. I have seen something which comes near to it in the cedar forests on the Yoshino hills, but Yoshino's winds, for Japan at least, are slight and gentle. In other words, Europe's trees are permitted to grow without any strong buffetting by the wind. So when the rare strong wind does blow, they are completely uprooted. In the "Hereditary Forest Office", Ludwig describes a discussion whether or not to thin a mountain forest. The argument against thinning is that once done, just one strong wind would bring all the trees down. This indicates just how rare is a strong wind and how unused trees are to it. The straightness of the trees is one of the main causes of the orderliness of the German landscape. While the trees in France are not quite so erect, even so, in northern France, for instance, you see a line of box trees all bent in the same direction and to the same angle. Thus, while curved, they are all in fact parallel. This is a good indication of the regularity of the wind.

Similarly, western Europe's rain is gentle. Even summer rain is hardly deserving of the term, being no harder than Japan's spring rains. Thus in normal circumstances an umbrella is not essential and on the few occasions when rain falls hard enough for one to need an umbrella and for one's trousers to be wetted and splashed, one need only shelter for a short while in a doorway before it stops. If rain of such violence lasts for half an hour, water inundates the city streets and floods basements; the fire brigades turn out and begin pumping frantically. And on such occasions you realise that drainage facilities are not very adequate. After a deluge of rain, lowlying meadow areas are flooded, because there are no small drainage ditches between arable fields or pastures to lead off the rain water to a nearby river. In Japan, where broad slopes lead down to a valley, there is invariably a stream at the bottom of this valley; but in Germany there is almost never such a stream; should there be one, you may be sure that the valley is on a broad scale. Further, some even of the well-known rivers appear to Japanese eyes as mere streams. The famous Ilm, for instance, flowing through Weimar, is like our stream running from Yoyogi to Sendagaya. The Rhine is a broad flow in that it carries the waters of the Alps, the roof of Europe, yet even so, there is nothing really startling about its size. Even the Elbe which takes in the waters of the wide mountain ranges from Saxony to Bohemia south of Berlin in the Dessau area, merely flows placidly and without dykes through the meadows. Neither town nor country, then, have more than insignificant installations for draining rain water—an indication that rainfall is gentle and slight.

If the continent of western Europe, with its gentle slopes, were to suffer the rain deluges of Japan, the rain water would not be easily drained. Although Berlin is a hundred miles from the coast, it stands only a hundred feet above sea-level. The Elbe and the Oder in north Germany and the Rhone, the Loire, the Seine and the Rhine in France are linked to form a canal network, with adjustments made in water level at a number of sluices; thus, there is a water network from the Mediterranean right through to the North Sea. The reason why the gently sloping plains through which these rivers flow never turn into vast lakes, but remain beautiful meadows or arable fields with just the appropriate degree of dryness is that, by nature, the need to drain is very slight. Even the rare exceptionally heavy rainfall does not succeed in disturbing this climatic feature.

In general, however, gentleness of both wind and rain mean that climatic change is tardy. The slowness of seasonal variation is indicated especially by the leisureliness of the growth of plant life. Deciduous trees begin to show their buds early in April, but the development of these buds is barely distinguishable. You watch them every day, but notice no progress and then, just as you are losing interest, they gradually advance and begin to show a lush fresh green in the middle of May. This is quite different from the rhythm of growth in Japan, where the spring green changes tone day by day and seems to grow almost overnight. Japan's spring green, in fact, seems almost to overwhelm you with the power of its growth; but there is no such rapid and vital advance in western Europe. Presently, by the time the summer comes, the corn slowly turns golden and though it is ripe by the end of July, it is left standing placidly and unchanging even until the end of August. The maturing of Japan's rice crop, by contrast, is extremely sudden.

Plant life is an exact reflection of the farmer's life. His wheat harvest is no doubt the busiest season of his year, yet it ambles along in a leisurely manner from late July until the end of August. So you can look over the extensive fields even at this harvest season and see only rare signs of reaping and gathering in. This is quite the opposite of the tenor of the dizzy bustle of the Japanese farmer's labours as he gathers his corn and plants out his rice. Man is not run off his feet by nature in western Europe; he can even make nature tread to his own leisurely pace.

So a docile nature, provided one takes into account only its docility, is very beneficial to man. But the picture has its other side, for this docility improverishes the land. As a result, the farmer must increase his holding; but he is able to do this, to put a greater area of land under cultivation with his own labour, precisely because of nature's docility. Anciently, when the Germans first built a semi-nomad proto-communist society, their land was no doubt overrun by gloomy and forbidding forests, but once these were cleared and the land was tamed to human control, nature here became obedient and submissive. It would not be untrue to say that the soil of western Europe is thoroughly tamed by man, for wide continent though it be, there is not one corner beyond the reach of man's arm. Deep in some remote mountain tuck trees are planted; roads lead to its very summit. This is facilitated by the gentleness of the slopes, and again, just by reason of this gentleness, trees can be transported by truck from every part of the mountain. Thus there is hardly any land in western Europe that is not put to some use.

The case with Japan is very different where a large proportion of the land is mountainous and not very readily directed by man. It would be wrong to claim that such mountain zones are entirely without utility; yet, even supposing that lumber for export purposes were required from Japan's mountains, production facilities are far from adequate in that the precipitous nature of the slopes makes transportation a complex problem. Further, afforestation in Japan is no simple matter, there being many tree varieties good for nothing but use as fuel. Mountain districts of this kind constitute the greater part of Japan; so most of Japan has yet to feel the directing hand of man. The Japanese exist by forcing a small proportion of their land to work at maximum capacity. Nor is this small proportion by any means docile for, given the slightest loophole, it attempts to slip back out of man's control. Yet the soil is rich; if carefully tended, it will retain and put forth its powers for as long as you ask it. It is this that makes the Japanese farmer the most skilful in the world. California was adduced by Herder a hundred and fifty years ago as the world's most barren land; now, through the labours of the Japanese farmer, it has become the richest. Yet this technical skill never led the Japanese to an understanding of nature; what it did produce was not theory but the kind of art best represented by Basho.

One realises thus that nature's docility is not to be separated from the development of man's technical knowledge about nature. Patterns can be deduced fairly readily from a nature that is docile; this discovery of a pattern in itself renders nature a stage more docile. Discovery of this kind was not easy in the case of a nature which was forever making unexpected assaults on man. In the one case, there is the endless striving in the search for law and pattern; in the other, there is the domination of the resignatory attitude which entrusts the whole of fate to Heaven. Here is the watershed which determines whether or not the spirit of reason is to flourish.

In this sense, western Europe has proved to be not specifically or distinctively western European, but has followed the general pattern of Europe as a whole. To understand this spirit of western Europe, and so the modern spirit, we must first consider the "gloom" of western Europe.

l)

The main constituent of western Europe's gloom is a scarcity of sunshine, particularly conspicuous in the winter half of the year. At this high latitude, the days are extremely short. On even a fine day in December it is growing dark by three o'clock; and fine days in December are extremely infrequent, dark and overcast skies being the norm. My own visit to London was in May, but I met there a Japanese who had spent the winter there, and annoyed him considerably with my remarks about the good weather London was having at the time. He had been made to suffer heaven knows how many dull and dreary days before he met a day as fine as this, and he rebuked me with the words, "Don't be so cheerful simply because you have happened to arrive in London on a fine day in May". The gloom of winter was extremely trying and oppressive for a Japanese. When it was cloudy, if you wished to read a book, you had to have the light on all day. In the gloom of the art gallery, you could only dimly discern the outlines of the figures looming on the canvas. In the library when there was no electric light you could hardly see to read even though you sat by a large window. You felt all the time, in fact, that the day had yet to dawn.

In which case, what of the summer? The well-known "merriment of May" is, of course, happy and graceful. Yet even in this month of May there are only two or three really clear, fine days; the rest form a procession of cool and dull days just like the gloom of a cloudy winter day in Japan. Even when the sun is at its most powerful, in July and August, its force cannot be described as really strong. At the very height of Germany's dog days, buds on the trees stay white rather than becoming green, and there is no parching or thorough shrivelling of the ground. However hot you may feel on the city asphalt, if you go on a country walk or for a hill climb, the atmosphere is no hotter than Japan's May. But it is just at this period that western Europe enjoys its best and warmest sunshine and the European, faced with the prospect of a long and gloomy winter ahead, is determined to get the most out of it and to enjoy it to the full. To a Japanese, spring is not a signal for sunbathing; spring is rather the budding of the trees, the blooming of the flowers, the lushness of the new green. But to the European, spring means most of all the return of the sun so that he goes out of his way to get into this sun. The Japanese, who does his sunbathing in winter, would feel the heat a little too much and would seek out the shaded route at times when the European sits himself in the full sunshine and steadily and resolutely basks in it. Occasionally you even see prams with babies in them put out in the full glare of the sun. I remember particularly a summer scene in one of Berlin's parks. Dotted about all over a broad stretch of grass, two or three kilometres, I suppose, in length, were men with their shirts and vests stripped and the upper half of their bodies completely bare. Such summer sunbathing was something quite new to me. If one can bask in the sun at the height of the summer, then the sun's force cannot be very strong. However that may be, this scene showed me very vividly just how much the Germans adore and prize the sun. And this indicates the scarcity of sunshine in western Europe.

But this is not the only effect of the limited amount of sunshine that the western European can enjoy. Anyone who has travelled from north to south through Europe cannot have failed to notice that as the sun's power increases so does man's cast of mind gradually become the warmer and more emotional. German melancholy loses some of its depth in southern Germany; the Frenchman may be quiet, but not to the point of melancholy; for the Italian, the adjective that applies best is perhaps boisterous. In other words, gloom in climate leads directly to gloom in man. Here is the core of the most notable difference between the tenor of civilisation in western Europe and in ancient Greece. In this matter, Spengler's distinction between the Apollon and the Faust mentality really hits the mark. Under the brilliance of Greece's bright sun, everything stands out in the most bold relief, the individual quite distinct and clear. From this phenomenal world it would not be simple to postulate uniform and infinite space which did not take due account of every particular. But on a dull cloudy day in west Europe, with everything indistinct or only dimly outlined, there is a strong sense of an infinity of space which absorbs all such ill-distinguished entities. This simultaneously acts as a pointer to infinite depth. There is a strong undertow here dragging inwards, and from this comes an emphasis on subjectivity and on soul. So while the spirit of ancient Greece was that of the static, of Euclidean geometry, of the sculptured and of ceremony, modern Europe could be described as active, with the spirit of differential and integral calculus, of music and of the will. The representative arts of western Europe are the music of Beethoven, Rembrandt's paintings, and Goethe's poems. All of these incorporate to the full an active Faustian character of infinite depth. The music of western Europe has its core in Europe's Greek education; but the Greeks gave far greater weight to the contents of the poems to which music was set, and never succeeded in exploring the world of pure sound divorced from visual forms. In the vivid and distinct world of Greece, it proved impossible to speak one's soul directly by means only of the rhythm and melody of sound, to the exclusion of all visual phenomena, and all symbols which required words. Only in the shrouds of Germany's gloom was the great undertaking of making pure music achieved. The most representative of the arts of Greece was her sculpture, a crystallisation of her vivid brightness; in contrast, it is Rembrandt's painting, the quintessence of western Europe's gloom, that is typical of the modern age. The delicate blend of gloom and faint light, of which none of the masters of the Italian Renaissance would have been capable, reaches a peak unexcelled in the whole of the world's art as a representation of unfathomable intensity of spirit. Yet this was work of genius that could only be created through the aid of Europe's gloom. In technical eminence, Velasquez is in no way inferior to Rembrandt, but his paintings embody the light of Spain. Painters create in accordance with what they see; even a Rembrandt could not have painted as he did under the Spanish sun. In the same way, Goethe's Faust, the hero, his cup of poison in his hand, going from that dim Gothic room to the field of the Easter Celebration, wrings illimitable depth out of the gloom of west Europe. I cannot think of a single instance in the art of the ancient period where this spirit of a ceaseless striving towards the light is so keenly embodied. If the epics of Greece picture the most typical nature-child of all, then Faust portrays the most typical man of soul. The character of this man of soul is, in a word, the "agony of gloom". The spirit is the same in the world of learning, for the scholarship that typifies western Europe is not that of the Renaissance but the power and quantitative physics taking its origin in the Baroque age, and the philosophy of *Sollen* having its centre in Kant. Both of these are active, engaged in an endless quest, and stand in pointed contrast with the static physics or the philosophy of being of the ancients. Kant's conception of space or form, tending towards abstraction and rejecting the particular, is a very pertinent example. Abstraction is a valuable ability, one offered to Germany's philosophers by the gloom of western Europe. Their climate denied this talent to the philosophers of the ancient world.

Western Europe, responsive to the mystic, was from the very first the most fertile soil for Christianity. This was, of course, not the only area to which Christianity spread, but in no other did it plant its roots so firmly and deeply. For here, the tendency to depth and the abstraction that were wrung from the gloom were exemplified most of all in faith in Christ. Judaism, the faith of a race resisting the terrors of nature in the desert, never took firm root in the land, although it did adopt the abstraction from land. Then came the Reformation, through the resurrection of the Christ, and, at just the same period, the realisation of a world state. So Christianity took on a dual abstraction, that of the land and that of the people. In other words, Christianity, though in origin the faith of the Jews, the product of the desert, was never from the very first formulated as a racial or even a national faith. So, in that they adopted Christianity as transcending race and land, the peoples of western Europe in the end moved to a way of thinking that was of the desert, of the Jewish race. Thus the Old Testament, the chronicle of the Jews, is read now as the history of mankind as a whole. The usages recorded there, while of the desert, have now become those of the European. The European conception of rites and of the world since time began has been replaced by that of the Jews. This complete spiritual conquest was only possible because Europe's agony of gloom responded to the terror of the desert. Probably no people accepted this wilful, personal one God as wholly as did the European; no one understood the wilful moral passion of the Old Testament prophets as well as he.

This does not mean, however, that the great cultural achievements of western Europe were based only in a Christian spirit. The learning of western Europe, or her art, could never have been created through Christianity alone. Just as the philosophers of the Middle Ages borrowed from Greece in their speculations about god and man, so Gothic architecture and sculpture depended on the Romanesque for their development. Even though the gloom of western Europe gave a local character to learning or art, they remained essentially of the meadow and thus stood on common ground with the ancient Greece. It was no mere accident that the modern West began with a revival of the spirit of the ancient Greece. Through an understanding of reason and a joy in human artification, both of them inheritances from the ancient Greece, the European was awakened to the meadow character that lay at the basis of his gloom. It was only by the agency of this awakening that the creation of a specific Western culture was achieved. So, at least in the matter of its great cultural creations, the gloom of western Europe and rationalism are not to be divorced. The establishment of the order of reason, the conquest of nature by reason—these are the fundamental trends guiding the spirit of gloom in its quest for infinite depth.

If we fail to take account of this and keep our eyes only on western Europe's gloom, we shall find there only a horrifying and dismal brutality. The inhumanity of punishments in the Middle Ages is perceptible even now in the instruments of punishment that still remain from the period. The lifelike brutality of religious art of the Middle Ages is enough to make us cover our eyes. The Gospels, of course, depict Christ's Cross in vivid detail, but the ancients did not create blood-stained figures of the Christ. Even when the ancient period was at its most bankrupt, the Ravenna mosaics picture Him as a robust young shepherd. But the Middle Ages represent the Christ on the Cross as a lifelike portrait of gloom so that the viewer will sense real ache and anguish. This is not the representation of the son of God or of God's love; it is no more than another expression of inhumanity and anguish. When we come to the bloodthirsty pictures of hell, these might even be described as expressions of exultation in inhumanity. Here and in such instances one sees the savagery of the West at its starkest. The same is true of the sense of gloom that exudes from the weapons of the Middle Ages. Sword and spear are in essence the tools of the killer yet their shape and aspect is not necessarily limited to such a sense of gloom. The eloquent curve of Japan's swords can even convey a sense of noble beauty. Yet the shape of western European weapons of the Middle Ages incorporates the repulsiveness of brutality itself. It was not with such gloomy weapons that the Homeric heroes fought.

Nor do the Middle Ages only give this impression. In the seventeenth century, with the Renaissance opening up the curtain on the modern age, with religious reformation achieved in Germany and with the sprouting of modern philosophical thinking in France, there occurred the Thirty Years' War, brutal and inhuman beyond all comprehension. Such atrocities were perpetrated in the name of religion, under the banner of the anti-reformists (*Gegenreformation*). In essence, the Reformation was a Renaissance conditioned by the gloom of western Europe. Whereas, south of the Alps, there had been the flowering of a beautiful art, north of the Alps there were the buds of humanism, of the ancient spirit intensified by introspection. But it was just in the countries of such humanists, and as a reaction to their humanism that there arose these civil disturbances unparalleled for gloom and cruelty in the entire history of the world. The whole of Germany was laid waste by this war; its population was reduced by three-quarters. Would any of her humanists have predicted such tragic mutual carnage? The war arose from the loyalty to his faith of the German; but was the opposition between the Catholic Church and Protestantism of such deep significance that either side could countenance such carnage? When I recalled one small episode in this war, standing on the very site where it took place, I was so overcome by the tragic sadness of it that, in spite of myself, I wept. I was in the old free city of Rothenburg in south Germany. This town has been by-passed by modern routes of communication, so, left lagging in the wake of the advance of civilisation, it remains a peaceful country town which has lost none of its mediaeval flavour and appears somewhat like a display of curios of the Middle Ages. There still exist traces, almost intact, of the long and desperate battle fought by this town at the time of its besiegement by a large Catholic force in the course of the Thirty Years' War. Through dexterous diplomacy on the part of the mayor of the time the town in the end managed to capitulate without very heavy damage; but, until this outcome, the townspeople, old and young, women and children alike, spent themselves in resisting to a man. Firearms had still to be fully developed so the townspeople fought with every stone or tile that could be found within their rampart. The men hurled stones from the walls on the advancing enemy; even the wounded refused to yield place. The women, to the utmost of their powers, carried these weapons to the side of their menfolk. Even three- and four-years-olds tottered under the weight of huge stones to the side of their blood-stained fathers. Even girls played a part in this battle. Until I went to Rothenburg, I had never thought of war in such terms; it should have been fought only by those with combatant qualifications, either as conscripts or by their own choice. This was how wars were fought in Japan, even in her "Age of War" in the fifteenth and sixteenth centuries. To the best of my knowledge, there has never once been a war in Japan in which children helped in the defence of a town or a village. So I realised for the first time how destructive that war proved and was able to judge why the German population was reduced to a quarter. Thus western Europe's gloom reveals itself once more in war, for the impression of dark barbarism here is common with that given by mediaeval weapons.

Yet, in spite of this gloomy inhumanity, western Europe's contributions to world culture are not to be underestimated. Though the gloom of western Europe could sink to such depths of degeneration, yet, working as an internal groping towards infinite depths, it began in the end to achieve the lighting of the beacon of reason. It is not by reason of her latent brutality but principally because of this light of reason that modern Europe has become the guide of the world's cultural progress. Thus seen, Western Europe's cultural contributions stem from her meadow character, the latter exhibited by way of her gloom. It is not at all unnatural that western Europe should play the role of the true heir of Greece.

m)

I have attempted to interpret European culture in the light of its meadow climate. But I do not claim that this climate was the sole source of European culture. History and climate act as the shield and buckler of culture; the two are quite inseparable, for there is no historical event that does not possess its climatic character, nor is there climatic phenomenon that is without its historical component. So, if we can discover climate within a historical event, then we can also read history within climatic phenomena. All that I have attempted to do is to examine these two factors, while restricting my attention primarily to climate.

Let me conclude this inquiry thus. When man becomes aware of the root of his being and expresses this awareness in objective fashion, he is restricted to historical and climatic methods. There has yet to be a spiritual awakening that was not thus restricted. But the climatic limitation is the superior, for by it the more percipient self-realisation can be achieved. Let me give a parallel; the man with the best sense of hearing recognises musical talent best of all; and the one with the finest physique recognises athletic prowess more readily than any other. Of course, with this realisation comes also a discovery of the superiority of the various faculties, but it would be wrong to maintain that this realisation from the very first made the faculties superior. In just this way the beacon of reason shines most brightly in a meadow climate, in the monsoon zone it is the refinement of "feeling" that is best recognised. This being so, in just the same way as we make music our own through the musician or are able to experience a game through an athlete, might we not learn to cultivate our own reason from the place where the light of reason shines the brightest and to perfect the refinement of our own feelings with the help of the places where such refinement of feeling is best realised? If climatic conditioning has affected every part of mankind and has given to each part its own peculiar merits, it is just from this that we can be made conscious of our own weaknesses and learn from one another. This is again the means by which climatic limitation can be surmounted. Neglect of nature does not mean to surmount nature. This is merely lack of awareness within climatic limitation. However, climatic distinctions do not disappear as a result of the surmounting of limitations through awareness of them. The opposite is the case, for it is precisely by this recognition that their distinctiveness is created. In one sense, a meadow land may well be heaven on earth, but we cannot turn our own land, wherever it may be, into a land of the meadow type. We can, however, acquire the meadow character and with this our own typhoon character assumes fresh and broader aspects; for when we discover this Greek clarity in ourselves and begin to nourish reason the significance of our own distinctive "perception" or "temper" becomes all the more vital. With this, the realisation of a supra-rational reason sweeps over us with the force of one of our own typhoons.

When we look back over Japan's history with these factors in mind, we cannot fail to realise the sensitivity of the intuition of our ancestors in the case of the events that affected them most vitally. The first of such events was the advent of Christianity and the uncommon devotion of mind and the strange terrors that it evoked. In one sense the invasion of Christianity was that of the desert; thus this devotion and these fears were the embodiment of the realisation that the Japanese lack elements of the desert type. The second phenomenon was the burning interest in European science which gradually infiltrated into Japan through the barriers of the period of isolation. This interest was no more than an expression of the craving for elements of the meadow type which the Japanese lack. No other land in the Orient displayed this yearning quite so intensely. However such intuitions on the part of the Japanese of the day were not accompanied by the realisation that Japan's climate cannot become either meadow or desert. The problem of such lack of discernment still faces the Japanese today.

(Drafted 1928; Revised 1935.)

Chapter 3 The Distinctive Nature of Monsoon Climate

(1) China

Interpreted in its widest sense, the monsoon belt includes the continent of China, for if the peculiar nature of the monsoon is defined in terms of its bringing humidity to land from a warm ocean zone, then such parts of China as are thus affected by the Pacific must be included as part of the monsoon belt. This influence, however, affects not only central and south China in that they are subject to typhoons, but spreads also even into the remote parts of the hinterland. The Yellow River and the Yangtse are no doubt representative of China's climate; but in addition the Yangtse at least may well be defind as a continental embodiment of the monsoon.

The first impression of the Yangtse, on a Japanese at least, is completely unexpected; for the whole of the day before the boat, covering a steady thirteen or fourteen knots, comes into Shanghai, the sea is a mass of mud. The Yangtse, which disgorges all this muddy water, has an overall length of over three thousand miles; it is four and a half times that of the Rhine and longer even than the whole of Japan. Thus this great output of mud is natural in the extreme; but even so, the sight is no less striking, for in one's concept of "sea" hitherto there had been no element of such a vast stretch of muddy water. Moreover, the estuary of the Yangtse is so broad that the distinction between river and sea is difficult to draw. Even when told that we were already going up the Yangtse, the only difference I could find was that the line of the horizon appeared rather thicker and better defined. The horizon, however, was the island of

Ch'ung Ming which flanks the estuary and the right bank of the river only; the other bank was completely beyond the field of vision. These factors are the ruin of preconceptions of rivers or seas. The Japanese concept of the sea is formulated on the basis of, for example, the Straits of Akashi. Yet this "river", the Yangtse, is as broad as the Bay of Osaka. Further, in the case of Osaka Bay, the hills of Izumi are visible from the coast of Suma and those of Awaji are visible from the coast by Sakai. But in the case of the Yangtse, there are no hills, only the horizon of the bank opposite.

Naturally this applies only to the estuary and not to the whole course of the Yangtse. But the Yangtse is just as surprising, whatever the width of its course. For the Straits of Akashi, the Japanese notion of "sea" no more than two miles across, are hemmed in by hills that beetle over its coastline. But the Yangtse flows through broad plains which give no impression of pressing in on the river. In other words, it is the Yangtse that dominates the level plain through which it flows.

There is an indication here of the nature of the Yangtse plain; for when the river boats come near enough to the bank for one to discern trees or arable fields, this flat plain is far too wide to be seen across. One can see for, say, a thousand or, at the very most, two thousand yards; beyond that, it is simply sky. The Yangtse plain may well stretch for a hundred, even a thousand miles, but one can see nothing beyond this thousand yard limit, with the result that there is no feeling that one is looking across a vast plain. The Japanese are accustomed to being made aware of the breadth of a plain by looking at the hills that flank it. Such hills may be no more than ten or twenty miles away, but this is sufficient for our intuitive capacities to be given the sense of distance. Yet, although the plain of the Yangtse basin may be too broad for such distant hills to be within sight, this broadness does not impress itself on us. This, then, is the aspect of the plain carved by the Yangtse; here again, though in the opposite sense this time, all one's notions of the vastness of a wide plain are destroyed.

The broad Yangtse valley has been created by water, water, in the main, brought from the Pacific by the monsoon. So it would not be exaggeration to argue that the Yangtse valley is a continental embodiment, in the concrete, of the monsoon. If this is true, what form do those characteristics of the monsoon belt, receptivity and passivity, assume here?

The immediate impression given by the Yangtse and its wide plain is not that of a vast grandeur appropriate to the word continent but that of an ill-defined monotony. The wide sea of mud gives none of the vivid feel of life appropriate to the sea, nor again does this river of mud, wider than Japan's "sea" in many instances, have any sense of smooth ease about its flow. In just the same way, the flat continent gives no feel of breadth. Again, to the Japanese mind at least, the plain that stretches from Yangtse to Yellow River may well be several hundred times the size of Japan's Kanto Plain, yet all that comes into the field of vision of anyone standing on it is merely an insignificant portion of this plain; however far he may walk across it, the only impression he has is of an endless reiteration of identical tiny portions. So the vastness of the Chinese continent is only revealed in the form of a vague and little-changing monotony. In other words, through contact with this continent the Japanese discovers the vague monotony within himself. But those who have lived with this climate for generation after generation have constantly discovered themselves thus and are never given scope to discover themselves outside of this limitation. Under such circumstances, the passive and resignatory qualities that are characteristic of the monsoon belt become a tenacity of will (from bearing up to this vague monotony) and an abandonment of emotion; hence they lead to a firm hold on tradition and a fining of historical sense. Here is the complete antithesis of the Indian character, for if the latter's distinctiveness is to be pinned to a fullness of feeling, then that of the Chinese must be found in his lack of emotion.

I do not claim, of course, that the Yangtse alone can be made to represent the climate of the whole of China. The northern half of the continent should be exemplified by the Yellow River, but I do not have any first-hand impressions of either the Yellow River itself, or of the area through which it flows, and such first-hand impressions are vital for study of climate. Since I cannot contribute anything constructive to do with the Yellow River, all I shall do here is to supplement my previous observations with second-hand information.

It has long been said of China, "Boats in the south, in the north, horses." The Yangtse basin, in other words, is a land of water; the Yellow River basin a drought zone. Modern times have seen the development of steamers and cargo boats on the Yangtse but there has been nothing of this nature in connection with the Yellow River. Again, the Yangtse basin is a rice area, that of the Yellow River a corn zone. But all such distinctive features can be summed up as deriving from the single fact that the Yellow River rises in the desert. The Yellow River, in other words, acts as an intermediary between desert and monsoon.

A similar argument could be based on the nature of the yellow soil of the Yellow River plain. The extremely fine particles of this soil, originally desert, are said to be caused by the effect of the cold. The movement of this deposit is started by the wind, water then conveying it even further. But if such water is regarded as originating in the Pacific, then the yellow soil belt is the product of the joint influence of desert and monsoon, and the Yellow River is the concrete fulfilment of such interaction.

In this light, the make-up of the Chinese is not without its desert elements. He has a strong streak of tension of the will which promotes a fighting spirit deep beneath his resignation and belies the coexistence in his character of elements of both monsoon and desert. But this is not an indication of a spirit of resistance in the Chinese character similar to that typical of the desert; it is rather a distinctive offshoot of the general monsoon nature—for the Chinese has none of the out-and-out submission that is the chief characteristic of the desert. There is here a close affinity with the anarchic tendency of the Chinese, who submits to no restraints other than those based in blood or regional association. The Chinese has no mind for tax burdens imposed by the state; he escapes his obligations in the matter of military service; he ignores orders and treats the law as scrap-paper; he gambles and smokes his opium. In short, he evades all state control and conducts himself at his own will. Of course, he acquiesces in any power that would be difficult to defy, but this is an outward acquiescence, a formal submission only; the heart remains untamed. This resignation that does not countenance submission is intimately linked with another characteristic of the Chinese—his lack of emotion.

Such were the impressions of the Chinese that I formed in Hongkong and Shanghai in 1927 or thereabouts. Looking down from the ship moored at the Kowloon side, I saw innumerable Chinese junks clustering round the foreign ships, loading and unloading cargo. These junks were, it seemed, the home of any number of Chinese families; four or five little children romped on the deck; young women and old grandmothers worked away, clinging precariously to the halyards. The sight was truly placid. Yet these same junks, when you looked again, had a number of old-style cannon mounted both fore and aft. This was armament against pirates—who would attack these junks with the same type of weapon. Here, then, were these people, in such flimsy craft, transporting cargo and working all the time under the threat and with the expectation of an artillery fight with pirates. This caused me no end of surprise, for the loading and transportation of cargo that envisages an artillery battle cannot be termed a peacetime matter. Yet these Chinese labourers treated it all as an everyday affair, going about their tasks composedly, their womenfolk and children by their side. I doubt if you would find such people anywhere else in the world.

I felt that in the attitude of these workmen one could read the whole character of the Chinaman. They lived in the midst of a blood-related group so closely knit that even the threat of bombardment did not cause disintegration of the group. No doubt, too, there were the links of a common territorial bond, which would prompt these junks to go to each other's assistance in the event of an attack. But beyond this there was nothing for their protection. State authority within Chinese territorial waters was non-existent; they only had their own power to protect them. Here they were, then, living a life with no law to it, not entitled to hope for or demand any safeguard from the state. This was what had created their closely-knit blood and regional association; this was what had fostered their attitude of resignation, their open abandonment of resistance to any force that transcended their own narrow grouping. Here is the outlook of the man beyond the law, passive and resigned, yet at the same time teeming with unfathomable spite. So one lives as normal together with one's entire family on a boat bristling with cannon. There is the risk that the whole family will be exterminated and it is for this reason that the boat is armed; yet this is no way to live, worrying one's heart over provision against and by anxieties concerning such potential peril. Danger is anticipated, so cannon are mounted, and the danger is not reduced in the least by further anxiety or emotion. As long as it remains only a possibility, the best defence against this danger is to refuse to become excited about it. At the same time, this danger is to be made to bring in its full share of profit, for the accumulation of cash is the accumulation of protective power. So the best safeguard against the danger is to defy it. The attitude of the man beyond the law includes both of these elements, a regard for self-interest and a lack of emotion. Herein lies his strongpoint.

I had the chance to observe this strongpoint of the Chinese very vividly in Shanghai in February, 1927. Russia's Borodin was just reaching the height of his influence in China and Chiang Kai-shek's army was starting to get control of the Yangtse basin. Chiang's northern forces had pushed to within a few miles of Shanghai and the sound of his guns was said to be audible in residential areas close to the suburbs. Shanghai workers at this point decided on a strike to show their sympathy with Chiang; post offices closed and trams came to a standstill; there were stories too that electricity and water supplies were to be cut off at any moment. The Communists seized their chance and rushed about the city, instigating and agitating. It seemed as though the general populace might respond at any moment. Foreigners other than Russians could not go near the Chinese part of the city without danger. Then the Northern Army, defending Shanghai, started to take all manner of emergency measures to suppress the Communists. Suspects were rounded up and put to death, their heads hung from lamp-posts for all to see. There were rumours that this may only be the start of such massacres. The foreigners resident in Shanghai feared most that the Northern Army, defending Shanghai from the outside, might be forced by pressure from Chiang's forces to retreat on Shanghai causing untold consternation. If this were to happen, then no matter which side won, an armed horde would descend on the city, pillaging and committing all manner of atrocities from robbery to rape and murder. This was how the foreigners saw the situation; extemely anxious and uneasy, they pinned their faith in the authority of their several governments to protect them. In response to such faith, war vessels of any number of nationalities were tying up at Shanghai one after the other and putting ashore landing parties. In consequence, the concessions at least might be protected; but it was felt that such protection would not be extended to those whose residences lay outside the concessions. So the talk among the foreigners was that families shoud be moved to a safe area near the harbour and within the concession limits. The prestige and power of their country was a great support and comfort to them. And, as a last resort, they could always get away from this troubled country and return to their own land where their government's authority would assure ample protection. To this end, large passenger ships lay waiting in the harbour, The foreigner, his nerves on edge, was so accustomed to the protection of his government that faced by the possibility that he was beyond the range of such protection, he could not shake off such nagging uncertainties and doubts.

But how about the Chinese, who could not appeal for protection, to his country—or, more correctly, to a band of dangerous coolie troops who might be transformed at any moment into a horde of armed hooligans? Naturally, the odd shop was closed and barred; but it was said that the aim of such action was, like the workmen's strike, to show sympathy with Chiang's troops. But beyond this one could discern nothing that reflected agitation or concern on the part of the Chinese. If you stood in the street to watch, their faces were quiet and unexcited; they came and went calmly and sold their wares composedly. In the exchange too, where it was rumoured that there would be control on quotations for the Japanese yen, Chinese swarmed and kept their minds intently on their gambling. There was not the slightest trace of any uneasy apprehension that even today one might lose one's life in some savage violence. As far as the

Chinese was concerned, as long as there was some chance of making money, there was still no emergency. When the emergency did come upon him, he would disappear, spirit himself away or flee with the greatest cunning of which he was capable. So until something did occur, there was no point in disturbing himself or wearing out his nerves. Such waste of emotion is not the way life is lived in China. These were the thoughts that were written all over their faces. The Chinese was not pricked by the stabbing fear that he might have strayed beyond the radius of the protective power of his state simply because he expected no such protection.

Still astonished by this striking contrast, I took my leave of Shanghai. After I had gone, apart from the gibbeted heads on the lamp-posts, there were no further disturbances, and the situation developed in a manner quite appropriate to the Chinese absence of emotion. So it was all to no purpose that the foreign residents had been alarmed at the sound of gunfire outside the city, and had become the victims of nervous impatience and anxiety. Here, again, one sees the strong points of a life beyond the law; such a situation would be undreamed of by a Japanese, every aspect of his life centred on the state.

While it is true that the Chinese are unemotional this does not mean that they have no emotional life; their emotional life may be called unemotional. Those who express themselves in terms of a dull monotony see no cause for change of the kind that would react on and agitate their emotions. Here Chinese and Japanese are poles apart, for the latter is possessed of a rich temperamental diversity which thrives on change. The picture of the Chinese, bird-cage in hand, gazing up blankly at the sky all day long is strange in Japanese eyes, for, to the latter such a leisurely rhythm of life seems to lack all sensitivity. Yet such absence of sensitivity is not without its good points; it comes out, for instance, in the form of a calm and unpushing attitude, which might well be a good target for the Japanese who is for ever pushing and pressing in some sense. But in China both farmer and merchant share this gentleness of pace. It might fairly be said that while the Japanese are fidgety and restive, the Chinese are calm and relaxed. Yet once arrived in circumstances calling for sensitivity of emotion or nervous tension, they do not remain completely unmoved. But since their nature is to be unperturbed, there is nothing of moral credit about their attitude to life.

The same quality characterises China's cultural products. Generally speaking, they possess an easy grandeur and while aiming at size, they are yet very much to the point. At the same time, there is a marked absence of emotional content, for there is here no delicacy of texture. This characteristic is best typified by China's palace architecture since the Middle Ages. The palace is built on the huge scale to give an impression of grandeur. But detail is insubstantial, for the aim of the architect is to make his work impressive when seen from a distance. However, it cannot be said that provided only the distant view of an artistic creation is good it matters not if detail is insubstantial. This lack of attention to detail is merely another manifestation of the Chinese lack of emotion.

Of course, it is no doubt unfair to make this architectural style represent the whole of two thousand years of Chinese art. As the finds at Lou Lan show, there can be fine detail in Chinese art. Intricate pictures painted on tortoise shell caskets particularly upset my thoughts, for I was considering Han art in terms of stone figures. The Ku-k'ai-chin scrolls in London also are truly intricate in tenor. Though they are somewhat later in date, the friezes at DaT'ung, Yün Kang and Lung Men include some which are rich in intricate detail. This characteristic was quite prominent in the art of the T'ang dynasty and was far from lost under Sung. But in our consideration of this grand art, there are two points that it would be wrong to overlook. The first is that all the finest art was the product of a culture area centred on the Yellow River valley; hence one ought probably to take a different view of Yellow River area art considered independently. The other point to remember is that this type of art went out of existence after Sung and Yüan and has certainly been extinct from Ming to the present. Yet even so there is an individuality that runs through the whole of Chinese art from the pre-Ch'in bronzes, the arts of Han and T'ang up to Ming and Ch'ing. The influence of the traditions of pre-Ch'in bronzes is evident in the style of modern Chinese furnishing or interior decoration. The insubstantiality of palace architecture, with its stress on distance, has elements which it shares with the abstraction of Han stone paintings or the grandeur of the great stone Buddhas of Yün Kang or Lung Men. There is a quality of grandeur and a rough texture about the mellow sculpture of T'ang; indeed, if one exempts works of real excellence and considers only mediocre products, the latter are not by any means unrelated in character to those of Ming and Ch'ing. Yet if one seeks in modern China for something akin to the delicate and intricate detail that characterised the art of the period between Han and Sung, one will no doubt find nothing that corresponds. So it would be fair to regard lack of emotion as a feature common to the whole of Chinese culture.

No doubt exactly the same can be said of the vast compilations, such as the Buddhist canon or the Ssu-k'u-ch'uan-shu, which are a characteristic of China. These great collectanea in that they have facilitated the preservation of China's literature are of untold value for later generations. But in the matter of the contents of such vast collections, there is little of merit; the Buddhist canon, for example, was, in the first place, an attempt to bring together in comprehensive form and with no omissions the whole of Indian Buddhist literature in

Chinese translation; there was no spirit of criticism through selection or arrangement. Later, however, when the collection came to comprehend works originating in China, strict and critical selective tests were applied, although, even at this juncture, the primary purpose, at least as far as concerned the translated sections of the canon, was all-inclusive comprehension. The consummation of such labour was reached with a great compilation of the T'ang dynasty which comprised 1,716 volumes, in 480 sets, and which first achieved printed form under the Sung. From the outset works included in the canon were classified according to a single scheme, but this was, so to speak, no more than a string holding the contents together from the outside; it did not effect any internal unification or adjustment of the kind that would distinguish wheat from chaff. Thus it would not be unfair to argue that in contrast with this apparent system and order on the outside, there is a veritable mountain of unclassified and miscellaneous material as soon as one examines content. With the Ssu-k'u-ch'uan-shu, this tendency reached the extreme—so much so that it was unable to fulfil the function of a collected series.

An even franker display of this Chinese characteristic is to be found in the form taken by her empire. In Europe, only the Roman Empire at its greatest reached the heights attained by China's imperial centralisations; and the latter followed each other in close succession from the periods of Ch'in and Han until Ch'ing, in times near to our own. If this were the only consideration, China might well appear to have produced a rich crop of surpassing statesmen. But her imperial organisation was not centralised and perfected in every intricate detail, nor did its authority penetrate to every corner of the land. Although the Chinese empire may well seem from the external viewpoint to have been a well-regulated and intricate organ of government, the people, essentially, were without the law. There were as many as a million—or even two million—bandits.

The facility of communication across China's plains offered no hindrance to economic relations; as a result, we see economic cooperation achieved over a wide area already in Ch'in and Han times. This was a development conditioned by China's climate and a far more natural condition than the feudal autonomy that preceded imperial unification. The feudal kingdoms, from the very first, were castle cities, with man-made walls surrounding and protecting their territory. In other words, without rigorous efforts directed at maintaining forced and unnatural partition, China does not permit the coexistence of a multitude of petty kingdoms. Since the Sung dynasty especially, a reciprocal economic organisation has penetrated the length and breadth of the land. The Chinese does not lean on the authority of the state; instead, he has skilfully handled such wide-range commerce on the basis of the activities of area groupings. So the fact that the Chinese was without the law was no hindrance to such economic unification. China's administration was no nation—wide structure embracing the people as a whole. Originally the bureaucracy was recruited from noble families, but from Sung times selection was from commoners by examination. The latter were not soldiers; they were well-read and of the intelligentsia, but backed by autocratic lords, they wielded immense authority. And, in most cases, these officials used such authority to line their own pockets. In the Sung dynasty, in addition to state monopolies, government and officials alike, the latter as individuals, engaged in a variety of economic and commercial activities. Scholar-officials of Ming and Ch'ing, while pouring scorn on the merchant and his money-making, yet themselves channeled the wealth they had accumulated into not only land, but a variety of commercial ventures. In the China of today, similarly, there is a surprising number of officials and even of scholars connected with commercial activities. So one might even say that the state, the government itself, was without the law.

After the final collapse of empire, its bureaucracy split and formed financial and military cliques which strove to enrich themselves by linking up with foreign capital. The fact that before the beginning of the recent war, Shanghai and Hong Kong were the very nerve centre of China reveals the absence of the law in China. The power of those who drove China derived from the banks in Shanghai and Hong Kong and even in cases where such banks were not foreign, they were yet protected by the prestige of foreign powers. So the kingdom of China was in fact a superimposition of elements external to China over the Chinese people. Yet the latter, essentially unsubmissive to state authority, were not unduly disturbed by this fact and only rarely did percipient leaders of the calibre of Sun Yat-sen feel it keenly. According to a statement made by the latter in 1924, China was undergoing such pressure from the great powers that she was, in all but name, a colony. More than that; she was in a much more disadvantageous position than a colony proper. But the Chinese people felt no strong concern about this economic pressure. Sun Yat-sen's diagnosis was correct—but he and those with whom he worked, in their efforts to free China from this stranglehold, entangled her even more deeply with foreign capital and even permitted her to become the focal point of world capitalist competition. This tendency even had a part, perhaps, in the dawning of nationalism in the people of China, but as long as the power that drove this movement was directed to intensifying the colonial nature of China, this nationalist awakening could not develop into a true movement for the liberation of China from her colonial status. The Chinaman's lack of emotion finally drove him to extreme distress.

An awakening to the nature of one's own character brings knowledge of how to overcome its limitations; it further opens the way to an understanding of characters different from one's own and facilitates the supplementation of one's own failings through the adoption of another's strong points.

For over a thousand years until the Meiji Restoration, the Japanese despised their own culture and looked up to that of China, trying their best to assimilate it even in the every-day matters of food, clothing, housing and the like. But in the same way that Japanese food and the rest ended up conspicuously different from the Chinese, so the less material culture adopted from China was no longer Chinese. For the Japanese appreciates a delicate fineness; he is unmoved by the sweep of grandeur that characterises Chinese culture. Outward order is not as vital to him as is an out-and-out inner refinement, conventional formality is not as attractive as inspiration in the heart. However much of Chinese culture he absorbed, he did not succeed in assuming a Chinese character. This notwithstanding, Japanese culture does keep alive the genius of the China that existed between the Ch'in and Sung dynasties. By acknowledging this, the Chinese could restore the power and grandeur of their noble culture of the past, lost from the China of today. It is here that could be discovered the way out of the impasse in which the Chinese nature finds itself today.

China's revival must come. There must be a return to the greatness of Han and T'ang culture, for the reconstruction of Chinese civilisation is an integral and essential part of any new advances that world culture achieves. The financial and military juntas that persist in a course of turning China into a foreign dependency are the real enemies of the people of China. When China's people stand squarely by their own strength, then will begin the revival of her greatness.

(Drafted 1929; Revised 1943.)

(2) Japan

a) Japan's typhoon nature

Man's way of life has its own distinctive historical and climatic structure, the individuality of which is shown with the greatest clarity by climatic patterns governed by the limitations within a climate. Climate, essentially, is historical; so climatic patterns are at the same time historical patterns. I have applied the term "monsoon" to man's way of life in the monsoon zone; the way of life of the Japanese is also of the monsoon type for the Japanese is receptive and resignatory.

But the Japanese are not to be typified by this category alone. Superficially, Japan and India have a number of features in common; plants flourish as a result of the blessings of a vast ocean, rich sunshine and a plentiful supply of water. Yet whereas India lies between the screens of high mountains to the north and the Indian Ocean and enjoys seasonal winds regular in the extreme, Japan, sandwiched between the broad continent of Mongolia and Siberia and the even broader Pacific, suffers from seasonal winds that are most fickle and the very opposite of regular. Both are washed by water absorbed in great volume from the ocean; yet, although this water, in the form of the typhoon is in a way seasonal, it has no parallel in the world in the matter of its savage and sudden outbursts; and in the form of heavy snowfalls, it again assumes an aspect of a kind rare in the world. In virtue of such heavy rains and snows, Japan's climate is by far the most distinctive within the whole monsoon zone; its nature can be said to be dual, combining both that of a tropical belt and that of a frigid zone. Temperate areas to some extent exhibit this dual nature, but only in the climate of Japan is the latter revealed so forcefully. It is evinced most distinctly in plant life. Tropical plants like rice, the most appropriate example, which require hot sun and plently of humidity, grow profusely in Japan, so that the summer scene is hardly distinguishable from the tropics. On the other hand, plants which require a cold atmosphere and only a small degree of moisture, such as corn, flourish just as well. So in winter Japan is covered in corn and winter grass; in summer, in rice and summer grass. But a single tree variety, incapable of such alternation, displays this dual nature in itself. The picture of the bamboo, a native of the tropics, covered in snow, is often quoted as a scene peculiar to Japan. But, accustomed to bearing this weight of snow, the bamboo has adopted a nature different from that in the tropics and has become a curved and flexible variety distinctive to Japan.

Features such as these, discovered by a consideration of climate in the abstract, are concrete factors in the history of man's life. Men cultivate rice and tropical vegetables, corn and the various cold-zone vegetables, so the rain and the sunshine essential to such cultivation affect and influence man's livelihood. Typhoons destroy the rice ears and so threaten man's existence. Now the typhoon, while seasonal, is also unexpected and sudden; thus it contains the dual nature of man's way of life. So on top of the dual nature of the monsoon climate, which, at one and the same time, in the form of copious moisture blesses man with food and threatens him in the form of violent winds and floods, and on top of the passive and resignatory way of life that corresponds to this monsoon climate in general, there is a further distinctive addition in Japan—the distinctive duality of tropical and frigid zones, and the seasonal and the sudden.

Monsoon receptivity assumes a very unique form in the Japanese for it is, first of all, both tropical and frigid. It is neither the constant fullness of feeling of the tropics nor again the single-toned tenacity of emotion of the cold zones. Although there is a plentiful outflow of emotion, there is a steady tenacity that persists even through change. Just like the changes of the seasons, the receptivity of the Japanese calls for abrupt switches of rhythm. So the Japanese is full of emotional vitality and sensitivity, lacking all continental phlegm. Such vitality and sensitivity lead to exhaustion and an absence of tenacity. But the recovery from this fatigue is not the effect of an unresponsive repose; it is rather brought about by constant changes of emotion resulting from abrupt switches of stimulus and mood.

But there is no alteration in the nature of emotions at such times of exhaustion and recovery, so that behind this lack of tenacity there lurks a certain dogged continuity. In other words, emotions may change but, inwardly, they persist.

Japanese receptivity, in the second place, is seasonal and abrupt. For in that a tenacity underlies emotional changes, and because, through the constant switches, the same emotion persists, the change is not simply seasonal and regular nor is it again entirely abrupt or haphazard. Rather, while the changes are always unexpected, they are switches to a new emotion conditioned in part by the old one. Emotions can alternate with the unanticipated and abrupt intensity of a seasonal yet savage typhoon. This emotional power is not characterised by any tenacious sustention, but rather by a savagery akin to that of Japan's own searing autumn winds. This has led often to historical phenomena of the character not of a sustained struggle but of a complete social overturning. And it has further produced the distinctive Japanese cast of mind that exalts and sets great value on emotion and abhors all tenacity. It is of deep significance and highly appropriate that this mood of the Japanese should be symbolised by the cherry blossoms, for they flower abruptly, showily and almost in indecent haste; but the blooms have no tenacity—they fall as abruptly and disinterestedly as they flowered.

Monsoon resignation also takes its own distinctive turn in Japan. First of all, it is both tropical and frigid. In other words, it is neither unresisting acquiescence of the tropical zone nor persistent and patient doggedness of the frigid zone. For, although essentially resignation, through resistance it becomes mutable and quick-tempered endurance. Violent winds and deluge rains in the end enforce resignation on man, but their typhoon nature provokes in him a fighting mood. Thus, while the Japanese thought neither to submit passively to nor to resist nature, he did attain an ill-sustained acquiescence. This is the passivity that is evinced in Japan's distinctive self-abandonment

In second place, this resignation is seasonal and abrupt. A resignation that includes resistance, precisely on account of this resistance, is not a seasonal or a regular reiteration of resistance; nor again is it an abrupt or haphazard resignation. Rather, within the reiteration there is an abrupt suddenness of resignation. Resistance, lurking behind this mask of resignation, can erupt with the unexpected savagery of a typhoon, yet once this storm of emotion has died down, there remains an equally abrupt and calm acquiescence. The seasonal and the abrupt within receptivity correspond directly to those within resignation. Fight and resistance are admired almost to the degree of savagery yet they do not develop into dogged persistence, for graceful abandonment or acquiescence enhance such spirited resistance and fight. In other words, an abrupt swing to resignation, open forgetting and forgiving, are considered virtues by the Japanese. The cast of mind that is symbolised by the cherry blossom is based in part on this abrupt resignation and is revealed most explicitly in open-hearted throwing away of life. This, in the form of the attitude under persecution of Japan's Christian martyrs, and again more recently in the Russo-Japanese war provoked European admiration. Anything that is grounded on resistance or fight is a clinging to life. For all that, when this attachment to life was exhibited in its most intense and objective aspect, the most prominent and central feature of this attachment was the attitude that was the very opposite—a complete contradiction of this tenacity. This is shown to perfection in war. The spirit of Japanese swordsmanship is the harmony of sword and calm meditation. In other words, the spirit of war is heightened on account of this dogged attachment to and transcending of life. These qualities all stem from Japan's "typhoon resignation".

This, then, is the distinctive Japanese way of life—a copious outflow of emotion, constantly changing, yet conceals perseverence beneath this change; at every moment in this alternation of mutability and endurance, there is abruptness. This activity of emotions sinks to resigned acquiescence in resistance, and underneath the exaltation of activity there lies a quiet and suddenly apparent abandonment. This is a quiet savagery of emotion, a fighting disinterest. Here we discover the national spirit of Japan. And we shall only find this natural character manifested through the events of history, since in fact it was built up by historical influences.

Man is essentially social, or relational. So his distinctive way of life is manifested best of all through such relations and through the associational attitudes formed in the process. The most familiar of these relationships, as Aristotle pointed out, is that between man and woman. The distinction made by the very use of the words 'man' and 'woman' is already understood in terms of this basic relationship. In other words, man plays one role in this relationship, woman the other; a person unable to play one of these roles can become neither man nor woman, and however much one unites such individuals, one will still not effect a relationship of male and female. Thus by the very use of the words 'man' and 'woman', we ascribe to the individual his function in this relationship. So though 'a person' can be an individual entity, 'man' and 'woman' do not exist independently of each other.

This relationship between male and female in Japan can be traced by reading Japan's love poems, starting from those in the *Kojiki* and the *Nihon Shoki* and proceeding through this most rich of all source materials. Here is found a calm love concealed behind a violence of passion, a love that is at once fighting yet selfless and acquiescent. This Japanese type of love and the many artless and disappointed loves pictured in the *Kojiki* possess a calm found neither in the Old Testament nor in the Greek epics. Yet, at the same time these loves have a typhoon savagery and a fighting power of a kind that could exist neither in India nor in China. But it is in the lovers' suicide that this calm and selfless resignation is shown at its most clear and concrete. As time passed, this artlessness was lost; yet this form of love is still discernible in the *Heian* period which saw in love the "sadness in life" and in the *Kamakura* period, when love was united with religion, and even in the *Ashikaga* period which glorified the fundamental power of love. Buddhism in no way bedevilled love's position. Rather, with its notions of worldly passions, it checked the divorce of soul and body. In the same way, the lovers' suicide, the favourite theme of *Tokugawa* literature, did not rest purely on a spiritual belief in the other world; rather, it displays the affirmation of love through a denial of life; the heart yearning for an eternity of love is crystallised in this momentary exaltation. Even if it is a departure from the way of man, in that, for the sake of the man-woman role, it tramples on man's other roles, it yet still evinces the character of the distinctive Japanese type of love.

There is, then, in the Japanese type of love, first and foremost an exaltation of love rather than a yearning for life. Love is not the handmaiden of desire—it is the latter that acts as love's handmaiden. So it is in love that there stands out an inseparable bond created by desire, a completely insoluble bond between man and woman. Here, there is a complete harmony of character expressed in terms of a gentle love. But, secondly, love is always of the flesh, and never a union of the spirit only. Love is never able to dispense with fleshly desire as its tool so that a calm love of personality becomes at one and the same time a burning passion. A bond never to be slackened is attempted through the agency of the flesh which is separable; an eternal longing of the soul explodes in a flash in the flesh. Thus, thirdly, love becomes a valour which does not cling to the life in the flesh; and, fourthly, there lies underneath all this an abrupt resignation—resignation that an indissoluble bond is hopeless in the flesh;

then fleshly love selflessly denies the flesh. Not only is this shown at its height in the lovers' suicide; it is further indicated by the fact that the Japanese, who always understand love as of the flesh, are selfless in the flesh. So Japanese love preserves a quality of emotion more refined than any such type of love as will selfishly cling to fleshly desire while it understands love as a matter of the soul.

But to limit the 'relationship' between man and woman only to one of unmarried love is to consider the abstract only. For this relationship must of necessity also include that between husband and wife and between parent and child. But this relationship of parent and child is not only that between husband and wife and the child they have born; for this husband and wife, as well as possessing the role of parent, are themselves the children of their own parents. So, in addition to being man or woman, there is also the factor of a person's status, as husband or wife, as parent or child. There can be no man or woman who has not fulfilled the role of child. So the male–female relationship is based in the associational attitude of the family, in the relationships of husband and wife, parent and child and so on. So the functions of these relationships developed in the first place within the unit of the family as a whole; it is not the case that the family comes into being through the association of man and woman, husband and wife and so on.

Relationships between people as family members differ openly between meadow, desert and monsoon climates. Meadow culture began with the piratical adventures of the Greeks. Adventurous males who had become separated from their native pastures made attacks on the Aegean coastlines; they began to build a rudimentary *polis* and took as wives the women of the lands they had conquered. Here there was the beginning of a new family, its constituents men who had escaped from their native houses and women whose housholds had been slaughtered. This is the historical background of the frequent stories of a wife killing her husband in the old Greek traditions. Hence although from the very first the Greeks had a firm tradition of ancestor worship and steadfastly clung to rites honouring the *hestia,* once the *polis* was created, its significance came to dominate that of the house. The family was understood in terms of husband and wife; in the matter of lineage, descent was traced only back to the father at the very best. In contrast, the desert family was regarded in terms of a traditional existence which bore the burden of the whole lineage from the very first ancestor. So even Jesus, born of the Virgin, is the "son of Abraham", the "seed of David". But in the way of life of the desert, this exalted state of the family yielded place to the tribe, for it was the latter rather than the family that was the unit of nomad life. Community of family life under the strict surveillance of tribal solidarity strengthened this sense. However, it was the monsoon family, particularly in China and Japan, that laid the greatest stress of all on the community of family life. As with the desert, there is the same power of lineage, but this was not dissipated in the tribe.

"House" signifies the family as a whole. The latter is represented by the head of the house, but it is the family as a whole that gives the head of the house his authority; it is not the case that the house is brought into existence at the whim of its head. The "house" is given a substantial and distinctive character by the fact that its unity is understood in historical terms. The family of the present shoulders the burden of this historical house and undertakes liability for its unity from past down into future. So the good name of the house can make a victim even of the household head. The household member, then, is not merely parent or child, husband or wife; he is also a descendant of his ancestors and himself an ancestor to those that are to come. The 'house' thus evinces most starkly the fact that the family as a whole takes precedence over its individual members.

The "house" in this sense stood out prominently as part of the Japanese way of life; the family system was stressed as being an elegant and beautiful custom. But where does the special character of this family system lie? And will Japan's distinctive way of life disappear as the family system falls into disuse?

What has been said of the specific character of Japanese love holds good in entirety for the family way of life. Here, the point of enquiry is the relationship not between male and female but between husband and wife, parent and child, elder and younger brother or sister. This relationship is, above all, that of gentle affection, aiming at a completely frank union. The artless ancients, when speaking of quarrels between husband and wife or of jealousy, already display this sense of warm and unreserved family affection. Again, the fine poem of Okura, the Manyo poet—"Silver or gold or jade, none are as precious as my child"—has long been regarded as entirely appropriate to the heart of the Japanese. Okura's family affection is revealed even more directly by his poem "On Going Home From A Party";

"My sobbing child and his mother
Now wait for me to go home."

Such gentle affection can even be seen in the Kamakura warriors who effected a great social revolution; Kumagaya Renshobo's reversal of heart, for example, sprang from his affection for his child. Again, in the No chants of the Ashikaga period the love between parent and child is conceived as of a deep and fundamental power. It goes almost without saying that the literary arts of the Tokugawa period used the affection between parent and child when they wished to draw tears. Through every age, the Japanese strove for the sacrifice of selfishness within the family. So there is a full realisation of the concept of the fusion of self and other. But while this affection is calm it is at the same time full of passion. The calmness of affection is not a mere fusion of emotions sunk in the depths of gloom;

it is a durability of emotions which lies behind fullness of feeling and the mutations brought by the latter. But this calm is only achieved at the cost of the purge and the purification of powerful emotions. So the force that is directed towards unreserved unity within the family, in spite of its outward calm, is essentially very intense. Thus the sacrifice of the self does not stop short at the needs of convenience but is carried through to the extreme limits. Whenever it meets with an obstacle, this quiet affection turns into ardent passion, forceful enough even to overwhelm the individual for the sake of the whole family. So, in third place, the family relationship takes the form of a heroic and martial attitude, unsparing even of life itself. Notions of vendetta carried on for the sake of parents in, for example, the *Tales of the Soga,* indicate just how much such sentiments stirred the hearts of the Japanese. A man was ready to sacrifice his life for his parents or for the good name of the house, and, for the individual concerned, this sacrifice was felt to possess the greatest significance in life. Such was the heroic *samurai,* prepared to lay down all for the good name of his house. The house as a whole was always of greater import than the individual, so, as a fourth feature, the latter threw away his life with the utmost selflessness. The most striking feature of Japanese history is this readiness to stake one's life for the sake of parent or child, or to cast away life for the house. So the calm of family affection contains the sacrifice of self-centredness; thus valour for the good of the family, in that it is not grounded in selfishness, is not a dogged clinging to life.

Hence, the Japanese way of life regarded as that of a household is none other than the realisation, through the family, of the distinctive relationship of Japan—the fusion of a calm passion and a martial selflessness. This relationship further became the basis of the conspicuous development of the 'house' itself, for this calm affection did not permit man to be viewed either artificially or abstractly, and, as a result, it was inappropriate to the development of a larger community of men built on the consciousness of the individual. So the concept of "house" in Japan takes on the unique and important significance of, if you like, the community of all communities. This is the real essence of the Japanese way of life and the Japanese family system, built on this foundation, has roots more deeply laid than any ideology.

It will be readily acknowledged that the family system has no longer the prominence or power that it possessed in Tokugawa days. But it would be harder to argue that the Japanese way of life today is divorced from the house. Modern European capitalism tries to see man as an individual; the family, too, is interpreted as a gathering of individuals to serve economic interests. But it could not on any account be argued that the Japanese, in spite of the adoption of capitalism, ceased to see the individual in the 'house' and came to regard the 'house' in an association of individuals.

To cite the most everyday phenomenon, the Japanese understand the house as "inside" and the world beyond it as "outside". Within this "inside", all distinction between individuals disappears. To the wife, the husband is "inside", or "the man inside" or even "the house". (These are the actual terms used of a husband.) To the husband, the wife is "inside the house". The family, too, is "those within"—distinguished clearly from anyone outside; but once within, all distinction disappears. Thus the "house", or the "inside" is regarded as the family as a whole, a relationship admitting no discrimination, but very strictly segregated from the "outside" world. A distinction of this nature between "inside" and "outside" is not to be found in European languages where, although one may speak of "inside" and "outside" in reference to a room or a house, these terms are not used of this family relationship. Contrasts between "inside" and "outside" that possess a significance weighty enough for them to correspond to

Japanese usage, are, in the first place, that between inside and outside of the heart of the individual, secondly between inside and outside of a house, regarded as a building, and thirdly, between inside and outside of a country or town. Hence, in this kind of distinction, attention is focussed primarily on the confrontation between spirit and flesh, between human and natural, and between the communities of men on the broad scale; there is no thought of making family relationship the standard of distinction. Thus it would not be unfair to say that the concepts of "inside" and "outside" in Japan lead directly to a comprehension of her way of life.

Exactly the same phenomenon is revealed by house structure. In other words, the house regarded as a structure of human relations is reflected in the layout of a house regarded simply as a building. Above all, the house exhibits an internal fusion that admits of no discrimination. None of the rooms are set off from each other by lock and key with a will to separation; in other words, there is no distinction between individual rooms. Even if there is a partitioning by *shoji* (sliding doors) or *fusuma* (screens), this is a division within a unity of mutual trust, and is not a sign of a desire for separation. So the close and undiscriminating unity of the house does permit such partitioning by *shoji* or *fusuma*; but the very fact of the need for partition within this undiscriminating unity is an indication of the passion it contains. So such partitions indicate the existence of antagonisms within the house; yet their removal is in itself a show of a completely unbarriered and selfless openness.

In second place, the house is quite unmistakably distinguished from "outside". Even if there is no lock on the rooms, there is always one on the door that leads to the outside; there may also be beyond this a fence, a wall, and, in extreme cases, a protective thicket or a moat. When a Japanese returns home from the "outside", he removes his *geta* or shoes, and by this very act he draws an explicit distinction between "inside" and "outside".

Thus the "house" continues as ever in Japan,—and continues not just as a formal entity but as a determinant of the Japanese way of life. The degree to which the character of the latter is unique becomes clearer with a comparison with the European way of life. A house in Europe is partitioned off into individual and independent rooms which are separated by thick walls and stout doors. These doors can all be secured by intricate locks so that only key-holders may come and go freely. In principle, this is a construction stressing individuality and separation. The distinction between "inside" and "outside" as understood first and foremost as one of the heart of the individual is reflected in house construction; it becomes the "inside" and "outside" of the individual room so that to go out of a room in Europe has the same significance as to go out of a house in Japan. Inside the room, as an individual, that is, one may strip naked; but once one goes from the room and joins the family as a whole, one should always be neat and tidy. Once one takes a step out of the room, there is little difference whether it be to the dining-room inside the house or to a street restaurant. In other words, the dining room, within the house, is already the equivalent of "outside" to the Japanese; yet, at the same time, "outside" in Europe, a restaurant or the opera, plays the same role as the tea-room or the living room in Japan. Hence, in one aspect, the unit equivalent to the house in Japan is narrowed down to the individual room with its lock and key; but, in another aspect, the family circle in Japan is broadened in Europe to extend to the whole of the community. In Europe there is no indissoluble relation, but merely a loose social grouping of individuals which does admit separation. Yet although this extends beyond the room as the unit, it is still "inside" from the aspect of a common livelihood, as are the parks or the town streets. Hence, while what corresponds to the wall or the fence of the Japanese house is narrowed down to the lock on the individual room, in other aspects this same equivalent is broadened to become the city walls or the surrounding moat. The city gateway in Europe corresponds to the Japanese house doorway. So, in Europe, the house, midway between the two units of room and city wall, is not of great significance. Man is individualist in the extreme; so, in addition to segregation, there is social intercourse, cooperation within division. In other words, the house has no prescriptive functions.

In outward aspects, the Japanese have copied the European way of life; but it would not be unfair to say that they remain almost entirely uninfluenced by Europe in the matter of their inability to base their social and public life on individualism. Who would think he could walk on an asphalt road in stockinged feet? Who would walk in his shoes—even if they be western shoes—on Japanese *tatami* matting? Where then is to be found this identity of "inside" the house, (in Japan), with "inside" the town, (in Europe)? It is not European in spirit to consider "the town" as completely alien to and outside of "the house"; and only in that he lives in an open, unpartitioned house is the Japanese still prescribed, as he always has been, by his house.

So it must be allowed that the way of life as seen in the house does very strikingly exhibit the distinctive character of the people. And it was by way of the concept of the house as a whole unit that the Japanese came to be aware of themselves as a whole. Mankind as a whole was understood first in terms of *Kami,* the Japanese spirit or deity; and in historical terms, this *Kami* was the ancestor of the house as a whole. This was the exceedingly plain and homely conception of wholeness or unity in early times, but, surprisingly enough, even as Japan's history progressed, this homely vital force continued to stay alive. The Meiji Restoration was achieved as the result of an awakening of Japan's people expressed in the form of the cry, "Revere the Emperor; expel the foreigner". But this awakening was in actual fact grounded in a revival of the spirit of the myths that regarded Japan as the land of the *kami,* the latter faith growing from the worship of the deity enshrined at Ise, the sanctum sanctorum. There can be no parallel in the rest of the world for this phenomenon; for a religious concept of wholeness was able, even in an age of the advance of culture, to act as the driving power of social revolution. So even the awakening of the Japanese people which blazed at the time of the foreign wars of the Meiji period was not a topic of theory in and for itself but was rather interpreted in terms of the analogy of the old traditional family unity. The Japanese, it was said, were one great family which regarded the Imperial House as the home of its deity. The people as a whole are nothing but one great and unified house, all stemming from an identical ancestor. Thus the entire state is "the house within the household" and the fence that surrounds the latter is broadened in concept to become the boundaries of the state. Within the borders of this state as a whole, there should be the same unreserved and inseparable union that is achieved within the household. The virtue that is called filial piety from the aspect of the household becomes loyalty from the standpoint of the state. So filial piety and loyalty are essentially identical, the virtue prescribing the individual in accordance with the interests of the whole.

The claims of this loyalty and filial piety, viewed as a single virtue, include a fair degree of patent irrationalities, whether regarded theoretically or historically. The family is the *alpha* of all human communities, as being a unit of personal, physical, community life; the state is the *omega* of all human communities, as being a unit of spiritual community life. The family is the smallest, the state the largest unit of union. The building up of the connection is different in each. So to regard family and state in the same light as human structures is mistaken. Further, speaking now historically, the filial piety that was stressed so heavily in the Tokugawa period does not by any means exhaust the sum total of the prescriptions laid on the individual in virtue of his membership of the house as a whole. In China, the relationship between father and son was denominated by a separate term but "filial piety" in the Tokugawa period signified only the son's relationship of service to his parents. In the same way, loyalty was understood in the narrow sense of the personal relationship between retainer and feudal lord, and had no connection with the state as a whole. Hence the reverence for the Emperor which symbolised the reversion to the state as a whole was essentially different from loyalty as it was understood in the Tokugawa period. Thus, the fact of the correspondence of the relationship of service to a parent with that of service to one's feudal lord is no proof of the correspondence of loyalty is the sense of reverence for the Emperor (loyalty that is, in the significance not of an individual relationship but of a reversion of the individual to the whole) with filial piety understood as the prescriptions laid on the individual by the family as a whole.

Even so, there is a deal of historical sense in the assertion of identity between loyalty and filial piety, both of them directed towards an understanding of the nation as a whole in terms of the analogy of the house. This is the familiar trait of the Japanese; the attempt to interpret the nation as a whole in terms of the distinctive Japanese way of life. And the simple fact that this particular and unique way of life was feasible hints that while the distinctiveness of the Japanese was best exemplified in the way of life of the household, at the same time in the way of life of the nation as a whole a similar distinctiveness was reflected.

In Japan, the one-ness of the nation was first interpreted in the religious sense; this is a circumstance of primitive society that can be understood only by way of myths. Before man felt or thought as an individual, his consciousness was that of the group; anything disadvantageous to the livelihood of the group restricted the actions of the individual in the form of a taboo. In a society of this nature, mankind as a whole was conceived in terms of a mystic force, so that a reversion to this mystic force was nothing other than a return to the whole; worship was merely the expression of the whole in terms of the rite of worship. Hence those who directed such rites came to be invested with a god-like authority as being representatives of thi, whole. The rainmaker became Zeus. This is a trend common to primitive religions; but in Japan we can see it in model fashion. As well as *kami* (deity) *Amaterasu Omikami* was also the superintendent of ritual. The most explicit expression of such conditions is to be found in the fact that ritual became government.

Thus the primitive Japanese were a unified religious group secured and guaranteed by such rituals. Although there were sad deficiencies in military and economic organisation and capacity, yet the religious bond created a highly compact solidarity and was primarily the source of their ability to send a considerable military force as far afield as Korea. This is also evident from the nationwide discoveries of tomb-period relics, which indicate the existence of the worship of mirror, jewel and sword. And this community of men as such a religious grouping, just as that of the household, was the community of a fusion of feeling that demanded no awareness from the individual of his identity as an individual. So this religious grouping came to be the most outstanding embodiment of the Japanese way of life.

Japan's myths may well show trace of all manner of primitive faiths. Yet the achievement of a compact unification through the agency of a single religious ritual has no parallel in the myths of either Greece or India. In this particular, only those of the Old Testament stand comparison. However the latter make clear distinction between god and man, whereas in Japan there is an affinity between the two, understood in terms of a blood connection. In the Old Testament, God's dealings with man are imbued with a strict and wilful authority; but in Japan, when *kami* approaches man, he never commands or wills; he is, rather, characterised by a gentle and emotional affection. This character is shown in true form by the descriptions of *Amaterasu Omikami* (the Sun Goddess). This is no more or less than a proof of the indissoluble unification and quiet affection that characterise the relationship of man within his religious grouping. The gods of Greece are not dissimilar in the fact of their proximity to man; but, in addition, they already reflect a relationship based on intellect and on the characteristics of a republican polity. They indicate, in other words, the Greek incapacity of unification within a single ritual.

Indissoluble unification within a single ritual was not of the same kind as the union of the spirit of the Christian Church. For, it was a union both in religion and of man, man who is flesh. Hence it was exemplified in the form not of the church of a God that transcended national division, but of a national unity. In the Church of God ritual was concerned in great measure with the soul and did not develop into the handling of the affairs of this life on earth; but ritual in the context of national unity easily became, in another aspect, administration of that nation's affairs. The Emperor, like the Pope, was the representative of the whole; but, unlike the Pope, he was at the same time the sovereign of the state. Hence, the inseparable union of the religious group, as being that of man who is flesh, was realised above all in separation. So it was inevitable that passion should be evident. *Amaterasu Omikami*, characterised by calm affection, could turn into the resolute god of fire and thunder. Here is an indication of the dual-natured "calm in passion" of the national way of life.

While being the unity of a religious grouping, this was also very much a union of, and not transcending, this world. It was for this reason that this inseparable union was realised in separation. So this coming together always contained the elements of confrontation and of struggle. War had already broken out between the *kami*—the myths are full of stories of war—so that union founded on a religious grouping could never be characterised by harmony only and achieve complete elimination of such elements of antagonism. This character is what people call the Japanese martial spirit.

But this latter did not lead the Japanese to anything in the form of a disintegration into innumerable *polis*. It was through war that a single ritual had been attained and in the same way war showed the path to inseparable union. The achievement of the latter was made possible by the selflessness that lay beneath the martial spirit. The wars that are the subject of the myths were all selfless—though this did not of itself eliminate the spirit of fierceness and fury from such fighting, but resulted rather in the fact that such fierce wars could switch abruptly to unity and harmony. Here again we find the duality of a martial selflessness that characterises the life of the nation.

Thus the ancient unification of the nation within this religious grouping has a distinctive character capable of interpretation by the house analogy. It was a passionate and yet placid union, a martial and yet selfless fusion. Because of this distinctive character, the Japanese warrior, even in the fiercest of fighting, could still look on his opponent as a brother, for it was not a part of the Japanese spirit to feel unremitting hatred for an enemy. Here we can see the ground in which Japan's morality took seed. Before the evolution of moral concepts, men's actions and minds were evaluated in terms of 'noble' or 'clean', 'dirty' or 'mean'. In this evaluation, there is already a reflection of the distinctive national character.

From this distinctive evaluation, we can pick out several outstanding elements. In first place, we see here the religious belief that directed the life of the nation towards that of a religious grouping. Nobility was recognised above all in the *kami* who presided over the ritual; so the motive force that led to unity was the source of all values. It is expressible in terms of reverence for the Emperor. In second place, value is set on the indissoluble union of man. A gentle heart and quiet affection were attributes indispensable for the great man and such qualities were understood not merely in terms of personal affections within the family circle but as the basis of mutual relationships reaching through the nation. In one sense, then, this was esteem of affection between men; but in another sense it became esteem for social justice. In third place, value was set in the nobility that characterised the warrior's selflessness. Valour was noble and beautiful, cowardice mean and unclean. But sheer brute force was ugly and unbecoming, brutality the ugliest of all. For though valour might well exist in it, there was also a strong taint of tenacious and selfish lust, and the nobility of valour lies in its disregard of self. Thus the bravery of the warrior must on all account be accompanied by a selfless resignation. In this sense, nobility and meanness came to be of higher value than life itself.

Myths and traditions show that these were the three prime virtues of the ancients. However, in that this characteristic of ancient times was based on the primitive faith of a union through religion, is it still discernible after the swift advance of culture? Could this indissoluble union of the nation still persist even after the dawn of a clear awareness of the individual as an entity in himself?

The period of which we have been speaking, that of the myths and traditions, and that of the tumuli, culminated in the construction of tomb-mounds of vast grandeur and military contact with Korea. It was, again, the age in which a stout and nation-wide union of the Japanese was achieved as a unification by way of ritual. In this light we can examine also the ages that followed, using as a link for this examination the great social upheavals of Japanese history The first such upheaval, nationwide unification in a ritual, achieved a society based on a feudal and religious structure. The feudal lords, in virtue of the religious authority of the Emperor—that of mirror, jewels and sword, that is—represented the entirety of the people of their territories. However, contact with the Chinese and their culture in Korea gradually drained the freshness from these primitive faiths and military and economic power took the place of religious authority as the force by which the local lord exercised sway. At this point unification by ritual came to include elements of unification by administration, a process heralded by a trend towards the centralisation of authority through an increase of shrine officials. Thus it was the very Chinese culture that had undermined the authority of religion that was taken up as the weapon to fashion a new administrative unification. As a result, the formation of centralised authority followed on the overthrow of a primitive feudal society. The Taika Reformation achieved a social structure of national socialism based on the principle of public land ownership; and even such drastic reform could be effected without even the smallest civil disturbance because of the religious authority that lay behind economic power.

The third of the great upheavals brought a recrudescence of feudalism in the form of the Kamakura Shogunate. A social system based on joint land ownership was unable to satisfy the natural urge to own something privately and the powerful and the mighty, concealed behind their vast manors, the curse of common ownership, worked away quietly for the establishment of private ownership; finally, the military power fostered in such manors brought the second age of feudalism, constituted by a Shogun and the protective manorial lords dependent on him. And even while there was no repeal of the legal system current in the period of public ownership, the military dictates of the Shogun came in practice to have the validity of law.

The fourth major upheaval was that of the Age of Civil Wars (or Fighting Barons); although feudalism itself was not upset, the controlling class was overthrown and its place taken by a force emanating from the people as a result of insurrectionary movements. At the same time, with the development of the town, the economic power of an urban population began slowly and quietly to overrun power of a military nature.

The fifth upheaval, the Meiji Restoration, saw the overthrow once more of feudalism and the achievement again of a centralisation of authority. The Emperor, who had possessed no physical power throughout the long years of feudalism, took precedence as of old over the Shogun and became again the symbol of the nation as a whole. Primitive faiths died hard.

Using these several upheavals as a mirror to the age in which they occurred, we can discover to what extent there was a historical realisation of the distinctive national character and of the moral thinking that grew from it. Reverence for the Emperor, the symbol of unity of the religious grouping, was indeed the motive power behind the Meiji Restoration. Feudal princes attempting to resist this by military power alone could achieve no division among the forces working for the Restoration and they disintegrated eventually in the face of the nation as a whole. Again in the fourth upheaval, that of the Age of the Fighting Barons, "nobility" as it was understood in antiquity, appears prominently in the guise of *bushido*. The essential spirit of *bushido* was to know shame, to feel ashamed in face of meanness, cowardice, baseness and servility. Here is a model instance of morality understood in terms not of good and evil but of the noble and the mean. Again the esteem accorded by antiquity to affection reappears in the age of the Kamakura Shogunate during the ascendancy of the all-powerful Kamakura Buddhist tenets of benevolence and charity. The concept of indissoluble union was understood in terms of a practical realisation of unconditional altruism and the goal of action became an affection of the kind that would throw away life selflessly. High regard for this same affection and the sense of social justice that grew from it are reflected in the theories of joint land ownership of the Taika Reforms, the second upheaval. With the national unity of a religious group backed by the newly adopted Buddhism and its ideals, this was an attempt to realise such ideals in practical form.

Moral thinking of this nature must be given special attention in our enquiry, for though essentially, of course, it is in no way peculiar to Japan, yet it was understood with a distinctive power in Japan. And it was in the distinctive national traits of the like of a stillness of passion and the selflessness of the warrior that the peculiar character of this realisation was based.

(1931)

b) *The Uniqueness of Japan*

When asked for my impressions of anything unusual after my first visit to Europe, all that I could do was to reply with a very firm "No". There was a great deal that impressed me deeply, but in the matter of the rare or the unusual Europe offered nothing of the standard of the Egyptian or Arabian deserts that I saw en route. However, on my return to Japan at the end of my travels, I was made suddenly and keenly aware of the strange character of Japan, a strangeness in no way inferior to that of the Arabian desert, a strangeness which makes Japan unique in the world. I propose to discuss here the nature of and the reason for this strangeness of which I became aware so suddenly.

The word *mezurashii* (strange) is said to derive from *mezuru*, meaning "to prize" or "to value"; but, judging from its everyday usage at least, there seems to be no essential connection with the latter. For example, even though there might be some sense of "prizing" the 'warmth' in the context "It is strangely warm for winter", this is certainly not true of the 'cold' in "It's unusually cold". So in essence "strange" and "value" must be set apart. The basic sense of *mezurashii* is "unusual" or "rare". On the basis of the premise of "the usual" or "the normal", it appears as "the unusual" or "the abnormal". Some degree of appreciation of the normal and everyday are essential for the recognition of the abnormal or the strange. Again the abnormal and the strange are not to be found where everything is as usual in what has already been recognised as normal. Thus for one who had understood the normal appearance of a landscape as covered in plant-life, the desert was strange or abnormal in the extreme. But, at the same time, to one who had understood the normal appearance of European architecture from examples seen in Japan, European cities, where buildings were as they should be, had nothing strange to offer. Whereas a text-book definition of desert in terms of the absence of plant-life gives no understanding of desert conditions, the Western architecture of Japan's cities did give me a concrete and positive insight into the conditions of Europe's cities. However, the strangeness that I felt on returning to Japan meant one of two things; either Japan where I had lived for so long and to which my eyes were accustomed, had come to possess qualities different from what I had hitherto considered as normal, or else Japan remained unchanged and it was in my interpretation of the normal that there had been the transformation. Or perhaps it was not just one of these factors but both of them that were at play. In other words, the normal condition in which I had lived and which I had grown used to seeing through the years remained identical; but there was exposed a much more fundamental condition lying underneath the surface which I had failed to perceive hitherto and which was now interpreted as rare or abnormal in contrast to what I had come to understand previously as normal.

Let me clarify this with the aid of a familiar example. Cars and trams are an everyday sight in Japan, so much so that it would be rare for a Japanese, nowadays at least, to marvel at these imports from or copies of the West. So it is not a matter of sensing anything strange about the cars or trams in Europe; rather it is a case of the Japanese being startled at the dirtiness of the taxis, the small dimensions of the trams and so on. The latter, for instance, in every town, give an impression of skimpiness (with the sole exception, of the window glass) far greater than the Japanese is accustomed to seeing at home. The underground railways too seem to be on a lighter scale than the Tokyo Government Line. Whether they are in fact smaller in size and lighter in weight is not in question here. (Perhaps, in point of fact, they are. The carriage ceilings on underground railways always seemed to me to be much lower than in Japan.) Anyhow, the fact remains that this is the impression we are given and there is nothing of the strange or the abnormal about this impression. Yet when I came back to Japan and looked at the cars or the trams in the streets, I did indeed feel that I was watching a wild boar rampaging through fields. When a tram surges through the houses that line the tracks, they seem to crouch and bow spiritlessly just as the commoner would grovel in face of a feudal lord's procession. The tram is taller than a single-storied house, longer than a house frontage and so stoutly built that if it were to run amuck, one has the impression that it would be the flimsy wooden houses that would be smashed into smithereens by its powerful onsurge. When a tram passes, it completely blots from view the houses on the opposite side of the street and only the sky can be seen above its roof. Even a car seems to loom large in Japan; in a narrow street it appears to block the way like a whale in a canal and it can even seem both taller and somehow longer than a house. But in Europe these means of communication are dwarfed by the houses; they are treated as tools of communication, as retainers in the service of city or individual, and their appearance fits their status perfectly. Yet in Japan these tools or servants overwhelm and overbear man, his house and even his town. Cars and trams are the same in both cases only in the matter of appearance and, roughly speaking, size; yet it is indeed remarkable and unusual that these identical objects can have inherent in them such a different balance—or lack of it—with their surroundings, be it house or town. Previously, I had not noticed any such disproportion, and when I went to Europe and saw these objects in their original proportion I felt only that they were small and did not spot any basic difference in balance. In objects seen everyday no absence of proportion was noticed; in addition, the original proportion, as being customary, was regarded as the most apt. However, after the return, this absence of proportion was both recognisable and strange, for there was now the realisation that although one had understood what was regarded as the most apt proportion, its defects had not been noticed even though they stared one in the face. So, working from it as a basis, one made a patent discovery of the defects of what was originally regarded as in proportion.

The absence of balance thus discovered (a true condition of the urban scene in Japan) was already a part of what has been for long felt to be the tangle and the disorder characterising Japan's modern civilisation. But we never appreciated that it was exemplified in such open, naked, candid and laughably strange terms. We, the Japanese, approached the problems of widening roads and facilitating car or tram transport only from the aspect of convenience, which only served to magnify the lack of balance between car, tram and road on the one hand, and house or town on the other. We are given modern, first-class roads one after another by our new city-planners; in dimension and the matter of pavements they are up to the standard of those of any European city. But in Europe, roads of this kind are lined by rows of tall tenement houses, a hundred of them even lining a short street. The ratio of street area to house then is very small. The same length of street in Japan would be lined by only a dozen or so houses, even allowing for the houses to be of the same frontage. Japan's houses, flat and low in the urban areas at least, seem to bite the ground; only the roads, open to the sky, give any sense of spaciousness and as a result their most obvious functions seem to be to offer free passage to the wind and to act as a collecting place for swirls of dust. In Europe's cities, even though there is little rain and wind to bring rubbish, the matter of keeping roads as clean and tidy as a corridor within a house is no light burden economically, even when the ratio of road surface per house is as insignificant as it is. The cost of the same task in Japan, where rainfall is heavy and mud plentiful, where the rubbish output is high—because of humidity—and where again the area of road surface per house is several times larger, would no doubt rise to ten times the figure for Europe. Roads as extravagant as this, broad and open to the sky, holding back rows of houses far meaner than any in Europe—these are Japan's wonderful, perhaps too wonderful, roads. In Japan the road is no longer a practical tool used for purposes of communication; it has become an extravagant luxury for which, for some reason or other, man is prepared to make his life miserable.

Such roads, to seek for a more basic origin, spring from the unduly wide and sprawling structure of the Japanese city. If New York is the best example in the world of a city suffering from height, then Tokyo is the most appropriate instance of a city suffering because of its sprawling character. The area covered by Tokyo's houses is said, for instance, to be several times that of Paris; even if the areas were identical, the drains that are adequate for Paris (to confine ourselves to the matter of the difference in rainfall only) would be far from satisfactory in the case of Tokyo. And since Tokyo's area is several times that of Paris, Tokyo would require several times the amount of public facilities that suffice for Paris, with the result that it would only be at a fantastic outlay that Tokyo could be equipped with merely the basic and essential facilities of a modern capital. To change the wording; Tokyo's sprawling nature is the precise antithesis of the character most suitable to the installation of facilities appropriate to the modern city. It is not only a question of drainage; the remarkable extension of roads and tram routes, the vast amount of electric cable and gas piping that is required, the time and the nervous energy consumed in travelling—all these, it could be alleged with reason, stem from Tokyo's sprawling character. In Japan, in other words, the greater the city the greater the inconvenience. Both economically and mentally, urban life demands tremendous outlay, yet life does not become in the least any more pleasant. And in the last analysis, this all comes back to the absence of proportion between city and house.

Then why do Japan's houses, completely out of balance with cars, trams, even with roads and cities, still continue to grovel almost at ground level, truly and grotesquely small in the midst of a great city? It will be said this is all rooted in an economic cause; that Japan is not as rich as Europe and that this is why high-storied buildings do not soar upwards toward the sky above Tokyo. But when one considers the immense waste as a result of the sprawling, it is difficult to accept this reason. If one totalled the construction cost of several dozen grovelling little shacks and added in land expenses and those of the various sources of waste mentioned above, it would be difficult to say which were the cheaper—this, or a tall and imposing ferro-concrete building. So it is not because of the lack of economic power that the Japanese do not build such tall buildings in their cities. The true reason is simply that the latter are not constucted by associational or cooperative methods. So we must ask now why the Japanese fail to choose this method when it is the more convenient, the more pleasant, and the only method which achieves results worthy of the word city.

One must look to the house itself to discover the reason. So our next problem is the character and the circumstances of the Japanese house.

The house in most European cities, with the exception of the homes of the rich, is not an individually inhabited and separate structure. You enter a building and there are doors to your right and left, each a "house"; you climb a staircase and again there are "houses" to right and left, each with its door, ten of them on the fifth floor, twelve on the sixth and so on, each leading off from the corridor and each a "house". Again if you go from the entrance through the garden to another entrance way, you find an identical staircase and an identical passage with the same significance leading up and through the same building. This passage is, so to speak, an extension of the road; its original purpose, in fact, is to serve as a road or a pathway. So if you go along this "street" and go through any of the "house" doorways, you come to another corridor or passage, leading through the centre of the house, on to which open the doors of individual rooms. These doors can all be locked so that each room by one motion of the hand can be made into an independent and self-contained "house". Such a room can be lived in as a house, with those who do not belong to the family unable to cause any trouble or worry. In this sense, then, even the passageway inside a house has all the qualifications of a street, as is shown very distinctly by the fact that when the postman delivers a registered letter to a person renting a single room, he must go through the corridor in the middle of the building and then through the passageway inside the house to reach the addressee's room. Nor is it only the postman; it is the same in the case of the errand-boy from the book shop or the department store. In this instance, it is the interior of the individual's room that corresponds to the porch of the Japanese house. If this be the case, then the street reaches right up to the door of this room and its occupant thus has direct contact both with street and town.

But this can also be regarded from completely the opposite point of view. The occupant of the room goes into the house passageway in the same clothing as he wears customarily in his own room; to go into the next corridor, he may just stick on his hat. He goes down the stairway and out of the building into the "corridor" beyond—the street—with no further change of or additions to his clothing. This street is washed by the rain in the mornings so that it is no dirtier than the corridor inside the building; (indeed, there are instances where it is the latter that is dirtier than the asphalt road). In fact the only differences between the two are that, in the case of the street, the sky appears and there are no means of keeping it warmed in winter. Someone may go across the street to a restaurant or to a coffee shop to listen to music or play cards. There is no difference between this action and that of walking along a long corridor to the dining room or the reception room of a large mansion. Nor is this restricted to someone living alone in a single room; it occurs every day in the case of a whole family. The gathering of the Japanese family in the living room to gossip or listen to the radio has the same significance as the visit of the European to the coffee shop to listen to music or to play cards. Coffee shop equals sitting room; street equals corridor. In this light, the entire town is the equivalent of a single house. If a man locks his door and goes thus beyond the one barrier that separates him from society, he enters public restaurants, public tea-rooms, public libraries and gardens.

Thus corridor is street and street corridor; there is no distinct barrier between the two. For, in one aspect, the scope of the meaning of "house" is narrowed down to a single room, in another it is broadened to include the whole of the town. In other words, house is not duly significant; only individual and society are left.

But in Japan, where there is no question of corridor becoming street or street becoming corridor, the house stands out most distinctly of all. Its barrier, be it porch or door, establishes a positive separation between street and corridor, between without and within. A Japanese takes off his shoes as soon as he enters a porch and does not put them on again until he goes beyond it. Nor does postman or errand-boy pass further than this barrier. Coffee shop and restaurant are entirely different buildings, in no sense the equivalent in purpose of the dining room or the living room within the house. The latter are private to a degree with not the slightest character of the public about them.

This is the type of house that the Japanese prefer to live in and in which only they can relax. However small it be, this is the sort of requirement they ask for in a house. Now what is the attraction that prompts such attachment? On the outside, the house is quite detached from the street; but within, there is nothing of the nature of the independence of an individual room. *Fusuma* and *shoji* do act as partitions but they have no atmosphere of an indication of a desire for antagonistic or protective separation of the kind expressed by the turning of a key in a lock; nor indeed do they possess the capabilities of becoming such. *Fusuma* and *shoji* have no power of resistance against anyone desiring to open them and their function as partitions, in a sense that is, always depends on the trust of others and their respect of the expression of the wish for separation indicated by the simple fact that they are drawn. In other words, within the "house", the Japanese feels neither need of protection against others nor any distinction between himself and others. A key indicates a desire for separation from the desires of others while *fusuma* and *shoji* show a unification of desires and are no more than a means of partitioning a room in this spirit of absence of separation. They have only the significance of a screen in the centre of a Western room. Within the house, there is no brandishing of keys as protectors of the individual's property. Thus the characteristics of the Japanese house are an absence of internal partitioning and the variety of the forms of key (including tall fences and formidable thickets) as protections against the world outside. So the attraction lies in this tiny centre of unity in the middle of the wide world.

But, it will no doubt be asked, is it not possible also to preserve such a tiny world in the European tenement house? However, this kind of building demands common action when it is under construction and again for its very existence it anticipates an attitude of those who live in it. Even if a room does not look immediately on to a passageway and has no means of direct intercourse with that next to it, yet it is still only a part of a much larger structure and sharing of facilities—for heating, hot water, the elevator—is inevitable. Such sharing, such community living is just what gives the Japanese his greatest misgivings and leads him to create his firmest partition between his house and the world outside. Europe's strongest partition in the past was the city wall; now it is the state frontier. Neither of these exist in Japan. Castle towns came to have a perimeter moat and dyke in the years just before and after the Momoyama period, but these were defensive works built by a group of *samurai* in preparation for attack from outside and were not the symbols of a desire on the part of the town to create a barrier or partition between itself and other such urban centres. So it is the fence or the wall round the house or the locked door in Japan that corresponds to Europe's city wall. Thus in the same way as the European has been conditioned and disciplined over the years by the world within his city wall, so the Japanese has been moulded within his much more confined world inside his house. Within the city wall men came into a group directed against the common enemy and protected their lives by their combined powers; any danger to joint interests was a danger to the individual's and to his neighbour's very existence. Cooperation became the basis and the keynote of life and prescribed every detail of life. Recognition of duty stood far in the forefront of that of any moral claims. Yet at the same time, cooperation, the submergence of the individual in most other cases, here gave a strong stimulus to individuality, so that the individual's rights, the correlative of his obligations, stood in the same way in the forefront of recognition. So the symbols of this way of life are "wall" and "key". But inside of the small world within the fence in Japan, cooperation did not envisage a common enemy endangering life but sprang rather from a natural affection so strong that it would readily call forth a spirit of complete self-sacrifice. Affection stands in front of awareness of obligation in the relationships between man and wife, parent and child, elder and younger brother; for though the individual gladly effaces himself yet in such effacement he still feels fullness in life. If cooperation depends on the individual for its full development, then it was only natural that it made little advance within this small world where the individual effaced himself so readily. In such circumstances, the individual never thought of standing on his rights nor did he come to the point of recognising the obligations involved in associational life. The environment prompted the advance of the delicate feelings appropriate to it, sympathy, modesty, reserve and consideration. Such feelings only had currency within the house and lost their validity in any relations with the unfriendly world outside; so the reverse of the picture is that one step beyond the porch of the Japanese house brought the preparedness for dealings with an aggressive enemy that went naturally with an outlook so unsociable. Hence the fence round the Japanese house corresponds exactly to the European city wall and the key. Thus the more insistent the demand for the abolition of reserve within the house, the more intense becomes the repugnance for cooperation outside.

The Europeanisation and Americanisation of Japanese society is indeed too plain to be gainsaid. Yet however conspicuous this be on the surface, as long as the old Japanese house continues to sprawl and grovel stubbornly in the midst of Japan's cities, in other words, as long as there exists this absence of balance that must be unique in the whole world, Japanese society will never succeed in breaking away from its roots in the past. Japanese wear Western clothes; they walk, in Western shoes, on asphalt roads; they ride in cars and trams and work in offices on the n-th floor of a Western style building which has Western furniture, electric lighting and steam-heat. One is tempted to ask, "Is there anything of Japan left?" And when it has all been listed, with Western fountain pen in Western style account book, it all comes back again to the house. "But is not this house, even, a building on Western models?", it may well be asked. Externally, it is. But it has a gate, a fence, a hallway; and, after all, funnily enough, the Japanese must still remove his shoes at the doorway. Here, not one of the qualifications of the Japanese house has been lost. So that the problem concerns not so much the size as the circumstances of this house. If a man wished to live in a house of this style in a European city, then, if nothing else, he must at least be rich. Why should it be then, that the man with the kind of income that in Europe would force him to live in a not very high-class terrace-house can live, not with any undue sense of distress or stringency, in a house with this kind of qualification? The answer is simple; the so-called Western style Japanese house, at basis, is not European in the least.

Let us follow the man who wears his Western clothes in his European style house. He has a lawn and flower beds in his front garden; sometimes there may even be a gardener to tend them. These are all for his and his family's delectation. Yet he shows not the slightest concern for the city park, for it is outside of his own house and so belongs to someone else. And this is the outlook of everyone else; the city park belongs to some other person, it is not "mine" and so it receives no loving care or protection. It is run by the city so that apart from the officials whose concern it is, noone feels any obligations in respect of it. So a matter that affects the city jointly does not attract the interest of the citizens generally but is left in the care of a handful of not too honest politicians. So there may be any amount of mismanagement, yet to the man living in his Western style house this is beyond his own four walls and so beyond his own ken. He, instead, in that he lives Western style, has "new" interests, such as his children's education. The moment his child blithely commits some dishonesty, then he sets his whole heart to the matter and is intensely concerned. But a piece of dishonest practice on the part of a politician in a matter of public concern does not even spur a hundredth part of such zeal. Again, even when he watches society, managed by these politicians, heading gradually towards a crisis as a result of their evil and corrupt practices, his reaction is that, after all, this is outside of his own house and that no doubt someone somewhere is assuming responsibility. Thus he has no determined or even clearly formulated attitude to such a problem. In other words, he does not regard the affairs of society as his own; which, of itself, indicates how little he is Europeanised.

In spite of the Western clothes in which Japanese parliamentary government has been conducted from the very first, the Japanese do not concern themselves in affairs of such public moment with the same zeal that they show for matters affecting their own person. There will always be something laughable about the Japanese parliamentarian as long as he tries to imitate a style of government conditioned by the discipline of communal life within a city wall while yet trying to do away with this basic discipline. The Japanese lavished most concern and value on his house; the lord of the manor could change and provided that the new lord, whoever he might be, in no way menaced his home, the Japanese gave the matter not the slightes concern. Even if there was a threat, it might be evaded by resignation and acquiescence. Thus, however servile the labours he was forced to perform, they did not impinge upon his intimate life within his own family circle. But, in contrast, within the city wall any resignation to a threat meant to the individual the loss of his all, so that common and aggressive resistance was the only method by which to preserve individuality. In the former instance, then, the development of acquiescence went hand in hand with indifference to public matters while in the latter, together with a keen interest and a ready participation in public affairs there arose an esteem for the claims of the individual. Only in the latter case was democracy really possible; only there did the election of representatives have true significance and only there could there exist public opinion—of the people as a whole. The red flag hanging from one window on the day of a Communist demonstration, the Imperial flag hanging from that next door on the day of a nationalist demonstration—such clear manifestations of a formed attitude together with a readiness to recognise one's duties as a citizen by a ready participation in such demonstrations are elements that democracy cannot afford to lack. But such concern on the part of the people at large just does not exist in Japan and, as a result, politics have become the specialised occupation of power-mongers. One of the most outstanding instances of this is that what goes by the name of a proletarian movement is in fact merely that of a coterie of leaders; it includes hardly any or at best only a handful of people to be led. It is not that this indicates a basic hollowness in such movements; rather, just as the Japanese show no care for a public park, so also the people at large view anything of a public nature as something outside themselves and so the concern of someone else. So there is no heartfelt or deep concern in something like economic revolution which, after all, is a public problem. Instead a far greater wealth of concern is lavished on matters confined to their life within the walls of their own house. So just as parliamentary government does not truly reflect general opinion, proletarian movements are in the same way, strictly speaking, those of proletariat leaders only and are in themselves no indication of the existence of a crystallised public opinion among the proletariat at large. There are close affinities in this particular between Japan and Russia. Russia is autocratic and its people in general have never participated in government; this is closely paralleled by the indifference of the Japanese to matters of public concern and their lack of a cooperative attitude to life. So this further instance of Japan's rarity or strangeness—the fact that there are movements with leaders only—can be said to be based on the distinction between "house" and "outside".

Many more examples of Japan's rarity could be adduced. They all stem from the character of the Japanese house and they all, in the last analysis are reducible to the old familiar street scene of the strangely tiny house cowering and grovelling in the path of the oncoming tram, rampaging like a wild boar. This is a sight the Japanese sees every day; whether he is aware of its full significance or not, he no doubt feels in his heart of hearts that it is something of a forlorn spectacle.

(Drafted 1929)

Chapter 4 Climate in Art

"Art forms of every kind, of every age and nationality press in on us. Distinctions and conventions of literary forms all appear to have vanished. As if that were not enough, a primitive and formless literature, music and art bears down on us from the Orient. These arts are semi-barbarous; yet even now they are still replete with the sturdy-hearted vitality of the people among whom they were created, as if their spiritual struggle were being fought out in a long romance or on a twenty-foot canvas. Amidst such absence of control, the artist is divorced from all convention and the critic is left with one standard of value only, reliance on his own emotions. Hence, here, the public takes charge. The crowds who elbow their way into vast exhibitions and theatres and lending libraries are the arbiters who make and break the artist's name. This lack of control on taste shows an age in which new feelings are breaking down the forms and conventions observed hitherto and are giving shape to new art forms. But this is not sure to be lasting. One of the pressing tasks of the philosopher and the historian of art or literature today is to build anew a sound relationship between art and aesthetic thinking".

This is the opening of Dilthey's "The Imaginative Power of the Poet", written in the 1880's. But, when one stops to think, this was already thirty years after "Madame Bovarie" and nearly twenty years after "War and Peace". Cezannes, the doyen of nineteenth century artists, had already perfected his style. The new art form that Dilthey hoped and waited for was already in existence. And now, the styles that this form led to have altered so much that they seem already to be of the past. Again, the neglect of the differences between art forms and conventions is not to be compared with the state forty years ago. In particular, there has been a development unprecedented since the beginning of human history. With world communication made outstandingly facile, political and economic developments promptly influence the whole world. In just the same way, cultures are all interlocked and influence each other. Even in the old European cultural world the leadership of the Greek and Roman artistic zone is a matter of the past. Tastes in weird African savageries or in Stone Age crudities occupy the show windows of department stores. Interest in the Far East, in the ancient traditions of Japan, China and India does not pass beyond the exotic but it stands alongside the rest nevertheless. Dilthey's words fit the present, with its confusion, even more than they did his own time. And for this reason the question he tried to answer takes on fresh significance for us. The question he asked was, "How does artistic creativity, set in play by all manner of circumstances in that it is rooted in man's nature, come to produce different arts, varying with both race and age?" This is a question which touches on the problem of the historicity of the spiritual life that is exemplified in the different cultural systems created by man. "How is the identity of human character, exemplified in the identity of forms of creativity, to be reconciled with its mutability and with its historical substance?"

The question clearly includes two problems, the "time" and "place" factors controlling artistic difference. In essence, differences in "place" contain within themselves time differences and both factors, closely interwoven, condition the distinctive character of a work of art. Again, with the world-wide cultural contacts of this modern age, the whole world seems to have coalesced into a single "place" so that only the single problem of "time" is now prominent. However, precisely because of this shrinking of the world, it has become much more easy to consider the time when it was still divided into any number of "places", and the degree and the depth to which local differences, which were marked, affected forms of art. Again it can no doubt also be shown that works of art that ignore such local difference of "place" are in effect mere transplantations which give no taste of and have not drunk deeply from the life of the "place" where they were created. This is a problem that in particular concerns the Orient, for only in so far as its artists continue to look back on and retain their long and distinctive traditions will differences of locality remain the focus of interest. Even recent European artistic scholarship, born of studies of the history of art and literature and the like, from the very first treated the problem of time as fundamental and gave only secondary consideration to problems of the kind of a people's distinctive character. However there gradually grew an awareness of the importance of the problem of "place"; this brought equal emphasis for the differences of both time and place in discussions of the distinctiveness of artistic impulse. This difference in trend was no doubt spurred by the shrinking of the world. We also propose to follow this trend and to restrict the problem by posing the question, "How does it come about that creativity, rooted in the nature of mankind which is the same, has given birth to artistic products that differ according to locality?" No doubt this problem will lead to an enquiry into local distinctions of mental and spiritual activity.

With the problem thus narrowed, we come upon a matter which Dilthey perhaps did not have in mind. When he was seeking for a theory of art that would clarify the artistic principles of the literature of the naturalist period, the theories of this literature were still very much in their infancy; one might go even further and say that even at a later stage, the naturalists, in the matter of theory at least, never grew up. Thus attempts to formulate such a theory and to escape from this infancy arose hand in hand with the reaction to naturalism and became the heralds of modern art. Art is not the representation of a mere mutable and haphazard phenomenon; it should express a pattern. Landscapes changing with the seasons or the weather are no more than a momentary and unstable aspect of phenomena that are not durable. The artist should aim at capturing the immutable structure of this landscape, a task that includes more than the mere matter of visual observation; this structure is only caught by depth of artistic experience. It is not a problem of being faithful to nature, for the true expression of this artistic expression is the most important task. The artist is not the servant of nature, for it is nature that is formed by his experience. Dilthey's dictum that "all sensation is no more than symbol" may well have been influenced by his own aesthetic. But, in the last analysis, it created not superb works of art but metaphysics and epistemology. However proud one might be of the attempt, on a metaphysical basis, to overcome the external character of phenomena, it is not to be thought for a moment that modern European art has succeeded in this. Dilthey hoped at the end of the nineteenth century that aesthetic theory and art might go hand in hand; now, for a reason completely the reverse, there is still no sound companionship between the two. Dilthey had in mind a connection between these two on the pattern of the age of Goethe and Schiller; but his objective was something quite different. Whether Europe, in the near future, will summon sufficient artistic creativity to attain such an objective is still a matter of some doubt. In its place, perhaps some different target will come to have a more powerful significance, something that was considered unimportant by Dilthey when he surveyed the whole world, of which this Europe, after all, is only a part. People would have only to forget European *art*. How well would European *artistic theories,* with only minor modifications, fit some of the arts of the Orient. Why should the new theories of art, nurtured by the reaction of a dislike of the naturalists, and born of a vague and distant foreboding, be applicable to the far-removed art of the ancient Orient? What is the distinctive character of such art and of the mentality that produced it?

Naturally this problem did not exist for Dilthey who called Oriental art "primitive", "formless" and "semi-barbarous". Yet has the situation altered even today? What he meant by the Orient I do not know; it may well have been something on the lines of the long romances of Tolstoy and Dostoevsky which, though "semi-barbarous", awakened in him some recogition of the strong-willed vitality of the people. Hermann Hesse, for example, even after the Great War, admired the Oriental breadth of spirit in Dostoevsky; this indicates the vagueness—or, at least the "non-European" content—of the concept "oriental". The "Far East" is as "primitively vital", as "semi-barbarous" as ever it was; those who yearn after it love it for nothing other than this primitive quality. Such people ask, "Where is the graciousness in this busy life we call modern and civilised"? Cars rush hither and thither one after another and herd men, wearied by life, to the grave. Senseless information is flashed out in bewildering neon letters as if it were too vital for a single moment to be lost; people dance to jazz music, whose only function is to confuse life, and even the rare moment of quiet privacy, the breathing space for relaxation, is disturbed by the radio. Amidst all this, all the depth, the beauty and the gentleness of life is lost and all that remains is a mechanised existence. It would be good to break away, just once, from all this bustle of existence in a civilised city and visit Africa, Asia, the far-distant Pacific Islands. In place of all this refined and civilised existence, there will be found the peaceful and healthy life of antiquity that reveals the essential depth and beauty of human existence. Is it not here that there is true "life"? It is not that such yearnings entertained by some Europeans are not understandable; but they are no more than a longing for what is "un-European" on the part of one weighted down by the mechanisation of life in Europe. This longing does not in any way grow from a positive appreciation or understanding of the life of the Orient. How is it that what is "un-European" becomes automatically "primitive"? Life in Japan, for example, has no doubt lost a great deal more of its "primitiveness" than has Europe; one never sees in a Japanese the childishness that is still preserved in no small measure in the European, for all the mechanical aids in his life; in this particular, it is the European who could be said to have a greater store of "primitive vitality". Again the fondness for astringency in the Japanese, the elegant simplicity that characterises all his tastes in food, clothes and dwelling conditions, his attitude to the moderation and the charm in everyday behaviour—these are all far too refined and delicate for the European to appreciate. Japan is now in process of following on after Europe and building a machine civilisation; but in the matter of taste, or of ethical sense, it is the European who could be called the savage. This again is something that the European might not appreciate—the European who, despite all his love of the "un-European", deep down in his heart still thinks of Europe as the hub of the world. As long as such appreciation is lacking, so will the problem of the distinctive nature of arts of different origins fail to gain due recognition.

b)

The problem we are posing is why, when artistic creativity grows from human character and so works identically everywhere, does it produce a variety of arts differing according to locality. I propose to separate this problem into two parts; first, I shall ask in what way these different arts differ; and second I shall ask how the distinctive nature of an art is related to the distinctive character of its place of origin, and how the latter conditions artistic creativity.

I shall treat first the problem of the way in which differing arts differ. Here it would be best to take up the most striking of the differences, something that is representative, in each case, of the art of Europe and of East Asia; these should then be compared under the heads of their most salient characteristics, so that their differences will thus be brought into the open.

I have selected "conformity with the rules" as the most important standpoint from my point of view. This was recognised as the true character of art as soon as modern philosophy came into being. Leibnitz, who accomplished the formulation of a logic of aesthetics, adopting Cartesian theories that the aesthetic pleasures in sensuous impression grow from some rational or logical basis, tried to derive sensuous pleasure from that part within sense perception that is appropriate to the mind. It is the logic in the verse form, and particularly unity within diversity that is the source of the aesthetic pleasure given by a poem. Beauty comes of order. Thus the order of the notes in music, the regularity of movement in the dance, the method in the continuity of the rhyme of a poem—all such representations of order afford aesthetic enjoyment. The pleasure given by proportion in the visual arts is no different. Artistic creation, hand in hand with the mental faculties that grasp the order within the universe through a formal unification of thinking, creates and copies an object that possesses such order; it is, so to speak, a mental faculty creating as god creates. Beauty, then, is the revelation of the rational within the sensual, art is the sensual revelation of a harmonious world union. The artist sees this world union not logically but sensually, with creative and vital feelings. So when he expresses what he has seen by means of his own free creative powers, because this world union is rational, order is the basis on which everything is made to stand.

A rational aesthetic of this nature reflected seventeenth century European—and particularly French—attitudes and social conditions, where rationalism thrived. Yet even though the stains of rationalism have been washed away and there has come a realisation of the individuality of the domain of beauty and art, the tendency to give recognition to the logical and the methodical still persists. Even the analysis of aesthetics of the eighteenth century empiricists regarded, as ever, the elements of aesthetic value to be unity within diversity, symmetry, proportion, and the fusion of the parts within the whole. In spite of the rejection of ideas that aesthetic value is essentially the product of such order and method—for a combination of all these does not produce a work of art—yet there was still no refutation of the earlier recognition of aesthetic formal principle. When, in the nineteenth century, historical method in studies of art, setting out from an enquiry into man's creative powers and employing psychology for the interpretation of empirical phenomena, began to analyse aesthetic creativity, attention was centred more and more on depth of experience, something not to be clarified by rationalism alone. However, in spite of the attempt, with the aid of general concepts produced by analysis of the living history of art, to transfer to abstract theorems of the style of the unity or the method within variety, such unity and order was still recognised in terms of artistic law placed on top of the creative powers of genius. The only point of concern was the historical nature of the form of, the individuality of a piece of art revealed in its composition, the criteria being the same principles of unity within diversity, symmetry, proportion and the rest. Again, when psychological studies began to go deep into the matter of aesthetic consciousness, this unity was found no longer in the rational order of the universe but in the unity of mental activity. But in an enquiry on these conditions, the problem is where to base principles of aesthetics; the universal validity of the principles themselves was not called in doubt. Only in recent times has there come at last an attempt to consider the true essence of art independently of the principles of aesthetic form, recognising it in contexts of the "form appropriate to emotion".

We intend here to consider the problem that the distinctive composition of a work of art even encroaches on such formal principles as those mentioned above. Whatever art form is brought under consideration, the fact that the basic principle of art is unity in variety is no doubt not to be gainsaid. However, whether such unity is obtained only by method and whether balance is only achieved by symmetry and proportion and the like are matters that should indeed be called in question. This question is dependent on the distinctive quality of the works of art themselves, for theory, after all, merely tags along behind art itself.

The representative works of European art are so imbued with rationalism that they could not but make conformity with order their standard. The surpassing genius of the Greeks, of the kind to instigate mathematical investigation, gave being to an exemplary art; the one led into the other, for while the arts of Greece certainly are without a par in the world, they possess a character that is of an outstanding rational quality. Form is acquired by order; balance by symmetry and proportion. But my own opinion is that it is not this exemplary order that gives Greek art its superiority. So before we go on to define this distinctive art form as based on formal principles we should first consider what it is that lies at the root of the supremacy of Greek art.

Let me take Greek sculpture as an example. Polycleitus' "Doryphoros" has long been famous as the canon of the proportion of the human body. Polycleitus lived in an age when the Pythagoreans were finding infinitely profound significance in mathematical relation and were attempting to reduce all that interested them in the matter of music or any symmetry of the kind to such mathematical relation. Tradition tells that the sculptor, seeking for absolute proportion in the human body, reached the canon—the rule of abstract proportion—and embodied it in concrete form in this statue. It is dubious whether "research" of this nature could in fact be transformed into creative ability, but one must at least admit that this work does possess a perfection of proportion entirely appropriate to the tradition. The original is now lost; but if the marble copies in the Vatican and at Naples are true only in the matter of proportion, it would be fair to conclude that they are adequate transmissions of the original. Yet, like so many other Roman copies, the impression they leave is at best weak; they have little of the vivid, brilliant power that cuts the heart and is visible only in the Greek original. Perfection of geometrical proportion does not alone have the power to strike through to the heart. I would like to contrast this with the so-called "Daughter of Niobe of the Commercial Bank" in the Terme Museum in Rome. This has caught just the moment when the young daughter of Niobe, pierced in the back by Apollo's arrow, struggles to withdraw it and drops one knee to the ground. Her head faces upwards and her clothes, falling from her shoulders, reveal almost her whole body. The work dates from about the middle of the fifth century, earlier than the Parthenon, so that it is the first known figure of the naked female body. Because of a bold attempt to interpret the problem of an impetuous and unusual movement, there are, it must be allowed, traces of an archaic stiffness and immaturity and several failures in the execution; the left arm, especially, is cast in a posture that is anatomically impossible. Yet, these defects and this stiffness withal, the work leaves nothing to be desired in the matter of bringing into the open the surpassing qualities of Greek art. The vitality of the work really does strike through to the heart. I would sum up its characteristics as an "external revelation of internal content". Here, internal becomes external; we feel this in every particular. It is not that this figure has both internal content and distinct outward-facing surfaces; the composition is rather of undulations welling outwards from within. Such undulations are truly perfect in subtlety. This is particularly true of that sweeping down from the breasts to the waist. One can only follow it with one's eyes and gasp; its beauty defies all deseription. In that this subtle undulation is an outward expression of the whole content, one has no impression of the limitation of confining contours. From a profile angle these undulations, to be sure, come together into lines but these are only extensions of the welling from within and are not lines that express movement towards the side. The spirit of life itself, flowing from within, links up each of these points. So if, as a proof of this contention, one looks closely at the line of the infinitely subtle undulation sweeping from breasts to waist, the limitless variations in this undulation are felt to be not switches of movement towards the outside but changes in this undulation, the rhythm of the life spirit welling from within. This impression is supported by the marks left by the sculptor's chisel. There is an appropriate example in the folds of the flowing garments that cover the left leg. It may seem that these are to be understood in the normal sense of a downward flow because of the weight of the clothes; however the distinct chisel marks still visible show clearly the sculptor's intention to stress the unevenness of the surface, and his comparative neglect of the downward flow of movement in the clothes. In the parts not heavily chiselled, there is little attention to effecting a smooth connection between the points that are in relief. Here there is the expression of life of a different kind from that of the flesh, a striving to distinguish the life spirit welling from within. Thus although this latter may cling to the flesh and express the swelling contours of the flesh, it is shown very frankly that it is of a nature quite different from the flesh itself. This distinction is not discernible in Roman copies. The chisel marks left on the skin surfaces may not be as plain as those on the clothing but they appear as even more delicate and minute lines or points.

However delicate they may be, they are always open and frank; they display openly the sculptor's intention of creating unevennesses and they thus remove the impression of smooth movement over the surface from the skin and stress the impression of a gentle welling from within.

This distinctive characteristic is recognisable generally in Greek originals; the combination of symmetry and proportion, in most instances, leaves nothing to be desired. The so-called "Birth of Venus", for example, on Ludovici's throne, could be said to be an exemplary embodiment of the grace of symmetry. Two nymphs stand on the shore, one at each side of Venus, born of the sea, and bend their bodies as they stoop to lift her up. The postures of the two nymphs are broadly identical, their clothes flow in a similar pattern. Venus, both arms outstretched, allows herself to be supported by them and they, similarly, extend one arm. The other reaches down, holding dry clothing in which to wrap Venus. The blending of these six arms and the triple division of the limbs is in relatively strict proportion. Venus' head, which forms the centre line, is flanked by the nymphs' bodies to each side and the obtuse angle formed by Venus' outstretched arm and her breast corresponds to that made by the nymphs' knees. The swell of Venus' breasts, in particular, is truly beautiful in its development into and correspondence with that of the three entwined arms. The details all follow strictly this general proportion—the back foot of the nymphs, for example, the small round pebbles under their feet, the clothes that sweep down their shoulders, their waist and their knees. This is an excellent example of brilliance expressed in symmetry. However the root of the superiority of this work is less this symmetry than the execution by which the figures of the various subjects, in strict proportion, reveal openly and to the exterior what is within. How well the shapes are captured as undulations welling from the interior! There is a round pebble tucked away in one corner—a pebble more worn away and of a gentle roundness that one never sees in Japan; you see them everywhere in Rome, on the park paths for example. Even this pebble is not simply a lifeless exterior with nothing of internal content to reveal; instead, the tactile sense that is felt in the matter of this stone is captured as an outward-welling undulation. The distinct difference of workmanship between the soft wet *hiton* clinging to Venus' body and the dry clothes of the nymphs above Venus' raised arms clearly discloses the internal essence of the different clothes. Even more in the plain sculpturing of the flesh, in spite of the plain simplicity there is an abundance of talent in the expression of the outward undulation of what is within.

The friezes and the gable sculptures of the Parthenon, too, give a clear impression of this same distinctive technique. No-one can fail to be struck by the beauty of the clothes. These are executed by means of clearly distinguishable rough chiselling marks; there was obviously no intent to create an even outward-flowing surface. In the case of a hollow, sunken surface, the method is simply to hollow out, but extreme attention is given to the extent of the sinking. This is a clear indication that the only point of concern was the expression of undulation. So in spite of the very real and vivid distinction between the feel of the undulation in the clothing and that in the flesh, the two here become intertwined. In the famous "Three Graces", a composite statue of three headless female figures, soft clothes cling to the ample bodies of the Graces and one is given a very clear impression of the undulations of the clothes, and, expressed through the latter, those of the body.

It is in this external expression of what lies within that the superiority of Greek sculpture is to be found. There is no internal content other than what is thus given open and external expression. With the age of the Roman copyists this attribute was lost completely, for the copyists interpreted the surface where this undulation from within was expressed as a simple plane surface and copied it faithfully as such. Thus while such a surface becomes beautifully smooth, at the same time it comes to be one that has the function of enclosing an undisclosed content. However, as the sculptures of Greece—the rough drafts, if you like—did not have this function, an enclosing surface comes to take the place of one that, in origin, was intended to disclose. This is the basis of the hollow impression given by Rome's copies. Moreover, when such copies came to be admired for their geometrically precise proportion and symmetry, these formal qualities, which originally did little more than act as expressions of the inner life spirit in the Greek original, came to be understood as expressing something quite apart from the central life spirit.

Thus European art, whether masterpiece or trash, came to pay the strictest regard to conformity with order. This can be said also of Europe's architecture and literature. The greatness of Greek temple architecture consists in its treatment of its material, stone, as something thoroughly alive. The temple is not just a mechanical construction but an organic whole in which all the parts come to life in the being of the whole. However, the Greeks cast such living buildings in a geometrically exact mould. Thus even though it might not have been observance of mathematical law that gave life to such works, here too the fact of compliance with the law came to be given significance in and for itself. However many structures were put up in later ages all strictly in compliance with such law, not one of them reproduced the life that characterised the Greek original. Again the greatness of Greek literature consists in its vivid directness; there was open and intuitive portrayal of the state and the motions of men's hearts. But because the Greeks expressed their emotions within rigidly maintained prescriptions and the laws of unity, such conformity and order came to be valued as the true essence of poetry. This stimulated the composition of mountains of trash—but trash, nevertheless, that kept within the rules.

All these qualities came to stand out in Renaissance Europe with the revival of Greek culture. But just as modern learning, while inheriting from Greece, has been disposed to give more weight to the mathematical than to the artistic or the interpretative aspects of the original, (and has achieved remarkable advances), in the field of art also it is the mathematical character that has been given emphasis. This is the distinctiveness of modern European culture and it is in this light that we should understand the ordering of works of art on the basis of an acknowledgment of formal aesthetic principle. There is no gainsaying that the European of today has been nurtured on the culture of the Greeks; but he received his nutriment from practical Roman hands and digested it in a way that suited his own nature, his own fondness for abstraction. So it would not be unfair to say that when Greek artistic genius fired people with a nature different from their own, it became linked with products tending in a direction quite different from theirs, and one that was quite beyond their expectation.

The arts of Europe are distinguished by conformity with standard and with the rules. In contrast we find in the arts of the Orient works where one can trace no such rational order. Yet they do possess an essential order which must be based in some method. But this method is patently not something rational, or related to numerical or quantitative calculation. What, then, is the essence of this method?

As a guide to the answer to this question, let us take as an example the art of the garden. The ancient Greeks left no model in this instance. But in the Hellenistic age, public gardens were laid out with great artistry in the great cities of the East and the art developed still further in Roman times in Imperial palaces, villas the like. These, of course, more than garden pure and simple, were rather pleasure grounds with every kind of facility. Yet they were mapped out with intricate method—artificially shaped trees, flower beds geometrically perfect in shape and symmetrical waterways and ponds; the framework, the skeleton or the centre was always adorned sculpturally. So this art thus perfected by the Romans can be regarded as important in the matter of the problem of the garden.

It was because narrow *polis* life produced no call for it that the Greeks were not stimulated to the artistic construction of the garden. This does not mean, however, that the Greeks remained stolidly indifferent to the beauties of natural landscape. As Butcher says, "Never has there been any race so deeply impressible by the world outside them". This contention can be endorsed no doubt by the siting of the *polis*; in nearly every case, the *polis* commands a beautiful view. The grandeur of the Acropolis and the beauty of its prospect are known well enough; but the Greek settlements in Italy and Sicily as well—Pestium, Tormina, Syracuse, Agrigentum, Segesta and so on—are all on sites chosen for the extreme beauty of their views of sea, hills and fields. The choice of a situation on a slight eminence some distance from the coastline was no doubt necessitated by considerations of defence; but we can gauge the true motives of the *polis* founders by the fact that from a number of sites in the immediate vicinity which equally or better fulfil such necessary conditions, they invariably picked that with the most beautiful view. When you look up at Tormina, for example, from the coast, the site appears far from ideal for defence purposes. Indeed sneaking suspicions even are aroused by the half-measures that appear to have decided this situation. But once you climb up to the town itself and look out, you realise immediately how compelling this situation must have appeared. Down below, there is a beautiful curve to the white sand-dune beach; above hangs majestic Aetna, white and of a shape the elegance of which has no par in Europe. The pattern of this outlook would be lost completely if the town were moved a mere five or six hundred yards. In this land where, by nature, there is nothing wild and coarse, where the plains and coastlines in their natural condition seem to be tended and trimmed, the landscape is composed, as it were, of a succession of distinct views. It was this that guided the Greeks in their choice of sites. If I have not already proved my contention adequately, there is the additional evidence provided by the theatre of the *polis.* The aspect of these theatres that struck me first was their clever design accoustically. In the comparatively small theatre at Tormina, needless to say, and even in the fairly extensive one at Syracuse, we found it eminently easy to converse in a voice no louder than normal, one of us standing high up in the very back row of the arena, the other down in the orchestra. And this, be it remembered, was in an open-air theatre. But what surprised me even more was the view from the theatre seats. The panorama from the Tormina theatre was obstructed by quite large-scale additions made by the Romans; yet even so, if you look from your seat towards and above the temple, which seems to separate off the world in which the play is enacted, you see, almost as if it were a framed picture, the sea in the distance, the white sand, and Aetna's graceful peak. At Syracuse, also, where the site is fairly open, the theatre is built on a slope which the sea washes to the south and commands a fine prospect of a well-ordered landscape of beautiful plains, the sea and the headlands that jut into it. The theatre at Segesta is again on an open site that faces the sea; built on top of a hill higher than that of the temple, the theatre looks out on to the sea in the far distance, ten miles beyond the beautiful Gadella valley. When you look up from the neighbourhood of the temple at Segesta at the ring of encircling mountains, you would not believe that the sea would be visible from here and it is only when you climb up to the theatre that you come upon the wide and open panorama. This method of theatre construction and siting is the very opposite of an attempt to remove the stage from any contact with the world outside so as to centre attention on the playing. Just as on a festival day the ancient Japanese would climb to a height commanding a good view and there eat, drink and dance in communion with their god, so the Greeks enjoyed their drama—its origin in the ritual of religion—in an atmosphere enriched as far as possible by natural beauty. This all goes to prove that the Greeks could ill live without a beautiful view and that *polis* life was by no means cut off from communion with nature. But the Greeks stopped short at a love of scenic beauty; they felt no urge to elevate this love into idealisation.

The Romans, on the other hand, as is indicated by their inventions of the round theatre or the public bath, had a nature which allowed them to enjoy themselves in man-made surroundings with no thought for the beauties of natural scenery. Rome's aqueducts symbolise her achievement in breaking down, by the hand of man, the barriers that nature had placed on the expansion of the ancient city beyond a determined size. This delight in the man-made, the artificial, is further exemplified forcibly in constructions of the style of the detached imperial villas, quite separate from urban centres. Here, the Emperor had an array, all his own, of all the tools for amusement that the city could offer—temple, theatre, bath-house, library, stadium and the like. Another of these was a garden, entirely artificial and geometrically precise. So enjoyment of a garden was nothing but enjoyment of the artificial dominating the natural. No doubt the Italian of today has inherited this tradition, for he has built his art of the garden on the insertion of the formal and the orderly within the scenery that nature has to offer. Perhaps because the age coincided with that of the interest in botanical research and the building of zoos and botanical gardens, the art of landscape gardening was understood as little other than a carving up of nature in conformity with geometrical rules. The garden of the Este villa at Tivoli in the Roman suburbs is admired as one of the finest examples from the Renaissance. It is situated on a fine slope looking down over the distant plains of Campagna; the land is fertile and water is plentiful. But the admiration for this garden is based on its carving up of soil or plants by geometrical straight lines or by circular paths, for the use of the slope made by the stone steps that dominate the garden by their strong geometrical precision, and for the fact that fountains ranged in a straight line or grouped with consummate art impress on one the fact that man's power reaches to the remotest cranny of the garden. This might truly be called the artificialisation of nature. But could it be said that by this process the beauties of nature are refined and idealised? This lining of a perfectly straight path by trees arranged in a straight line and standing precisely vertical—so that the whole looks like a water channel perfectly angled—is in fact tantamount to the use of trees in place of stones. But the beauty of the trees grouped thus is not refined by such labours. In Italy the natural shape, even, of a pine or cypress is regular; any further refinement of such regularity is mere geometrification of the tree's shape. The regular shape of the tree in its natural condition, because of perhaps some slight accompanying irregularity, reminds us all the more of the order that is intrinsic to nature here. If even such slight irregularities are removed by artificial means, then the sense of apartness from the natural is intensified. This feeling of artificialisation is entirely different from that of the task which the Greeks set themselves—the open expression of the orderly proportion of the human body. The Greeks may well have refined and idealised the human body but, at least, they did not artificialise it. So, from this aspect, natural pastures or olive groves, not so artificially tended and trimmed, provided only they were suitably framed, could be said to be much more beautiful than the Renaissance garden. Hadrian's villa near Tivoli, for example, even when allowance is made for the fascination of the ruins, as a natural landscape enclosed in a set framework captures our imagination much more forcibly than the Este garden. When, in ancient Roman times, there was an assortment of Roman style architecture here, there was no doubt some sense that here was the work of man's hand. Now that these fruits of man's labours have decayed, and there are vineyards and green pastures and olives growing wild, nature has again come to exhibit her own beauty, far more attractive than the artificial. So the construction of an artificial garden is tantamount to the strangling of natural beauty.

In contrast, there is refinement and idealisation of beauty in the Japanese garden. The European would understand the latter as being of the same character as his own natural garden; but the latter, or the modern English garden, is nothing but the insertion of natural landscape, with no alteration, into a fixed framework. Although this is far superior to the artificial garden in the matter of giving life to natural beauty, yet the power of artistic originality employed is not very strong. The nature park at Munich can in all honesty be admitted as very beautiful; yet the beauty here is the beauty of the pastures, the trees and the streams of southern Germany; it is not that this beauty is the creation of the artist. The Japanese garden, on the other hand, is not simply nature untouched, for whereas nature in her own state never has the feel of the wild in Europe, in Japan nature left alone is indeed disorderly and desolate confusion. To achieve the neat and tidy feel of the European meadow in a Japanese hill pasture, constant attention and trimming must be given to weeding and draining and breaking up the hard clods of soil. So even the achievement of the effect gained in Europe by the mere framing of a natural landscape calls for a hundred times the effort in Japan. The degree of labour required to produce order out of the disorderly wildness of nature has led the Japanese to the discovery of an entirely different principle of the art of garden construction. The putting of some artificial order into the natural could not be achieved by covering up the natural by the artificial, but only by making the artificial follow the natural. And by the nursing of the natural by the artificial, the natural is, all the more, made to follow from within. In the matter of grasses, for example, if those that obstruct and those that serve no purpose are removed, nature then reveals her own order. Thus the Japanese discovered a purely natural form within the disorder and wildness of nature and this is what is reproduced in their garden. In this sense, the Japanese garden is indeed a refinement and an idealisation of natural beauty. It would not be untrue to say that the function is the same in method as the arts of Greece.

What, then, is the composition of such a garden? In the case of an austere garden, there may be nothing other than a single pine growing from a flat surface of moss or five or seven paving stones. (The door-yard and garden of the Shinjuan hermitage in the Daitokuji Temple, for example, or that in the Katsura Villa). There is no diversity to be unified here so that it could be described in essence as nothing more than a simple unity. The moss, however, does not grow naturally over the whole surface thus. It is artificial in that it has been achieved by tending. What is more, the moss does not form a simple plane cover on the surface of the kind that would be given by turf cut and trimmed. The gentle green of the moss has an undulation that wells subtly from below. This undulation belongs to nature, untouched by man; yet man, realising the true beauty of this subtle natural undulation, has given it life by his tending of the natural. So the garden builder gives close attention to the relationship between this soft undulating green and the hard stones. The way of cutting the stones, their shape, their arrangement, and even whether the surface be plain or whether the shape be square are all determined from considerations not of the achievement of a symmetrical and geometrical unity, but of a contrast with the soft undulations of the moss. Thus, when the moss surface is long and narrow in shape, the stones are distributed in a straight line; when the moss surface is loose and discursive, they are dispersed, large and small intermingled. Here is a unity gained not by geometrical proportion but by a balancing of forces which appeals to the emotions, a unity of a meeting of spirit. Just as spirits meet between man and man, so do they also meet between moss and stone or even between stone and stone. Every effort is made to avoid the orderly in order to achieve this "meeting of spirit". In such a style of composition, the more intricate the materials that make up the garden, the more prominent becomes this "meeting of spirit". Natural, unworked stones of a variety of shapes, all manner of plants large and small, water—these are assembled in a composition that avoids orderly method as far as possible and again without as much as an inch to spare between them. In the case of a pool, for example, while regular rectangles, cross-shapes or circles are avoided as far as possible, there is yet no attempt to copy the rambling disorder of the natural pond. The rare or the partial or sectional beauty of form that nature displays in a sea-shore, a river bank, a beach of a lake, are adapted as models and all combined and coordinated into a composite beautiful whole—yet still a whole that gives no feel of the artificial. Thus the pond in a first-class garden is never to be grasped in its entirety by a single glance, for it is composed of an infinity of complex aspects so that each angle affords a new impression of the composition. It is important to combine trees of different natures and shapes, for it is this that give colour composition throughout the changes of the four seasons. Thus there should be an assortment of evergreens with only a slight degree of colour change, deciduous trees with a much broader range of variation, trees which vary in the speed of the shading of the spring green and range from a light yellow to a deep crimson in autumn tints. In spite of the term "evergreen", there are those with a spring colour that has a dull gold lustre, or a dark silver flash, or even the beautiful greeny-blue of a pine in midsummer. Only when these different varieties are sited in accordance with their respective sizes and only with the achievement of a composition which keeps its harmony through the changes of the seasons can a Japanese garden be said to be of superior class. Here man takes as a model a harmony revealed haphazardly somewhere on hill or in valley and reproduces this as a unity that is not haphazard. This complex form of composition is not achieved by geometrical precision. If there is any order here it is not of the kind that men can grasp rationally. So what is to be regarded as the rule or the order in the art of the Japanese garden is not in fact rule as such but merely the fact of modelling on a garden already in existence and determined.

It is simple to progress from this distinction between East and West in the art of the garden to the distinctive characteristics of other arts. No doubt the garden builder learnt much from the art of painting, for there are many similarities between the latter and the art of the garden. Four or five differently shaded bamboo leaves done in ink in the top left corner of a rectangular canvas, a faintly-executed bamboo stalk leading from these down the left side, most of the rest of the surface left blank, but, exactly in the centre, a little below the bamboo leaves, a sparrow, heavily shaded. In the composition of a painting of this kind one can recognise no symmetry in any sense of the word, yet there is a sense of balance that reaches through the whole canvas; the surface left unpainted, wide and deep, balances with the dark shade of the sparrow and the power in the latter corresponds to that in the two or three bamboo leaves that are drawn particularly forcefully and prominently. Thus each of the components has its essential position which is not to be altered. Through this connection of balance, this meeting of spirit, even a painting of this nature, with only one corner actually filled, gives a feeling of great richness of composition. This type of composition is frequently to be found in the small works of the Sung and Mongolian periods imported from the Chinese continent, and also in the large sliding-door (*fusuma*) and screen paintings of the period from Ashikaga and Momoyama to Tokugawa. A small painting of a sparrow perching on a plum branch, a screen painting of plum blossom leaning to water, a small screen with figures crowding round the Imperial carriage; in all these there is a perfectly measured balance—between the shape of the plum branch jutting out irregularly from the edge of the painting, the distribution of the blossom above and the position of the sparrow perching on it; or again there is a delicately judged harmony of colour and line between the shape of a red plum tree laden with blossom and the water or the rockery that faces it; or again a well-measured balance of movement in the skilful matching of the figures round the Imperial carriage at the very edge of the painting and their gradual thinning and dispersal as one moves towards the blank part of the picture. This well-measured balance may well be clear at a single glance, but we can discover no order or rule lying at the root of this delicacy of measure; it was achieved intuitively and it is a "meeting of feeling" that would disappear with the difference of a mere inch.

The distinctive character of this style of composition is familiar to us in every-day life through its appearance in other artistic and industrial products. The Western plate or tea-cup has its regular pattern, but that of the Japanese dish or tea-cup, though at first glance it may seem haphazard, has a charm that transcends that of a regular pattern and which one never tires of contemplating; this type of pattern must be acknowledged as possessing, however unconsciously, a feeling of "Japaneseness". This feeling, if artistically heightened and intensified, turns into something like a Koetsu or a Korin ink-case.

There is a distinctive Japanese character to such "nuance" art, so far removed from order, yet truly of a distinct composition; in comparison, the Western ink sand or pen holder, however precious the metal they are made of, can only give a feel of the mechanical.

But the distinctive nature of the composition of a painting does not spring solely from this "meeting of feeling". In addition to a space technique form of composition which takes the place of symmetry and proportion, forms that can be grasped at a single glance, there is in Japanese painting a further distinctive composition which plays a vital part and includes time factors. This is to be found in the picture scroll. In Western art, it is the content of the story alone that links a series of paintings based on a story; each painting is an independent composition in itself, or the paintings, individually independent, are united to form a vast, decorative whole. But the Japanese picture scroll is conceived in such a way that the composition itself evolves in time. This evolution is not unlike musical development; beginning quietly, the degree of complexity is slowly accelerated, until it becomes at last a composition complex to a degree with countless subjects all mutually linked; then it gradually returns to simplicity and ends on a note that is the extreme of plainness. Alternations between association and dispersal often produce effects of startling beauty. In essence, each section of a painting of this kind no doubt has method in its composition in isolation; however, it was originally conceived as a determined part of an evolving whole and the significance of the part only becomes fully evident in the whole. This is naturally true of paintings based on a story, such as the Otomo Dainagon scroll; yet even in the case of, for example, Choju Giga by Toba Sojo, or Sesshu's landscapes, neither of which obtained any linking effect from their material, compositional evolution is indeed something of importance. The tone of the brush, too, alternates in sympathy with switches in composition, indicating a full understanding of the evolution of the whole on the part of the artist. There is, however, in development of this kind none of the order and regularity that characterise musical development, for here development is achieved by constant switches to another form not by the repetition of an identical theme. Yet there is the order of a whole; if one must seek for a parallel, it is to be found in the unified development of a life full of illogical factors.

There is a further example of this style of composition in the linking of ideas in the distinctive Japanese "linked verse" form. Each verse in a linked poem has its own independent existence, yet there is a subtle link that unites these so that one existence evolves into another and there is an order that reaches through the whole. As these developmental links between verse and verse are usually forged by different poets, the coordination of the imaginative power of a single poet is deliberately cast aside and the direction of the development given over to chance. Thus the composition of the whole is the product of chance; yet, because of this, it becomes all the richer, with the kind of twist and turn that could not be expected of a single author. Yet how can such chance create artistic unity? Here again the answer lies in "meeting of feeling", in this case a meeting of the heart. If there is no meeting between the tempers of a gathering of poets, no surpassing linked verse will come of the gathering. While preserving their own individuality, the poets combine their feelings and reveal their individual experience in a symphonic concord of each other's hearts. This form of poetry was no doubt something never thought of in the West.

Japanese literature has other aspects in addition to that of the "linked verse" form which display this same distinctive character. One of these is the delineation of a scene by means of the pivot-word. Objects seeming to have no conceivable connection in the matter of content are linked one with another in accordance with associations in the words themselves. This is truly the extreme of illogicality in comparison with the picture given where content provides a logical thread. Yet this marshalling of words according to an association of ideas does make one sense a strong flavour of compositional unity in the whole, for even though there may be no link of intellectual content between words, yet they are threaded together by emotional content. Representative examples of this kind of word picture are to be found readily in the *Taiheiki* or in the lovers' journey scenes in Chikamatsu's dramas, and there are instances even more striking in Saikaku who wrote with such reality and directness. Certainly Saikaku used the trick of the "linked verse" in certain parts of his works; there are not a few instances in which the words of the first verse, independently of their intellectual content, call up the succeeding verse and in which this type of linking takes the place of a direct description of an incident. This kind of pointillism by the word is likewise made possible not by a logical thread perceived in intellectual content but by a linking of the words that is felt in this "meeting of feeling".

This characteristic can be discovered also in the *No,* in the tea-ceremony and in *Kabuki,* all of them arts born of a "meeting of feeling". There are even a number of appropriate examples in Buddhist art which traces its traditions far back to Greece. The Japanese have long been recognised as an artistic people and they do truly excel in their ability to express openly and intuitively what is within. However, while the Greeks sensed through sight, the Japanese saw through sense, a difference that it would be wrong to disregard. Japan shares this characteristic with China and India; the only difference lies in the matter of composition in "meeting of feeling" and here Indian art is completely divergent. The composition of a chaotic grouping of nude statues in the reliefs as Amarāvatī, the confusion of pinnacles in a Hindu temple are born neither of logical rule nor this "meeting of feeling". What exactly was their basis it is difficult to say though at least it can be asserted that they were achieved by an overwhelming of reason and an enrapturing of the senses.

From this comparison of the arts of East and West from the point of view of conformity to rule, it is plain that while this is the character of the arts of the West, it is not so of the East. One could select many angles for comparison other than this, such as, in particular, that of humanism; but for simplicity's sake, I shall leave this question here and move on to the other problem, that of the connection between such characteristics and differences of "place".

c)

In this problem of the link between differences of "place" and artistic characteristics, the smaller the "place" divisions, the more intricate the details of form that come in question; the broader such divisions, the deeper the insight into artistic character. Here, the connection between the artistic differences we have discovered and a "place" differentiation conceived in terms of East and West should highlight this question in its most magnified form.

It is humidity that brings out most of all the differences between East and West. The hot season is also the rainy period in monsoon-influenced India, China and Japan; every form of plant, favoured by both rain and sun, flourishes and luxuriates. Rainfall is from three or four times up to six or seven times that of Europe and atmospheric humidity also is far greater. The Middle East, in contrast,—Arabia and Egypt—is a zone arid in the extreme and, unless there are special circumstances to prevent this, land reverts to desert; hill and plain alike, with no covering of plant life, are bare and stark as skeletons. In other words, in European eyes, the Orient represents the two extremes of humidity and aridity. In that winter and wet season coincide, Europe has only a slight rainfall and minimal atmospheric humidity. On the Mediterranean coastline, the summer is dry enough to shrivel pasture grasses, but this again does not permit the rank growth of strong-rooted weed-grasses and presently, along with the October rain, tender pasture grasses begin to grow again. In central and northern Europe where the sun has little power and there is almost no aridity, tender pasture grasses flourish the whole year round.

It is this interrelation between humidity and sun that brings the most marked differences in natural features. In the humid East, sun and water combine to bless plant life and are at the same time the source of the battering that plant life suffers from typhoons, deluge rains and floods. So while, in this humid atmosphere of the East, vegetation is luxuriant, it is also wild, promiscuous and ill-ordered. When Japan's natural features are said to be the scene of elegant growth, the reference is to a small-scale undulation rich in change or to the brilliance of colour or the light and shade of the atmosphere and not to the grace or gentility of aspect of the plant life. Indeed, if one speaks with an eye only to the latter, the landscape can only be described as disordered and wild. In contrast, in Europe, strong coarse weeds do not rampage as they do in Japan and, as a result, tender pasture grass carpets the land and trees, ignorant of trials and hardships, stand erect and well-ordered. Here there is indeed a sense of the gentle; it is only a matter of course that man should acquire hence his sense of order.

Humidity again is the source of a marked difference in the tone of the atmosphere. In Japan the light and shade of the atmosphere which gives an abundance of variety of the kind of the morning mist, the evening fog, or the spring haze which we experience as a matter of course has an important function; for in one aspect, it provides a sense of season or of time, of calm or of freshness, and, in another aspect, it is the source of the charm of the light and shade of the landscape itself. But even if the atmosphere of Europe with its meagre humidity content may give rise to monotonous fogs or mists, it is still not sufficiently rich in change to impress our feelings with any delicacy of light and shade variation. Dull and cloudy days succeed each other in northern Europe, clear and fine days are the rule in the south; this monotony, this absence of variation, may be said to be the mark of Europe. There is here also an intimate relation with temperature variations. The thermometer does indeed show temperature variations in Europe in the course of the same day; but such changes are mere physical phenomena and are not prominent enough to affect mood and temper. The variety of products, all of them rich in change, of the interrelation of humidity and heat, is not to be experienced in Europe; the cool of a summer's evening, for example, the freshness of the morning, the violent change, sufficient to bring a complete change of mood, between the noon warmth and the biting cold at sunset of an autumn day, the morning cold in winter, enough to shrivel the skin, and, after it, the balmy warmth of an Indian summer day. The summer heat of north Europe may well be moderate enough for one to wear winter clothes without discomfort, but even after sundown there is no refreshing cool and no sudden change on the style of the complete clearing of the weather that follows a sharp summer evening shower in Japan. If one might be permitted a little exaggeration, the feeling is of a single monotonous summer dragging along month after month. Even the European, inured as he is to this monotony, finds it impossible to tolerate and attempts to escape from it by a change of air. In winter, in both day time and night time—for there is little difference in this aspect—there is a steady stagnation, one might almost say, of the same freezing temperature. There is no difference whether the temperature drops to three or to ten degrees below zero; for in both cases, we are shrivelled by the cold. Even in a spot that catches the sun well on a rare clear day, its rays are just like the moon's and have no warmth; so there is not the slightest difference between being in and out of the sun. This is more readily tolerable than the Japanese winter where, even though it might well be warm in the sun with the north blocked off, yet if you take one step outside, the cold wind cuts right through you; the European winter is not only tolerable but is further of the kind to stimulate man's will to resist the cold. Hence man puts out all his efforts to vanquish this monotony by all the artificial stimuli of a warm life artificially created.

Climatic characteristics of this nature insinuate themselves into our experience to a depth far greater than we realise. This is exhibited particularly conspicuously in vegetation. In Japan the new spring green bursts and develops and increases colour with a speed almost too swift to give us a chance to seep in the freshness of the new buds to our hearts' content—our hearts that have longed so impatiently for the spring. You notice that the willow buds have begun to burst and almost in an instant the whole tree becomes a luxuriant green; there is a feeling almost of indecent haste. Europe's spring green, however, moves as slowly as a clock hand; it does grow, agreed, and in a month, say, there is a fair degree of change, but this is not a change swift enough to carry us away. The same is true of the autumn leaves. Already in August, the leaves are yellowing and give off a brittle sound as they rustle. Yet some trees with a lustreless and livid green remain unchanged and eventually, just as one begins to think that the change will never come, the green fades slowly into a frail yellow. There is nothing to capture our eyes until all the leaves turn yellow towards the end of October, nor is there any sudden and startling change of the kind of the leaves all turning colour overnight after a sudden fall of temperature brings the first frost. The relationship between weather and vegetation can be transferred to the description of men's minds and hearts. When I was among Europeans I could not help but be astonished at the degree to which the Japanese has need of minute and delicate switches of mood. The European, on the other hand, inured to the monotony of his climate, is as settled and stolid as the buds on his trees. Even the Italian, the most excitable of all Europeans, may well be richly endowed in the matter of change in the lilt of his words or his gestures, but he still does not demand minute switches in mood. But European composure is not by nature of the same character as that cultivated by the Zen sage, a composure that has its roots deep in a man's nature; it springs rather from the habit of a monotony of mood, a mere continuation, if you like, of mood. By comparison, the Japanese must have all manner of variation and shading in his life, to the extent, for example, that he is struck by a desolate sense of loneliness if he goes the summer through without hearing the cicada. In spite of their full and faithful transplanting of modern European civilisation, in the matter of their clothes, their food and their houses, the Japanese have been unable to achieve any real Europeanisation. The fact that they still cling fondly as ever to their *kimono,* their rice and their *tatami* is grounded in the reason that these are capable of expressing best of all changes of mood and temper that correspond to the seasons or to morning and evening.

It is not only that climatic characteristics limit temper; in a very practical sense they prescribe man's livelihood. To quote the most striking example, agriculture in Europe proceeds at a pace that is indeed easy-going; there is no call for a struggle against weed-grasses, little anxiety in the matter of violent winds or floods and no pressure from swift switches in season. There is not sufficient moisture to call for the building of ridges for seeds; corn, sown almost indiscriminately, can be left standing for a month even after it has mellowed. The farmer who begins to reap in leisurely fashion towards the end of July is still carrying on at the same leisurely pace in early September. But the Japanese farmer harvests his corn and plants his rice shoots all within ten days; after only a short interval, he begins to weed his paddy under the boiling sun and, before he has time for breath, he is worrying his heart out about typhoons and rainstorms, the violences of nature against which he is powerless. The intensity and the severity of the labours of the latter make them quite different from those of the European and lead inevitably to a divergence in attitude towards nature. The European who, out of his monotony, approaches nature aggressively, dominates the whole land to the remotest corner and enthusiastically contemplates the use of the machine to facilitate his domination. By contrast the Oriental, in order to produce his rich crops, makes use of the abundance of sunshine and moisture that are the reverse of the coin of nature's tyranny, a tyranny so violent as to preclude all thought of resistance. Instead of thinking up artificial devices to aid his labours, he tries ingeniously to harness and set in motion the forces of nature herself. This difference shows up eventually in the form of that between a technique of an eminently logical character and one attained merely by the mastery of a knack.

No doubt no-one could deny that in the course of the association between man and nature, natural characteristics come to be exemplified as features of man's life. When man first discovered himself standing in confrontation with nature—the world beyond him—man made nature's features his own. The bright and shadeless clarity and the aridity of Greece's "eternal noon" presently turned into a type of thinking in which man revealed his all. Nature's docility—the warm, humidity-free atmosphere, the tender pastures, the smooth limestone—presently turned into the Greek style of clothing, with its sense of freedom and its carefree scorn of the need for protection against nature; it turned into, again, the nude contest, the love of the statue of the naked body. This does not mean that natural phenomena gave rise to distinctive effects on the soul of man as if it were a piece of blank paper, for man did not and could not live thus in isolation from his natural environment. The brightness of Greece's "eternal noon" was from the beginning the clarity of the Greek; the method in nature was from the first the rational inclination in the Greek. Hence the characteristics of nature should be understood as related to the spiritual make-up of those who live with that nature.

Differences of place on the style of East and West come to signify differences in spiritual make-up. This is not merely a question of artistic characteristics; it concerns also methods of material production, forms of religion or world outlook; it concerns, in fact, every facet of man's cultural life. What I intended from the first by the word humidity was not simply a meteorological phenomenon but rather a principle governing man's spiritual make-up and acting as a dividing line in the matter of humanistic, intellectual or contemplative approaches to life between on the one hand the intensely strong-willed and practical way of life of the desert with its product of a faith in a stern god in man's likeness and, on the other, the highly emotional and contemplative attitude to life of the monsoon which created the belief that all life is one. Of course, such characteristics could be transwerred through historical agencies, for place characteristics are not by any means absolute as is shown, for example, by the fact that the Old Testament, the child of desert life, has laid its spell over Europe for a thousand years, or again, that the Koran, born of the same desert, maintains strong influence in India today. Yet, in spite of this, neither Old Testament nor Koran are to be fairly comprehended without an understanding of the character of desert life. The lack of this understanding may have read an esoteric interpretation into these desert products, but it cannot be said that this renders meaningless one's appreciation of desert characteristics.

Our problem, however, is limited to art. Just as place characteristics signify characteristics of spiritual make-up, so also do they signify artistic characteristics and, hence, those of the imaginative power of the artist. Artistic creativity, as being rooted in man's character, is no doubt not to be marked off into two or three divisions in accordance with distinction of place, yet within the limits in which it is exemplified concretely in one place as the originality of a certain artist, it is bound to assume the distinctiveness of the place as its own character. When Polycleitus fashioned his perfectly proportioned statue of man, it was a case of his inner experience compelling expression and being thrust to the outside. The human form that he had in front of his eyes every day was recast by his imaginative power, heightened and typified; even though it might not exist in fact, it lived and moved in and through his experience. This was no doubt also the process when the creator of the *Suiko Buddha* gave his figure a long and slender trunk and sinews that are not those of man. But in the case of Polycleitus it was the subtle quantitative relations within the body of man that, as a form significant within his rich experience of man, spurred his emotions and stimulated the transformative functions of his power of imagination. If the human body that he saw every day had not been the most regularly proportioned of the human species, if the docile natural environment had not allowed man to sport himself naked and to feel that he was the very hub of nature, this order might not have guided the functioning of his imaginative power. (If it be said that a human body so regularly ordered and proportioned was the product of the long physical regimen of the knightly age that bore its fruit in Homer, one must take into consideration the problem whether or not the life of the knightly age, with its kernel in the craving for glory and adventure was practical not within the gentle natural surroundings of the Aegean coastline so much as in the desert, for example, with all the threats of nature.) It is because his experience contains the order within nature that the artist is moved by the order in his experience.

Though of the same human race and with the same traditions of near-nudity, the Indian's imaginative power was entirely remote from such regularity. This is to be appreciated from nature's teeming force in India, which offers man no sense of order.

Thus we see that there are marked artistic differences which depend on whether it is the rational or the irrational aspect of nature that stands out most strikingly. Such artistic differences also reflect precisely what it is that man demands of nature. In Europe, nature with its docility and its discipline was treated as something to be mastered, as something in which rule was to be discovered. We are astonished, for example, as Orientals, by Goethe's passionate zest for nature, as naturalist. Man addresses prayers for eternal life not to nature but to god; and even when honour is paid to nature it is at best as god's creation or as something in which either god or reason is embodied. In the East, however, because of its irrationality, nature was treated not as something that is to be mastered but as the repository of infinite depth. Man sought consolation and assistance from nature; the poet Basho, who was typically oriental, came into aesthetic, moral and even religious association with nature; but he showed not the slightest trace of an intellectual interest. His concern was to live, to live with nature; so his view of nature was directed to religious salvation. This could only come with the protean fecundity of nature in the East. Seeing his own reflection in nature, man felt that he was being shown the way to infinitely deep abstractions and the best artists tried through their experience to seek out and express this way. Even in a landscape the artist made not the slightest attempt to capture in his experience the method or the immutability of the structure of the landscape; rather, just as the Zen sage expresses his mental tranquillity in deliverance in a simple nature sketch poem, so the artist tries to express illimitable depth using the landscape as a mere symbol. I am not saying, of course, that every artist in the Orient was and is capable of this. I am merely trying to point out that in the "meeting of feeling" of the artist who was capable of comprehending what was most significant in the savage disorder and the teeming abundance of nature there is a powerful expression of such a purpose—a purpose that it would be wrong to demand of European art.

But this is all of the past. Today, now that the world seems to have become one, the stimuli of differing cultures appear to be toppling the distinctivenesses of nature. Yet natural distinctiveness is not something to disappear without trace. As ever, man will be restrained unconsciously by its curbings, as ever he sinks his roots in it. Even the Japanese—like the Russians in this matter—who seem to have liberated themselves so valiantly and heroically from the shackles of the traditions of their past still reveal their national character explicitly in their impatient excitability. Perhape the volatile Japanese climate might prove in the end more difficult to subjugate than the *bourgeois*. But we must remain conscious of the significance of, and love, our destiny, our destiny to have been born into such a climate. In that this is our destiny we do not thereby become a chosen people without a match in the world; but we can, by maintaining and fostering this destiny, make contributions to human culture of which no other people is capable. By such contributions we would first give real significance to the fact that every part of the world has its own distinctive character.

(Drafted 1929.)

Watsuji Tetsuro, the Man and his Work

by Furukawa Tetsushi

1

On December 26th, 1960, Dr. Watsuji Tetsuro, the author of *Fudo,* came to the end of his distinguished scholarly career. He was always of the opinion that any translation of a book should be undertaken by those who wish to read it, and that the author himself had no need to undertake it. So when it was proposed to him by the International Cultural Association around 1939–40 that *Fudo* should be translated, he rejected the suggestion. But the time came when a plan for translating *Fudo* into English was again taken up by the Japanese National Commission for UNESCO and this time it succeeded in securing the author's full approval. What a pity it was that he should have ended his days in this world before the translation manuscripts by Mr. Bownas had time to reach his sick-bed!

Fudo was first published in 1935 when its author was forty-six years old, but it will be evident to any careful reader of the work that it was based on his studies and observations during travel abroad in 1927–28.

In his *Pilgrimages to the Ancient Cathedrals in Italy,* the only record of our author's European travels, in a passage treating of his experiences at Rome on January 30th, 1928, he points out that what most strongly strikes anyone newly come from the north is the dark complexion of the people, their smaller stature, the fidgety restlessness of their manner as compared with the apathetic sedateness of the northerner and so on. He continues, "There is perhaps no other adequate way of describing all these features than as climatic characteristics." From the northerner's viewpoint, Italy is a land of the sun, of azure skies, where the weather is mostly fine and the people, basking in the intense light of the southern sun, cannot avoid growing darker in complexion. Again, in cold countries the climate naturally has a bracing effect while in hot countries people are apt to fall into idle and slovenly habits. The former will serve to strengthen a man's physique, while the latter will tend to weaken it. In consequence, most Italians are of as poor physique as we Japanese, and among Italian women there are many who are slim and delicate just like Japanese. Further, the German is so tough and capable of long hard labour without showing any sign of fatigue that he sometimes seems as if his nerves are deadened, while the Italian is both readily excited and soon exhausted. In these points Japanese and Italians have very much in common, concludes our author. This is an attempt to account for the physical and mental similarities between Italians and Japanese from the standpoint of the climatic resemblance between their respective lands.

But between Italy and Japan there is a striking contrast in atmospheric humidity. For instance, a little to the north-west of Perugia, the ancient capital on a bold hill commanding splendid views of the Umbrian countryside, there lies Lake Trasino, the views of which, quite different from those of northern Europe, have something in them that will sometimes remind us of Japan. What is this "something that will sometimes remind us of Japan"? Our author explains that, as he was looking out from the train running a short distance from this lake towards Florence, he noticed some white moss—just like that commonly seen in Japan covering stone lanterns—growing on the stone walls alongside the railway track. Now moss is connected with atmospheric humidity. The higher the humidity, the more luxuriant moss grows; and in proportion to the luxuriance of vegetation, there come into being more and more features that remind us of Japan. Culture as well as nature in Japan has a great deal to do with atmospheric humidity. According to our author, the damp resulting from this high humidity of Japan's climate is to be counted among the causes that have prevented wars and struggles in Japanese history from becoming in any degree merciless or deadly. In Rome there are to be seen the catacombs where the early Christians fought their battles of martyrdom under the ground. Those were human struggles merciless and deadly to an extent that the Japanese have never experienced. In Japan, where the humidity of the atmosphere is very high, any such life underground would be out of the question. So it may be said that the dampness of Japan prevents human struggles from becoming merciless.

2

Now in contrast to the dampness of the atmosphere in Japan, the air in Europe is remarkable for its dryness. Thus weeds grow apace on the soil of Japan while they do not prosper well in Europe. Consequently, in Europe it is easy to maintain an immense expanse of grassland as a good pasture while in Japan this would cause almost endless labour.

Dr. Watsuji came to find the climatic difference between Japan and Europe in humidity and aridity. This leads direct to the ideas basic to *Fudo*. Thus in the history of the development of his "climatic" theory *Pilgrimages to the Ancient Cathedrals in Italy* has great significance. But the origin of his "climatic" theory must be traced to a still earlier source. In an essay *What Has Japan to Be Proud of?*, one of his youthful pieces of criticism collected and published under the title *Guzo Saiko* (Icono-regeneration) at the age of twenty-nine, there occurs the following passage: "Some ascribe Japan's resurgence to the ancient culture of the East. Tagore, for example, said something to the effect that the ancient culture of the East has long permeated Japan both physically and spiritually, and that this permeation has now revived and led Japan to her present glorious victory. This is a not implausible theory. It is very probable that had it not been for the powerful influence of Confucian teaching during the Tokugawa Period our post-Restoration culture would have been of a much more superficial and transient nature. But the matter is not to be so simply disposed of. Perhaps we must also give due consideration to our comparatively simple and light-hearted national character fostered under the influences of our natural and climatic environment, to our habit of obedience implanted through the six centuries of our mediaeval feudalism, to the naivety of our thought resulting from the lack of foreign stimulus, to the physiological and psychological uniformity of our nation achieved through racial mixture extending over long ages and to many other factors". Here we can recognize the seed of the ideas that were to mature into his later "climatic" theory, by which the simple and light-hearted national character of the Japanese people is to be ascribed to the natural and climatic influences of their native land.

Again, in his *Koji Junrei* (Pilgrimages to Old Temples), first published a year after *Guzo Saiko,* he writes of his impressions of a visit to the Toshodaiji Temple at Nara: "I found myself in front of the Temple and spent a few minutes of happy contemplation. A clump of tall pine trees surrounding the Temple gave me an ineffable feeling of intimacy. Between the pine-grove and this monument of ancient architecture there certainly is an affinity both intimate and ineffable. I do not think a piece of Western architecture, of whatever kind or style, would match so well with the sentiment aroused at the sight of the pine-grove. To encircle the Parthenon with a clump of pine trees would be unthinkable. Nor can we, by even the furthest stretch of imagination, conceive that a Gothic cathedral would in any way match with the gently sloping curves of these graceful pine branches.

Such buildings should only be contemplated in conjunction with the towns and cities, forests and fields of their respective lands. Just so do our Buddhist temples have something intimately connected with and inseparable from the characteristic features of our native shores. If there are to be found some traces of the Northern forest in Gothic architecture, can we not say with equally good reason that there are in our Buddhist temples some traces of Japanese pine and cypress forests? Do we not feel in those curving roofs something of the influence of the branches of our gentle pine or cypress? Is there nothing to be perceived in the look of the temple as a whole with its reminiscences of a stately old pine or cypress adorned with thick evergreen foliage? The traditional origins of our wooden buildings in the East are of great interest when we try to reduce differences in culture to differences in climate." And in the concluding passage in which he tells of the fascination exercised upon him by the sad and noble statue of Kannon, Buddhist Goddess of Mercy *Avalokitesvara,* in her sitting posture with one leg lying on the other, he records his reflections as follows: "The original source from which these earliest monuments issued was, I suppose, the gentle nature of our country. Nature in our island country, so lovable and easy of access, so gentle and beautiful, and for all that as full of mystery as that of any country in the world, could never be otherwise represented in human form than as this all-merciful Kannon. The sweet intoxication that comes from contemplation of our gentle nature is one of the most remarkable characteristics of Japanese culture, running through all the stages of its development. In the last analysis, this characteristic feeling has its ultimate source in the gentle nature of our native land itself. The delicate love of nature that feels keenly the beauty of the sparkling dewdrops lying ready to drop on the slender slanting leaves; the quiet communion with nature that we enjoy when, out for a walk, we cast ourselves heart and soul into her embrace; the ecstasy of a heart free and buoyant—all these might seem at first sight very different from this Kannon. But the difference lies only in the direction of attention. Though the objects that we catch hold of are different, our mental attitude itself in trying to catch them is not very different on each occasion. The peculiar beauty of Mother Earth in Japan has bequeathed the same beauty to the children born to her. All inquiries into the culture of Japan must in their final reduction go back to the study of her nature." All these observations are so many expressions of the author's attempt to reach a full appreciation of differences in culture by reducing them to differences of climate or nature.

3

But when he wrote *Guzo Saiko* and *Koji Junrei*, Watsuji had no direct experience of foreign life, nor had he any direct knowledge of foreign scenery. So when he talked of the Parthenon or a Gothic church, he spoke only on the strength of his book knowledge supplemented by such impressions as he could cull from pictures and illustrations. But in 1927–28 he stayed in Europe as a government student sent abroad for study by the Ministry of Education, and during this stay he stored up an immense stock of information direct through his own eyes and ears. For example, in *Fudo* we find the following passage:

> "In my direct experience of the Mediterranean, in neither March, May nor December was it what I would normally imagine as sea. This, you may think, is merely the vague impression of an individual; nevertheless, it is one that I did feel extremely strongly. I travelled from Marseiles by way of Nice and Monaco and then went on to stay in Genoa in the middle of December and early January. Even in mid-winter, the Riviera Coast was as warm as the south; in places bamboo varieties and other tropical plants

might have been transplanted from the South Seas. You came out in perspiration when you walked at midday even without an overcoat. But this south coast of the Mediterranean is quite alien in tone to Japan's southern coastlines. The pure white sand of the beach in the vicinity of Nice and Monaco, skirted by a concreted and buttressed road, had not one piece of dirt or rubbish on it; someone might just have swept it. There was a novel sensation about this sand stretching far into the distance; for while in the south of Japan the beaches are pretty enough even in winter, my feeling is that they are washed and covered much more by the tide. It is the same with the sea wind. Here in the Mediterranean, the wind is much drier than would be expected for an off-sea breeze. Presumably the tang of the beach is not as strong in winter as in summer, yet I felt the scent of the sea is stronger in Japan than here. This sensation that here was a sea that gave no feel of the sea was so strange that I looked round at this clear transparent stretch of water. The sea-bed close in to the shore or the rocks on this sea-bed bore no sign of plant life or of shell-fish varieties. It should not be thought for a moment that such things do not grow at all here, but I must admit that I never saw any. Japan's women divers plunge into the winter sea to peel off laver from the rocks and to collect turbo-shells. In Japan, if you are fond of winter-laver or a turbo-shell roast, you can even have a strong and unmistakable tang of the beach at your city dinner-table on a mid-winter night. But there is none of this feel about the Mediterranean; it is a sea with little life in it, a sea where marine plants do not flourish. I do not remember on a single occasion seeing boats putting out to fish in this sea. The sea itself was always calm and still and yet I never caught sight of even a single sail. There was an air of desolation about this scene. To someone who knew the brave sight of winter fishing for tuna and bonito in Japan's southern seas, this was truly a sea of the dead."

Such detailed observations would never be possible when you only look at pictures or illustrations. During his year and a half abroad Watsuji amassed with untiring assiduity such close and delicate impressions, the direct fruits of which were *Pilgrimages to the Ancient Cathedrals in Italy* and *Fudo.* As a rule, a student abroad spends most of his days attending lectures or joining seminars at some foreign university, or collecting books necessary for his further study. Watsuji, on the contrary, seems to have made a point of getting out and about to familiarize himself with the people and the things about him, or of making the rounds of every picture gallery, historical spot, old tomb or church that he could find time for. According to his *pilgrimages to the Ancient Cathedrals in Italy,* he made it a rule to "pay a visit to some picture gallery or church—not more than one on each single occasion—in the morning, and, after making a leisurely inspection, come home for lunch; in the afternoon, taking a short rest after lunch, I worked until dinner-time; between whiles, if tired, I go out for a walk to a near-by park, and sometimes, taking a book with me to the park, I read it there." Thus he went his daily rounds, visiting churches and galleries, and inspecting their pictures, sculptures and buildings. Sometimes he made his rounds in the afternoon, and again sometimes his inspection continued from morning till evening. But for fear lest "the impressions should lose their power and concentration as a result of a surfeit," he deliberately restricted himself to "a visit to some picture gallery or church—not more than one on each occasion—in the morning, and, after a leisurely inspection, lunch back at home."

But in Italy he found too many art treasures to allow him always to keep to such a slow and leisurely tempo of appreciation. There were "no end of wonderful masterpieces" that utterly overwhelmed him, and he complained that he had "no energy left at all to write down the impressions". And yet, making full use of his own peculiarly keen powers of appreciation, he successfully summed up each and every impression he received of all the art objects he was able to see.

4

For a better comprehension of Watsuji's character, we must return again to the question of climate. He was born in a part of the former Province of Harima which now forms a part of Himeji City, and we cannot understand his prolific literary output without reference to the climate of this part of the country. In modern times Harima has produced among others Yanagida Kunio, the celebrated founder of systematic folklore in Japan, and the late Miki Kiyoshi, well known as a vigorous philosophic thinker. When we consider the way these three eminent scholars went about their work, we are struck by the likeness that runs through them all. They are all remarkable as well for their indefatigable energy as for their rich endowment of poetic intuition and the robust, realistic outlook on life which is based on experience and is used to support their philosophical theories.

But not all authors hailing from the Harima area possess the qualities of this trio. So we cannot attribute Watsuji's rich endowment of poetic intuition and robust, realistic outlook on life entirely to the influences of climate. Accordingly, we must examine his early history. When he was a student of Himeji Middle School, he is said to have been fired with the ambition to become a poet like Byron. The deep impression left on him after the perusal of a history of English literature caused the boy to order from Tokyo the poetical works of such English poets as Byron, Keats and Tennyson. He even went as far as to contribute to the school magazine his version in

Japanese of *The Prisoner of Chillon.* When he went up to Tokyo to take the entrance examination of the First Higher School, he planned to read English literature.

Although he changed nominally to philosophy, the boy had no mind to make philosophy the subject of a life-long study, remaining as deeply immersed in Byron as ever and attracted chiefly to things literary and dramatic. At that time Natsume Soseki, who later became one of the representative novelists of the Meiji era, was a teacher of English at the First Higher School, and young Watsuji, when he had no other lecture to attend, used to stand just outside the window of the classroom where Professor Natsume was lecturing and listen with great enjoyment to the words of the famed teacher. He was also a member of the student committee of the Literary Club, and contributed to the school magazine two novels, *Pillars of Fire* (1907) and *The Romance of the Rape-Blossom* (1908), and one play, *Resurrection,* as well as several essays. This literary fervour continued after he entered university, and he published in September, 1910, in co-operation with several friends, who included Osanai Kaoru and Tanizaki Junichiro, a literary coterie magazine, the second *Shin Shicho*; to this he contributed a play called *Tokiwa* (1910) and a drama entitled *In the Neighbourhood of a Railway Station* (1911). In addition, he translated *Mrs. Warren's Profession,* and wrote essays in dramatic criticism. When Osanai Kaoru organized a new dramatic movement called *The Free Theatre,* Watsuji gave his full support. But, shocked by the complete failure of his *Kiyomori and Tokiwa,* he gave up literary creation and devoted all his exertions to the writing of critical essays and philosophical treatises. *Guzo Saiko,* published in 1918, was a collection of such early essays, and both *Nietzschean Studies,* published in 1913, and *Sören Kierkegaard,* published in 1915, belong to his early philosophical writings.

5

Nietzschean Studies was originally intended as a graduation thesis, afterwards retouched for publication. It was in July, 1912, that Watsuji finished the philosophy course of the Literature Department in the Imperial University of Tokyo. At the time the atmosphere in the Faculty of Philosophy was inimical to the study of a poet-philosopher like Nietzsche. Consequently, Watsuji's *Nietzschean Studies* was rejected as a suitable graduation thesis and in its place he was obliged to take up the study of Schopenhauer. His thesis was presented only just in time.

It is worthy of note that Watsuji wrote his *Nietzschean Studies,* which he followed up with a monograph, *Sören Kierkegaard.* In other words, Watsuji had a keen interest in such thinkers as are popularly called poet-philosophers. Neither Nietzsche nor Kierkegaard was to be found in any ordinary history of philosophy published around 1915, chiefly because they were not philosophers in any orthodox sense of the word, but were of the school of poet-philosophers. The zeal with which young Watsuji pursued such philosophers may go to prove that he himself was one of them. Indeed, in *Guzo Saiko,* a collection of critical essays published in 1918 and in *Koji Junrei* which came in the following year, there is to be found the touch of the poet-philosopher.

6

Ancient Japanese Culture, which Watsuji wrote in 1920, is a painstaking attempt to reanimate the ancient Japanese as depicted by our old chroniclers through a comparative study of the formative imagination revealed in *Kojiki* (Old Chronicles) and *Nihongi* (Chronicles of Japan) in the light of archaeological remains. It constitutes the first step in a series of studies of the primitive cultures of the ancients, and was followed by *The Significance of Primitive Christianity in the History of World Culture* (1926), *The Practical Philosophy of Primitive Buddhism* (1927), and *Confucius* (1936). The procedure adopted in this attempt to reanimate the ancient Japanese by treating *Kojiki* as literature, by dealing with the poems and songs found interspersed in ancient chronicles as pure pieces of literary attempt, and by paying special attention to the power of formative creation shown in the archaeological relics, is also that of the poet-philosopher. As an example, we might quote the following passage which points out that the imagination of the ancients, though wanting in rational unity, is given a kind of unity by the simple feeling of wonder; this is an idea born of an appreciation of *Kojiki* as literature.

"The imagination of the ancients was weak in unifying power, and in consequence, could not represent the great complexity of the world in bold relief. But this does not mean that it lacks richness of intuition. The descriptions in *Kojiki* give the impression of being fruits of rich intuition with a weak unifying power. If imagination might be called 'a speculative power thinking in terms of form and image', the imagination found here, too, might be called 'a weak speculative power thinking in terms of exuberant form and image'. Those descriptions are certainly devoid of power, but in point of their freshness of intuition they have a beauty of their own never to be passed over. For example, in the description:

'When the land was still young and as a piece of floating grease, drifting about as does a jellyfish, there came into existence a god, issuing from what grew up like a reed-bud. . .'

a superb use is made of the image of a piece of grease floating about without definite form like a thin, muddy substance far thicker than water, yet not solid, and of the image of a soft jellyfish with a formless form drifting on the water, and of the image of exuberant life of a reed-bud sprouting powerfully out of the muddy water of a swampy marsh. There is no other description that I know of that so graphically depicts the state of the world before creation. 'And the earth was without form, and void; and darkness was upon the face of the deep. And the Spirit of God moved upon the face of the waters.' This passage in Genesis is only a negative description of the earth minus form, matter and light, and not a positive one depicting the state of the world before creation. The *chaos* of the Greeks was of a more concrete nature. They imagined a uniformly chaotic state where the land, the sea and air were all fused into one, neither solid, nor liquid, nor gaseous. But this, too, belongs to the same category as the Hebraic Genesis. The ancient Chinese described it, as in a passage at the start of the *Chronicles of Japan,* in terms of sheer conceptual similies such as 'formless and unborn as a chick in its eggshell.' As compared with all these, how concrete and graphic is the description that we find in our *Old Chronicles*!"

Again, by examining the poems and songs of the ancient chronicles purely as literature, Watsuji discovered two characteristic features—that they unite the subjective and the objective and that fact is treated as fact. On the first of these features, he says:

"Some of the poems and songs in *Kojiki* and *Nihongi* are composed in regular style while others are irregular. Judging by the evidence of the poems in *Manyoshu* (the oldest collection of Japanese poems), the former belong to a later, and the latter to an earlier period. We shall begin our study with the earlier ones."

Then he goes on to say:

"The old poems and songs of this kind are, of course, all lyrics. But they are not quite the same sort of lyric as those in

Manyoshu. In *Manyoshu* most poems are so many expressions of sentiment 'from within', such as:

'Kaerikeru
Hito kitareri to
Iishi kaba,
Hotohoto shiniki
Kimi ka to omoite.'

They told me that
A man had come.
My heart jumping,
I nearly died,
Thinking it might be you.

But in the earlier chronicles we find no such subjective pieces. Again, in *Manyoshu* we find many poems where the poet is conscious of the separation of the subjective and objective world and then, uniting these two worlds, expresses his sentiments through the description of some scene of nature, as:

'Hingashi no
No ni kagerō no
Tatsu miete,
Kaerimi sureba,
Tsuki katabukinu.'

In the east
The summer-colts shimmer.
I look round–
The moon slants
In the western sky.

But in the ancient chronicles there are few such purely descriptive poems of nature, and these few, being of regular form, perhaps belong to the later period, such as:

'Saigawa yo

Kumo tachiwatari,
Unebiyama
Konoha sayaginu.
Kaze fukan to su.'
Over the River Sai
Storm clouds billow.
On Mount Unebi
The leaves rustle
In the whistling wind.

Among the earlier poems we find some simple and direct expressions of love for one's own native land, such as:

'Yamato wa kuni no mahoroba,
Tatanazuku aogaki yamagomoreru
Yamato shi uruwashi!'
Yamato, happy hollow of our land!
Nestling in the bosom of the blue hills
That cluster round its plains,
How beautiful is Yamato!

Here there is scarcely any separation of the subjective from the objective, and the poem cannot be regarded as purely descriptive of nature. Even the following piece,

'Chiba no Kazunu o mireba,
Momochitaru yaniwa mo miyu,
Kuni no ho mo miyu.'
When I look out over Kazu field in Chiba,
I see countless happy homesteads crowding,
And I see the lofty peak of the land.

is not so much the expression of the poet's sentiment apostrophizing beauty as revealed in natural scenery, as a simple confession of his personal experience as he looks over the land as a scene of life which includes busy human habitation."

After making this distinction, Watsuji concludes: "When we look at this distinction from a psychological point of view, we find that the poets of the *Manyoshu* concentrate their feeling upon themselves and gaze at it within themselves, or separate it from themselves and enjoy it in nature confronting them as beauty in the objective world, while the ancient poets, whose feelings still retain a virgin simplicity as a single undivided experience, are not yet troubled by this division of the subjective and the objective."

Ancient Japanese Culture is full of such interpretative observations. We may well call this a *philological* method of inquiry. In the Preface to his *Homeric Criticism* (published in 1946) Watsuji stresses the indispensability of European philological methods to the proper development of the study of Japanese and Chinese literature, and calls the attention of young Japanese students to the intimate relation between literature and philosophy as two forms of philology. *Ancient Japanese Culture* is, in fact, the product of this philological investigation applied to the study and interpretation of Japan's ancient culture.

7

But it was in the field of primitive researches that this philological tool was put to the most effective use. This is evident from an examination of his *Significance of Primitive Christianity in the History of World Culture, Practical Philosophy of Primitive Buddhism, Confucius,* and the like.

The Significance of Primitive Christianity in the History of World Culture is an attempt to interpret primitive Christianity as a product of Hellenistic civilization, instead of as a development that occurred in an environment totally different from the spirit of Greek civilization, and for that purpose, tried to trace, by a critical examination of the growth of the Christian myth, how the human Jesus turned into the mythical Jesus. As a result of a philological analysis of the Gospels, Watsuji discovered the human Jesus as the living source of the Four Gospels and the originating power of the belief in resurrection, and as the origin and prime mover of Christianity, giving vital power to the undercurrents of Hellenistic civilization.

In *The Practical Philosophy of Primitive Buddhism,* too, the tool of philology was employed with success in analyzing the life of Buddha. He proposed, for instance, that the Nirvana Sutra is not the work of a single synthesizing imagination, but a quite loose compilation of legendary stories current among monks and priests of the Holy Society about the last days of Buddha. Among these legends there are some that are of profound significance in that they give an account of Buddha's determination to enter Nirvana; others are of only a factual interest, such as the story of Chunda, who supplied Buddha with his last meal, and that of Subhadda, his last convert. The most numerous are the legends which centre on the sentiments of the disciples after Gautama's death, such as stories regarding Buddha's burial rites, his erection of towers and the rules of the Holy Society, or regarding the authority of Ānanda, and the like. The narratives treating of Buddha's internal life in his last days are, after all, limited to those telling of Buddha's determination and proclamation concerning the entry to Nirvana. Buddha's last teaching was that "all mundane things are liable to decay; you should exert yourselves faithfully observing the Law (Dharma)." When Buddha fell ill and was asked by Anonda to give his last directions to the Holy Society, his only answer on this occasion, too, was: "Let yourselves be guided by the Law (Dharma)!" This single idea—that what leads the Holy Society is not Buddha himself but the Law, and that regardless of Buddha's corporeal existence the Law is the only guiding star that eternally leads all men to Enlightenment and Freedom—this alone is perhaps the most ancient and most powerful teaching to be found throughout the whole of the Nirvana Sutra. The legends concerning Buddha's Nirvana, with this basic idea within themselves, constantly developed outwards. And on the external fringe, long before the compilation of the Nirvana Sutra, there were legends that had the sentiments of Buddha's disciples as their kernel which had already taken shape in an extremely mythical form.

The tool of philology was again given full play in *Confucius,* a study of primitive Confucianism. Here, a philological analysis of the *Analects* led to the discovery that the *Analects* is the only reliable source for the life of Confucius, and that among the Books of the *Analects,* on the whole, the first half belong to an earlier stratum. Watsuji discovered that the life of Confucius, as compared with those of the other three teachers of man—Gautama, Socrates, and Jesus—is remarkable for the lack of records regarding his death, and that the most prominent feature of Confucian teaching consists in the paramount significance given to ethical conduct.

Watsuji, then, studied first ancient Japanese culture, next primitive Christianity and primitive Buddhism, and, last, primitive Confucianism. But what provided the stimulus for this enquiry into the past? According to the Preface to *Ancient Japanese Culture,* it was not till 1917, when he was twenty-eight, that he became interested in the antiquities of Japan. That interest was first aroused by the question what sort of men it was who created great monuments of art such as the sculptures and buildings of the Asuka and the Nara Eras. It is impossible to say that he had no intention at all of reviving the old. Indeed, after paying high praise to the Kannon of the Chuguji Temple for its immaculate beauty and divine sweetness of expression, he says in his *Pilgrimages to the Ancient Temples*: "Of all the artistic representations of love does not this statue stand unique and peerless in the whole history of art? Specimens more powerful, or more dignified or profound, or expressing more intense ecstasy—

there may be not a few to be found in the world. But this masterpiece of purity of love and sorrow is perhaps unique in touching our hearts through its serene concentration and thorough softness. If in this sweet, pastoral feeling, imbued with infinite sadness, the mentality of our forefathers living in those far-off days is reflected, this statue is an expression of the national character of the Japanese. Japanese art, ancient and modern, whose soul is to be found in the consciousness, infinitely sad, of the transiency of all life, and in the quiet love, infinitely sweet, in this transient world, boasts in this statue its supreme and inimitable expression. The intoxicating softness of line of the colour-prints of the Ukiyoe School, the soul-enthralling sorrowfulness of tone in Japanese music, though they may contain some touch of fragile decadence, are, in the main, so many waves of a tide streaming from the yearning expressed in that Kannon. The religion of Honen and that of Shinran, and the tales and romances of the Heian Era, sometimes described as indecent and demoralizing, all have for their basic tone that yearning and the soft, sympathetic sentiment which takes its rise from it."

But it is plain that a mere "revival of the old" was not Watsuji's purpose or intention when we read in his Preface to *Guzo Saiko*: "But a mere 'revival of the old' is not my object. Even the old, when revived, shines with a new life, casting off its old crust. Here is no longer any restraint of time; it is eternally young and eternally new. What I wish to do is nothing more or nothing less than to advance such life as lives in the everlasting New." It was for this reason that Watsuji strove to elucidate not only ancient Japanese culture, but also primitive Christianity, primitive Buddhism, and primitive Confucianism.

8

We have seen Watsuji as poet-philosopher, philologist, and fervent admirer of the ancients. In 1925, however, he was called to

Kyoto to take the Chair of Ethics in the Department of Literature in Kyoto University, and from that time he spent the rest of his life in the study of ethics and morality.

To his ethics Watsuji himself gave the term *Ethics as the Science of Man.* The formation of his system began in 1931, with the publication of *Ethics* in the *Iwanami Philosophical Lectures,* but reconsideration from a new standpoint led to the statement of a new system in *Ethics as the Science of Man,* published in 1934 as a volume of the *Iwanami Encyclopaedic Library of Science.* This fresh statement of ethics as a rational theory of human existence was systematically developed and comprehensively described in *Ethics* Vol. I (1937), *Ethics* Vol. II (1942), and *Ethics* Vol. III (1949). This system of ethics is, in our opinion, an achievement not only unprecedented in the whole history of learning in Japan, but rarely to be met with even in the international world of letters.

What, then, is this "ethics as the science of Man"? How is it different from what is popularly known as "ethics" in the West? "Ethics as the science of Man", according to Watsuji, enables us to study ethics in the concrete. Man here means not a mere individual, nor mere society, but Man as an entity dialectically synthesizing the Individual and the World.

We find our ethical problems not in the consciousness of the individual in isolation, but in the relations between man and man. Therefore, ethics is the science of Man. Unless we deal with it as a problem of the proper relation between man and man, we cannot find a true solution to the problem of what makes our actions good or bad, what is our duty, responsibility, or virtue.

The Japanese word for ethics is *rinri,* a compound of *rin,* company, and *ri,* principle. The term means literally the order or principle that enables men to live in friendly community. In ancient China there were five "cardinal human relations" (or great companies)—parent and child, master and man, husband and wife, senior and junior, friend and companion. These were the most important *nakama* (relationships). The relation between parent and child is a kind of *rin* (or ordered company), a class of *nakama* (or companionate relationship). It is not that parent and child exist separately first and then are related to each other afterwards. Both gain their respective standing as parent or child by being a member of the same company organized in a definite relationship.

Rinri, the principle of ordering human action, makes the common existence of men what it is. The Japanese word *rinri,* the principle of social existence, shows that to the Japanese ethics is not a question of individual consciousness, but one of the relation between man and man. The Japanese term, in fact, is more akin to the Greek *politikē* than to the English "private ethics". The conception of ethics in *Ethics as the Science of Man* had been already propounded, at least in essential substance, in Kant's *Grundlegung zur Metaphysik der Sitten.* Hence Watsuji's explanation that it is not his intention to propound anything out of the ordinary, but that he only wishes to distinguish his system from the so-called *Ethics* of modern times, a system separated from, and opposed to, *Politica.*

According to *Ethics as the Science of Man,* the code of ethics propounds the principle by which all human relations are put on their true footing, and, while this demands that the Individual deny himself on the one hand and makes him return to the Whole, it is on the other hand a denial of the denial by which the Whole is denied in its turn, and thus it is life itself that marches on to infinity, nothing obstructing its sweeping course. In this sense, our author's ethical principle looks very much like dialectics tinged deeply with a Buddhist colouring. This code not only regulates all the relations between subject and subject, but it is also objectively expressed in all the cultures of the world. So through the understanding and interpretation of these expressions our ethical experience and ethical practice can be made both broader and deeper. Here Watsuji's method becomes interpretative. Each and every kind of human organization—family, blood-relationship, local community, cultural community, and national state—is dealt with in turn. The theory of national morality, too, is solidly systematized on the basis of Watsuji's philosophical survey of world history, where he turned to good account the vast stock of knowledge which he had gained during his researches into ancient Japanese culture, primitive Christianity, primitive Buddhism, primitive Confucianism, and so on.

9

The second of Watsuji's achievements as a student of ethics consists in his historical investigations into Japanese ethical ideas. The two-volume *History of Japanese Ethical Ideas,* published in 1952, is a comprehensive synthesis of all his labours in this field.

The original treatises incorporated into this work were first published in the form of a series of lectures in the *Iwanami Lecture Course on Ethics*: *Emperor-worship and Its Tradition* (No. 1), *The Idea of a Humanistic State and Its Tradition* (No. 6), *Morals of Devoted Loyalty and Its Tradition* (No. 3), *Bushido* (No. 12), *Merchant Ethics* (No. 13), etc. He worked to the over-all plan of making a topical survey of the history of Japanese ethical ideas, taking up successively for his theme an ethical idea that was brought to clear consciousness in each era, and following it up in its course of development in successive eras. In 1943, he retouched the earlier paper and published it in book form as *Emperor-worship and Its Tradition.* In this book he gives a historical outline of Emperor-worship, which he considers as the root of all ethical ideas in Japan, from which all other forms of ethical thought have been derived. The plan to make this the first of his serial works was brought to an unexpected stop by Japan's unconditional surrender in the Pacific War. In addition, Watsuji decided to abandon his method of treatment and to adopt the ordinary way of description that treats of each era as a synthetic whole. So his papers were reorganized under a new system, which was published in two volumes under the title of *A History of Japanese Ethical Ideas.*

It was only the method, however, that changed. There was no change or revision in Watsuji's views. Thus the ethical idea perceived in the old myths and legends, epitomized as the morals of a Clear, Bright Conscience; the ethical idea of the First Constitutional Era, epitomized as the Idea of a Humanistic State; the ethical idea of the Early Shogunate Era, epitomized as the morals of Devoted Loyalty; the ethical idea of the Mid-Shogunate Era, epitomized as the Rebirth of the Ancient Ideals; the ethical idea of the Late Shogunate Era, epitomized as the morals of Nobility or Gentility; the ethical idea of the Meiji Era, epitomized as the Union of Eastern and Western Morals—all are to be found in the same form in the original plan.

It was Watsuji's conviction that Japan occupies a very peculiar position in the modern civilized world, and that this peculiarity of position, inevitable under the pressure of world history, unavoidably imposes upon her a destiny to act as heroic defender of the freedom of the swarming millions of the East. When the Pacific War broke out, he felt that this historic development, imposed by destiny upon the shoulders of the Japanese people, took its start, and kept watching the progress of hostilities with the utmost concern. In about March, 1945, with the increase of the intensity of air-raids on Tokyo, he started a seminar to study the "re-evaluation of the Modern Age from the outset". This meeting, chiefly attended by the members of the Faculty of Ethics in the Literature Department of Tokyo University, where he was at that time the Senior Professor of Moral Philosophy, had for its object to find out the causes of the defeat that now faced Japan and to gain information and wisdom to provide for the future. Watsuji considered that the most fatal of the defects of the Japanese people lies, in a word, in their want of a scientific way of thinking: the Japanese put their sole trust on intuitive facts and make light of the conclusions reached by reasoning.

This major and widespread defect of the Japanese is, according to our author, not of a day's growth. Since they gave birth to a new science, European nations have spent three centuries allowing this scientific way of thinking to permeate every aspect of their way of life. The Japanese, on the contrary, closed their country to foreign influences immediately on the birth of this new science, and for two centuries and a half all the facets of this modern spirit were shut out by state authority. The rapid progress of science during these two hundred and fifty years made it that Japan's loss could not be remedied by a subsequent hasty importation of the fruits of that scientific progress.

Thus, in order to understand this major defect we must examine the implications of this closure of the country. This was Watsuji's motive in undertaking research into the "re-evaluation of the Modern Age", the fruit of which was published in book form in 1950, entitled *Sakoku* (The Closed Country), and subtitled *The Tragedy of Japan.*

10

This study, *The Closed Country,* was first delivered as a series of lectures in the Literature Department of Tokyo University in April, 1947, under the title of *World History from the Ethical Point of View.* This series continued for a year, after which it was published in the magazine *Tenbo,* this time under the title of *The Formative Process of a World Outlook.* In other words, *Sakoku* has two former names: *World History from the Ethical Point of View* and *The Formative Process of a World Outlook.* These four titles—*The Closed*

Country, The Tragedy of Japan, World History from the Ethical Point of View, The Formative Process of a World Outlook—give us a fair impression of the substance of the work. It was Watsuji's aim first to trace the process by which the European nations broadened their world outlook both towards the East and West as a result of their spirit of pursuit after the Infinite in the early days of the Modern Age, and then to show how negative and cowardly was the attitude that Japan adopted amidst such upheaval and excitement; lastly to point out that this closing of Japan led ultimately to her recent disaster.

But in the days when Prince Henry the Navigator, of Portugal, looking out over the Atlantic from his castle on the promontory of Sagres at the south-west end of the European continent, was striving to open up the passage round Africa, and when the great mariners were making a series of exploring voyages and, discovering the passage to India and the new continent of America, were beginning to build their colonies on those remote shores—in other words, at the glorious dawn of early modern Europe, we find not all our Japanese forefathers sleeping slothfully. Over the sea hundreds of marauding fleets of Japanese pirates ravaged all the coasts of South Korea and of China. At home, popular movements, called Peasant Uprisings, were shaking the tottering system of feudalism to its very foundations, and causing the temporary downfall of the successors to the Kamakura Shogunate and providing an indirect cause that led to the rival barons in the Age of Civil War becoming true heroes in their several ways.

There arose from among those heroes one Oda Nobunaga, hero of heroes, who put an end to the struggles of the rival barons. In *The Closed Country* Watsuji sees this Nobunaga as the solitary figure of the times eager and anxious to broaden Japan's outlook. The ordinary interpretation sees Nobunaga simply as a war-lord, fiery-tempered and cruel, well represented by his motto: "Kill the cuckoo if it will not sing". But in reality he was far more tolerant and broad-minded than the famed Toyotomi Hideyoshi, who might impress one as very large-hearted; he possessed, in addition, a strong curiosity to explore the unknown and an equally strong desire to broaden his outlook, qualities that Hideyoshi could lay no claim to. It was this curiosity that led Nobunaga to be a friend and protector to such foreigners as Valignani, Organtino, Frois and the like, and also to build iron-clad war vessels big enough to overwhelm the Mongol fleet. At this time the atmosphere favoured Japan's adoption of European civilization and there were chances enough for bringing Japan into the brilliant company of the progressive modern nations then taking rapid strides in spiritual development. But Nobunaga was a lone bright figure in the universal darkness of mediaeval Japan. The Japanese intellectuals surrounding Nobunaga were not so enthusiastic as their lord about broadening their outlook, and the Jesuit Fathers, on their part, though in a position to supply Nobunaga with much information about Europe and its culture, devoted themselves fully to their missionary work. So Nobunaga, "the spearhead of the creative power of the day", died before his time, his visions unrealized.

This novel portrait of Nobunaga in *Sakoku* is derived, in the main, from the observations and testimonies of Frois and other Jesuit missionaries. This alone would make the work worthy of attention.

11

Among Watsuji's other works, *Studies in the Spiritual Development of the Japanese People* (1935 and 1945, two volumes) constitutes a continuation of *Ancient Japanese Culture* and is a collection of essays on the culture of the successive ages since the first historical records. It contains, among others, *Political Ideals in the Asuka and the Nara Era, The Adoption of Buddhism in the Suiko Era, Fine*

Arts in the Suiko and the Tenpyo Era, The Tale of Taketori as a Fairy Tale, The Pillow-Book of Seishonagon, The Tale of Genji, On "Mono no Aware" (Poetic Beauty of all Transient Life), covering an extensive field of historical investigations into Japanese culture. It is of special interest for us to find here an essay of considerable length on Dogen, the founder of the Soto Sect of Zen Buddhism. This is our author's first serious attempt at a re-evaluation of Buddhist philosophy, a field of study that occupied an important part in his life work.

In the Preface to the *Studies in the Spiritual Development of the Japanese People,* Watsuji confesses that in the course of his historical survey of the spiritual development of the Japanese people he discovered how deeply the spiritual life of the Japanese is rooted in Buddhist teachings. This led him to a special study of Buddhism, the fruits of which are to be seen in *Practical Philosophy of Primitive Buddhism* as well as in the treatises on *The Transplanting of Buddhist Ideas in Japan* and *Japanese Literature and Buddhist Thinking,* both part of the *Studies in the Spiritual Development of the Japanese People,* Second Series.

In *Guzo Saiko* Watsuji confesses that he once dreamed as a boy that he "should write his *Faust* from his own experience". What, then, was his *Faust*? His three-volume *Ethics*? His two-volume *History of the Development of Ethical Ideas in Japan*? It may be. But from the fact that it was not his dream as a youth to become a philosophical expert, a work such as *The Closed Country* or *Climate and Culture*—the latter, perhaps, rather than the former—is best called his *Faust.* For no other work reminds us so strongly of our author's character as a poet-philosopher, one in whom intellect and imagination go hand in hand and head and heart sing in such perfect unison!